A Handful of
BULLETS

A Handful of BULLETS

HOW THE MURDER OF ARCHDUKE FRANZ FERDINAND
STILL MENACES THE PEACE

HARLAN K. ULLMAN

NAVAL INSTITUTE PRESS
ANNAPOLIS, MARYLAND

Naval Institute Press
291 Wood Road
Annapolis, MD 21402

Library of Congress Cataloging-in-Publication Data

Ullman, Harlan.
  A handful of bullets : how the murder of Archduke Franz Ferdinand still menaces the peace
/ Harlan K. Ullman.
     pages cm
  Includes index.
  ISBN 978-1-61251-799-5 (hardcover : alk. paper) — ISBN 978-1-61251-792-6 (ebook)
1. World politics—21st century. 2. World politics—20th century. 3. World War, 1914–
1918—Influence. 4. United States—Politics and government. 5. United States—Foreign
relations. 6. United States—Strategic aspects. 7. Strategy. I. Title. II. Title: How the murder
of Archduke Franz Ferdinand still menaces the peace.
  D863.U55 2014
  327.1—dc23
                                                    2014026725

♾ Print editions meet the requirements of ANSI/NISO z39.48-1992 (Permanence of Paper).
Printed in the United States of America.

22 21 20 19 18 17 16 15   9 8 7 6 5 4 3 2

Contents

PART ONE

Deus ex Machina: How the Murder of an Archduke Began the Unraveling of the Westphalian Era, Created Four New Horsemen of the Apocalypse, and Transformed the Nature of the International System in the Twenty-First Century

PART TWO

Many Archdukes, Many Bullets

PART THREE

A Brains-Based Approach to Strategy: Corralling the Four Horsemen

Foreword

Writing a foreword for *A Handful of Bullets* is a particular pleasure. First, this is a must-read book with highly provocative and captivating ideas, analyses, and recommendations. Second, and I shall return to this theme, the call for a twenty-first-century strategic mind-set is both a serious challenge and a necessity if the United States is to remain a global leader.

Harlan Ullman is well known as a sharp and clear-eyed observer of global events, and his work on shock and awe is widely regarded as fundamental to understanding twenty-first-century geopolitics. I have known and followed his work closely for several decades and am proud to pen a foreword to this fascinating volume.

The absolute necessity for a new strategic mind-set has been made clear over the course of a hundred years of history dating back to June 28, 1914, and the assassination of Austro-Hungarian archduke Franz Ferdinand and his wife Sophie on the back streets of Sarajevo at the hands of Gavrilo Princip that precipitated the First World War. The book argues that September 11, 2001, and the attacks on the World Trade Center in New York City and the Pentagon in Washington, D.C., have become the new June 28 and Osama bin Laden the twenty-first-century equivalent of Gavrilo Princip.

Harlan posits four new Horsemen of the Apocalypse as arising over the past century as the major dangers and threats to global peace, prosperity, and stability. I shall focus only on the most dangerous rider—failed and failing government, evident from Afghanistan to Zimbabwe, with Brussels and Washington in between. And over the past years, I have had particularly close association with Afghanistan, Brussels, and Washington in my previous assignment as Supreme Allied Commander Europe.

The future of Afghanistan, and for that matter of most states, rests in the ability to govern. Nothing has been more difficult during our more than dozen years in Afghanistan than trying to help the Afghan people bring a system of fair, free, and open government to that war-torn country. And quite frankly, as I look at our own government and its failure to address some of the most fundamental issues we face economically, politically, and socially, as well as regarding our security and well-being, I find *A Handful of Bullets* a powerful diagnosis of what ails us and what needs to be done.

Not all of Harlan's tough medicine will be easily swallowed, nor do I agree with it all. But this book offers some unconventional ideas that can spark a debate with authority, from the idea of mandatory voting to a Sarbanes-Oxley–like law for Congress.

Here you will find ideas about how to structure our national defense, demand accountability from national leaders, and structure U.S. foreign policy to achieve best advantage in a difficult and demanding international world. It offers ideas that challenge much of conventional thinking and in that sense serves us all best.

—Adm. James Stavridis, USN (Ret.)

Preface

The Great War—or, the "war to end all wars," as promised by President Woodrow Wilson—was neither great nor ultimately conclusive. Precipitated by the assassination of the Austro-Hungarian archduke Franz Ferdinand and his wife in the streets of Sarajevo on June 28, 1914, World War I demolished the order established by the Congress of Vienna, an order that had maintained the peace in Europe for almost a century. The ensuing carnage laid the foundations for a second world war and a cold war that followed.

World War I also left in its catastrophic wake three transformational legacies that remain largely unnoticed today. These legacies have provoked and will provoke massive and even tectonic change to the international order. But containing, mitigating, and preventing these disruptions from exploding into major crises will prove no less difficult a challenge than did restraining the forces that ignited the chaos and violence of the last century.

The first legacy would create an excess of potential archdukes and an abundance of bullets, any combination of which could detonate a regional or global crisis. The second began the unraveling of the Westphalian system of state-centric politics that had been in place since 1648. And the third was to seat "Four New Horsemen of the Apocalypse" as the major threats and challenges to global peace and prosperity. The four riders are failed or failing government; economic despair, disparity, and dislocation; radical ideologies; and environmental calamity.

In a sentence, these legacies would make Osama bin Laden into a modern-day version of Gavrilo Princip, the archduke's assassin, and turn September 11 into an event like June 28, 1914, but in many different and frightening ways. Instead of using a Beretta 9-mm pistol, bin Laden orchestrated the crashing of three airliners into New York's Twin Towers and the Pentagon in Washington, D.C., starting a global war on terror.

This book tells this story.

Unfortunately, our current strategic mind-set in place to deal with the twenty-first century remains firmly anchored in the past. That mind-set must change if aspirations for peace and prosperity are to be met with decisive and effective actions.

Hope is not a strategy. But we must hope that politicians and publics will finally recognize that engaging man's better angels rests on thinking and not spending, talking, or politicking our way clear of danger—a wish that will require more than divine intervention if a new mind-set is to have any chance of taking hold.

—Harlan Ullman
Washington, D.C.
March 15, 2014

Introduction

I deas for books spring from many sources and inspirations, even from seren-
dipity. June 28, 2014, marked the hundredth anniversary of the assassination
of Archduke Franz Ferdinand and his pregnant wife Sophie in Sarajevo after
his driver took a wrong turn. Of course, not all assassinations, even of heads of
state or government, have equal impact.

The assassinations of three presidents—Abraham Lincoln, William
McKinley, and John F. Kennedy—did not provoke wars or supercrises. Each
death raised the question: Had the assassinations not taken place, what might
have happened differently? Perhaps reconstruction of the South following the
Civil War would have proceeded more compassionately. Perhaps McKinley
would not have been as interventionist as his successor, Theodore Roosevelt,
was in settling the Russo-Japanese War of 1904–1905. And perhaps JFK would
have kept America out of Vietnam.

But that is speculation. Ferdinand's death had the most disastrous and
immediate of consequences: world war. Given the many thousands of splendid
histories, memoirs, and analyses written over the last century, it would seem
that little new could be written about that war. World War I did not resolve the
great power rivalries in Europe. That war merely postponed the day of reckon-
ing when a rearmed Nazi Germany would seek expansion and revenge and send
its army to war, conquering most of Europe.

World War I also planted, with the secret Sykes-Picot Treaty of 1916, the
seeds for the unrest and violence across the Middle East that persist today, and
for instability in Asia as well. World War II continued the unfinished business
of the Great War. A cold war, one that itself lasted four and a half decades after
the Allies defeated the Axis enemy, followed.

So, bluntly, does this centenary warrant yet another book? The answer borrows from General of the Army Dwight David Eisenhower's recipe for solving problems. Make them bigger, the general and later president always advised. When planning for the Normandy invasion, Ike's "bigger" problem was how to occupy Europe and destroy the Nazi war machine. The invasion was step one.

On the basis of Ike's advice of expanding the problem, the answer to a single "bigger" question explains the need for this book. Did the archduke's death bequeath other, less visible legacies that have transformed and even revolutionized the geopolitics of the twenty-first century? The response forms the foundation for *A Handful of Bullets*.

June 28 eviscerated the order imposed by the Congress of Vienna in 1815. That order had generally kept the peace among the great European powers for a century—this, the first of these hidden legacies, would bequeath an excess of potential archdukes and a surfeit of proverbial bullets. This volatile and lethal combination can ignite (and has ignited) crises and detonate ticking political time bombs without necessarily shooting at or killing specific targets such as the lamented archduke.

Next, and a legacy that is still largely invisible and not fully appreciated, June 28 and the wars it would provoke began the unraveling of the Westphalian system of state-centric politics. That system had governed the conduct of international relations since 1648. And third, Four New Horsemen of the Apocalypse were saddled to ride out to threaten twenty-first-century society.

Consider only a few examples of how much these three legacies have changed and challenged international and domestic politics over the last hundred years.

In 1914, the political power to overthrow governments, win or lose wars, and defeat enemies belonged to states. Power was measured in numbers of capital ships in the line of battle, army divisions, and the time it would take to mobilize those forces. A handful of bullets were sufficient to start the First World War. That war in turn left in its ashes the ingredients for a second world war and a cold war

In 1917, it took a violent revolution to end tsarist rule in Russia and create the Union of Soviet Socialist Republics. Six decades later, an exiled Shia ayatollah living in Paris could incite a revolution to overthrow the Iranian government without the need for an army. A decade after that, the Soviet Union would implode, collapse of its own weight, without a shot being fired in anger.

In 2001, an exiled Saudi radical living in Afghanistan—a country few in the West had ever visited, let alone knew anything about—ordered two dozen acolytes on a suicide mission to America. On September 11, four civilian jet airliners were highjacked—two crashed into New York's Twin Towers and one into Washington's Pentagon, starting a global war on terror that continues.

Indeed, September 11, 2001, will prove to have been a critical inflection point, one that redefined the nature of American and global politics and added great momentum to the forces unraveling the Westphalian system. And Osama bin Laden would become the twenty-first century's first Gavrilo Princip.

By 2014, social media and information technologies have accelerated the effects of these legacies. A hundred forty characters, the maximum tweeting allows, have the political power to move societies, generate revolutions, and overthrow regimes and governments. A single person (Edward Snowden) can release secret documents about U.S. and British surveillance systems directed against not only hundreds of millions of people but also heads of friendly governments. The ramifications of that revelation have shaken to the core America's reputation as an honorable ally, and they have yet to run their course.

Concurrently, economic and technological revolutions were under way with equally profound impact that would complicate and accelerate the erosion of the Westphalian system. In 1914, it was inconceivable that a teenager might invent or create an idea that would be worth hundreds of millions of dollars or that a single weapon could wipe out an entire city in a fraction of a second. Yet, the nuclear revolution produced the latter. And regarding the former, the "dot-com" and information revolutions have made many youthful multimillionaires and billionaires commonplace by 2014.

Many more extraordinary transformations are occurring with potentially unbounded effects and influences on society. Three-dimensional (3-D) printing, genetic research, and other technologies are suggestive of extraordinary future possibilities for the world as we know it. Climate change, among other issues that recognize no borders and respect no boundaries, obviously will heavily shape politics and future well-being.

No example guarantees that an excess of archdukes and bullets will trigger major crises or a world war. Nor do any examples condemn the Westphalian state-centric system (and traditional government as the ultimate arbiter of power through use of military force) to irreversible obsolescence. But each underscores the centripetal forces pulling away from traditional state-centric relations and toward crosscutting challenges to society at large.

Further, growing interdependence and interconnectivity of states, fueled by the information revolution, have imposed additional norms, laws, and requirements on domestic societies. These effects, generated by globalization writ large, have eroded national sovereignty by necessitating compliance with suprastate organizations or international agreements. In the European Union, member states agreed to forego for their collective benefit elements of national authority and sovereignty.

A final point about the magnitude of change: in 1914 and inflated into 2013 dollars, using official U.S. budget figures, U.S. gross domestic product (GDP) was about $848 billion. In 2013, U.S. GDP was about $17 trillion, a real twenty-fold increase or, on a per capita basis, a gain of a factor of seven (leading to the question of where that money went). In the case of China, the differential is vastly larger and probably incalculable, demonstrating the extraordinary force of the diffusion of economic power. But what these order-of-magnitude increases mean for the future or for the role and reach of government is by no means self-evident or obvious.

In the United States and many other countries, government seems incapable of understanding and keeping up with these and other consequences arising from a more complex, complicated, globalized, and tightly interconnected and interdependent world. As will be argued, failed and failing government is the greatest single danger and threat facing publics and politicians today.

What is missing and is desperately needed is a critical mind-set that recognizes current twenty-first-century realities and proposes appropriate intellectual, strategic, operational, and organizational solutions for dealing with them. Otherwise, peace, prosperity, and stability in the twenty-first century will remain elusive at best and in grave jeopardy at worst. While the focus for creating a new mind-set is the United States, clearly the need and application is far more widespread.

This book tells the story of how these three legacies have induced profound transformations, created new vulnerabilities (and opportunities) while exacerbating older, traditional threats. Analyses of these newer dangers are essential if publics and politicians are to be able to understand them better. More important, specific remedial actions and steps are desperately needed to lessen or mitigate the risks that another June 1914–type incident, inadvertent or not, will erupt into cataclysmic consequences.

The starting point is recognizing that the Westphalian state-centric system no longer fully fits today's world. In this unraveling, many potential "archdukes" and "bullets" exist. The assassination a century ago in the Balkans ultimately led to the emergence of today's Four Horsemen of the Apocalypse, who constitute the major threats and challenges to global and regional stability. As they emerge, an alternative strategic paradigm or major readjustment of the Westphalian system will take shape. As the reader will see, the greatest danger to the United States (and many other states as well) is failed and failing government.

For much of America's history, its security rested on the ability to spend more money than potential adversaries, while relying on the protection of geography (until intercontinental missiles and bombers overcame that advantage) and the good fortune of a superabundance of natural resources. However heroic the contributions of millions of soldiers and citizens, it was the expenditure of virtually unlimited resources that overwhelmed the Nazis and Japanese and turned the tide of World War II.

During the Cold War, Vietnam, two conflicts in Iraq, and the war on terror, writing checks to allocate vast resources was fundamental to the strategy. More was better. Absent a threat as palpable as Hitler or the Soviet Union and short of a catastrophic crisis, and given fiscal and economic constraints imposed by rising debt and deficits that are redefining national security, the only viable solution is to reject that past solution of more money and think, not spend, our way clear of danger.

To accomplish this transformational response, the best, even only, recourse is to exercise our brains and generate a "brains-based approach" to strategy and to a twenty-first-century mind-set. Injecting brains and intellect into a broken and failing political system resistant to any intervention is a daunting but perhaps not insurmountable task.

A last point: to make this book an easier read, footnotes are not used, although I am happy to provide any documenting information on request. Wherever any reference is needed, it is included in the text. And, of course, any errors are my responsibility.

PART ONE

Deus ex Machina: How the Murder of an Archduke Began the Unraveling of the Westphalian Era, Created Four New Horsemen of the Apocalypse, and Transformed the Nature of the International System in the Twenty-First Century

By themselves, centenary anniversaries celebrating events, great or small, too often have only symbolic or cynical rather than transformational value. The centenary anniversary of the archduke's assassination and the start of World War I will be commemorated for many reasons this year. But more notable is the passage of a hundred years since the "Guns of August" set Europe and much of the world ablaze.

As with many great events, some of the more profound consequences of the Great War are still hidden by the veils of time. As China's urbane prime minister Zhou Enlai quipped when Henry Kissinger asked him about the impact of the French Revolution of 1789, "it is too soon to tell." The same observation need not apply to the First World War.

Historians often overestimate the relevance and significance of historical inflection points, as economists have (mis)predicted hundreds of the past two or three actual recessions. World War I ended the relative stability in Europe brought about by Napoleon's final defeat and the Congress of Vienna of 1815. To avoid this historians' (or economists') trap of (mis) prediction, let me assert that the start of World War I did far more than end the construct for a century of European stability and create the enmities that would erupt into a second world war.

What has been largely overlooked or ignored is that from the ashes of World War I three unintended and unexpected legacies arose. The first would create many potential archdukes and bullets and thus breeding grounds for new crises. Second was the erosion of the Westphalian system of state-centric politics that had governed the conduct of international politics since 1648. And a third led to the emergence of Four New Apocalyptic Horsemen.

Over time, the revered notion of sovereignty, central to the concept of state supremacy, would be challenged to its core. As President Woodrow Wilson found to his detriment, attempts to reinforce or replace the dented notion of sovereignty with a supranational body, in his case the League of Nations, would fail, ultimately leading to a second world war and then a very dangerous cold war.

The reason that the legacies of World War I extended far beyond ending the Congress of Vienna era and were the seeds of future conflicts remains obscured in plain sight. The Great War served as an unintentional but convenient extension of and accelerant to the phenomena of globalization and the diffusion of all forms of power, turning both into a collective deus ex machina. The effects would profoundly and irreversibly transform the future character, nature, and structure of global politics.

This transformation would weaken and begin dissolving the state-centric nature of international politics. The diffusion of power would empower individuals and nonstate actors with far greater means to influence, create, and affect events at the expense of traditional states. In this process, new threats and dangers to society would be created. And globalization and growing interconnectivity and interdependence among states and populations for trade, finance, investment, labor, and social interactions would further erode and complicate national sovereignty through greater external intrusions into domestic life.

Among these complications, governments now confront a seemingly endless array of intractable problems, from providing for the general welfare to protecting their publics against violent acts, whether of man or nature. As a result and irrespective of their democratic or autocratic character, most governments today are failing in the ability to govern. As the legitimacy and especially competence of even democratically elected governments are increasingly challenged, history is not being kind to those states that have been unable to respond accordingly.

Had Ferdinand not visited the hospital where wounded from an unsuccessful bombing attempt against the entourage earlier that day were recovering; had the driver not made a wrong turn that afternoon; or had the archduke's open touring car been armored—who knows what might have happened differently. But, of course, none of those possibilities happened.

Even sophisticated observers at the time failed to recognize the legacies of the murders. Today, these legacies are often ignored or blamed on other factors. As with many great events, Premier Zhou was correct. The full effects and consequences of this erosion of the Westphalian system have still not fully emerged into public view a century later.

Neither the concept of globalization nor the diffusion of power is new or was considered new in 1914. However, catalyzed by the assassination and war, both would eventually create replacements for the infamous riders of the apocalypse. Simply put, a century later the old horsemen have been replaced by four new riders, riders who represent the greatest dangers and threats to the international order and peace, prosperity, and stability.

The first new rider is failed or failing government from Afghanistan to Zimbabwe, with virtually all other nations in between, the United States topping that list, at least among advanced states.

The second rider comprises economic despair, disparity, and disruption.

The third rider is radical and violent ideology, often provoked by and aligned with religious extremism.

The fourth rider is environmental calamity and climate change.

All the riders race at the speed of light, connected by the Internet and information technologies instantly available to vast numbers, irrespective of physical location. These horsemen did not spring instantly into existence, as mythology claims the goddess Aphrodite emerged from Zeus' brow. Nor have the range, interconnectivity, and complexity of the issues facing governments and publics multiplied overnight. These riders took decades to mature. The horsemen should be the strategic centers of gravity and focal points for politicians and publics alike in providing good government. But that is not the case. Instead, and indeed, current (American) strategic thinking is still grounded in the twentieth century, and the riders remain distant if not invisible to both observers and officials in high office.

Recognition of the decline, possibly the end, of the Westphalian system and the assaults on state sovereignty has not yet taken hold. Governments and citizens face the twenty-first century with mind-sets and experiences often fixed in the past. A key belief or unspoken assumption, perhaps by default, is that nearly four hundred years of the state-centric Westphalian system will remain the basis for the conduct of international politics for decades and possibly centuries to come.

An alarming conclusion and warning must be heeded. The intellectual and organizational foundations for the conduct of both geo- and domestic politics must reflect this dramatically different world. Unless the still partially hidden consequences of the archduke's assassination are fully assimilated, peace, prosperity, and stability will remain as elusive as they were on the early afternoon of June 28, 1914.

1

Globalization and the Diffusion of Power

A t a time when monarchs, princes, and presidents were regularly targeted for assassination, a handful of bullets killed an archduke and his pregnant wife in the Balkan city of Sarajevo. The deaths became the casus belli for World War I. Many fine histories have been written to explain how a tragic but seemingly minor event had such a shattering impact, disrupting and fundamentally reshaping the trajectory of history. Tens of millions were killed. The seeds of a second world war were laid. Two and a half decades later, World War II would bring even greater destruction. And that monumental conflict would be followed by a cold war that could have annihilated much of mankind.

In 2014, legacies from a century ago have transformed politics and society. The notion of state sovereignty has been challenged by globalization's breaching of once-sacrosanct international borders. Trade, investment, the electron, and the Internet, among other daily manifestations of human intercourse, recognize few boundaries.

To suggest an even more stunning change, bullets like those fired a century ago to kill a lone archduke today no longer need to be aimed at a particular victim to have great effect. In fact, no direct relationship or causal connection between targets and assassins may be needed to provoke crises and even wars. An impoverished and desperate Tunisian street vendor could set himself afire and precipitate the so-called Arab Awakening. That act of desperation demonstrates this phenomenon and the differences that separate the twenty-first century from the past. But governments are still largely unprepared for and unable to respond proactively to such unexpected events.

The deus ex machina is globalization and the broad diffusion of all forms of power, accelerated over the last few decades by the information and electronic revolutions. Both revolutions provide unprecedented global and instantaneous access via computers, smart phones, and the Internet. Beginning in 1914 and the Great War, these forces have over decades eroded, challenged, and transformed the 350-year-old Westphalian structure of international politics based on state-centric relations.

In large part this transformation has been driven by the empowerment of individuals and nonstate actors with far greater influence, authority, and power, at the expense of traditional states, for which they were once reserved. As globalization binds many disparate states and regions more closely, many laws, rules, and regulations that once were limited by borders have become borderless. This phenomenon has been amplified by the complexity and intrusiveness of extraterritorial-governmental controls, rules, and regulations covering the conduct of business, economic relations, and international intercourse, all challenging the concept of sovereignty.

In the past, when disputes became politically or diplomatically unresolvable, the ultimate arbiter was military force. Wars, large or small, were controlled and won or lost by states. Revolutionaries of the day had to seize control of government first, through a coup d'état or an insurrection, in order to win and exercise power through the mechanism of the state. Examples included America in 1776, France in 1789, Russia in 1917, and Germany in 1933. In the twenty-first century, the Westphalian model wherein states maintain sole or total control over the use of force is no longer essential or a prerequisite for the outbreak of a major conflict or war.

War by accident or miscalculation has been a persistent historical theme. But what happens when the state no longer exerts full control over the use of force and the principal adversary (or adversaries) has no organized army, navy, or air force, and yet war still breaks out? Those possibilities challenge the Westphalian state-centric political order to its core.

Unlike the past, when armies, navies, and later air forces, with their huge armored formations, warships, and fighter aircraft, were the tools of war, today ideas and ideologies have become the new weapons of choice. The reason is that ideas and ideologies do not require military strength equivalent in kind or in number. The irony is striking. How do the most powerful armies and navies defeat enemies that have no military forces? This question forms today's major geostrategic contradiction.

As Lenin and many authoritarian rulers before him realized, the purpose of terror is to terrorize. Violence and terror do not need armies to be effective. In fighting a war of ideas, even the strongest militaries in history cannot alone guarantee a successful outcome against adversaries who lack powerful militaries, who are disciplined around ideas and ideologies, and who use terror and violence to achieve their ends. The recent wars in Iraq, Afghanistan, and against global terror have shown agonizingly that vastly dominant armies are not sufficient to ensure victory, no matter how defined.

In its study of the global war against terror a decade ago, the Pentagon's prestigious Defense Science Board issued a prescient warning to the secretary of defense, Donald Rumsfeld. The only way to win the war on terror was to win the war of ideas, "*and* [emphasis mine] the U.S. is losing the war of ideas."

Throughout this transformational and perhaps revolutionary period, the major threats to peace, security, stability, and prosperity have been radically altered. These have shifted away from state-centric, nation-versus-nation politics and conflicts to other, more immediate, ubiquitous, and yet discrete dangers. Unfortunately, the only thing more difficult than teaching a bureaucracy to unlearn an idea is to teach it to learn a new one.

State-versus-state conflicts and wars have not been made obsolete by this transformation. But the reach and influence of nonstate actors and individuals have been magnified by this diffusion of power. While state-versus-state conflict cannot be ignored or dismissed, the old Westphalian system will not alone suffice as the basis for ensuring future peace, prosperity, or stability in the international system.

Some wars start for trivial, even foolish, reasons; others arise from irreconcilable strategic, political, or economic clashes over incompatible interests, or personal, cultural, ethnic, or religious misunderstandings, animosities, and hatreds. Aristotle believed that love, greed, and honor were fundamental causes of war.

History has never lacked reasons, ranging from ideology to idiocy and incompetence, to send armies and navies and later air forces into battle. Unique in history and of immediate concern is that many of today's potentially explosive modern archdukes, however inconsequential or trivial, no longer need an obvious or immediate combustible mixture, or even 9 mm parabellum bullets, to generate a spontaneous catalytic event like that of June 1914. These archdukes or, to mix metaphors, fuses need not in essence bring with them, or create their own, fuel for conflagration in order to detonate unexpected or unintended explosions.

The now-famous Tunisian street vendor self-immolates, and a revolution breaks out across the Arab Maghreb, causing a succession of dictators and autocrats to fall from power. An inadvertent burning of Korans in Kabul erupts into massive demonstrations of protest throughout Afghanistan that threaten the government's stability. A video of a young Pakistani woman being beaten in Swat provokes a military offensive to punish the offending Taliban.

A rogue trader in Paris nearly collapses one of Europe's oldest banks. East Asia's most powerful states contest a few specks of rock in the South China Sea, their respective military forces operating in potentially dangerous proximity. In each single event there is nothing immediately earthshattering. However, taken collectively, these individual and often simultaneously occurring events are symptomatic of the post–post–Cold War world, or what President George H. W. Bush meant by "a new world order" over two decades ago.

In an interconnected and instantly wired world, will seemingly insignificant events, perhaps deemed unworthy as news, produce disproportionately large, possibly uncontrollable effects? If the answer is yes, that marks a major departure from the last century, when state-led aggression was the major cause of war. Hitler's 1939 invasion of Poland, Japan's attack on Pearl Harbor in 1941, Korea in 1950, the Tonkin Gulf incident (which proved largely invented) in 1964, and Iraq's invasion of Kuwait in 1990 were the principal instigators of war in the last century. Despite many who blame World War I on German ambitions, that war was a relevant exception to the pattern of the past century. The war was started not by a major military attack or extreme political crisis but by a lone assassin and a handful of bullets.

Today, the explosive fuse for igniting a crisis, or worse, does not need to be directly connected to a triggering event. The modern equivalent to the bullets that killed the archduke and his wife are far too plentiful, and they exist not only kinetically but also in cyberspace, with potentially devastating effect.

The likelihood of major conventional war, including contingencies in Iran, North Korea, the South China Sea, India and Pakistan, and conceivably Ukraine, cannot be ignored. In addition to dealing with these fairly obvious possible crises that threaten the international order, what can be done to identify potential archdukes and separate them from destructive bullets they might fire from unexpected directions or at entirely different targets?

Against this transformational context, is the international community capable of dealing with the often hostile and destructive effects wrought by the empowerment of individuals and groups? If this empowerment neutralizes or overwhelms the state-centric system for traditional politics and diplomacy, can that force be overcome? If not, the utility and relevance of the Westphalian state system will indeed decline. The answers are central to determining the safest and surest means for navigating these very unexplored, dangerous, and uncharted waters.

The ability of the Westphalian system to nurture peace, stability, and prosperity as inoculations against violence, chaos, and disruption is further impeded and complicated by another factor. Today's international order remains a legacy, in many ways a relic of the post–World War II era and the Cold War. The United Nations (UN), World Bank, International Monetary Fund, and the North Atlantic Treaty Organization (NATO), among others, grew out of World War II and the Cold War. Not even such newer structures such as the G-20 et al., the World Trade Organization, the Shanghai Cooperative Organization (SCO), and other regional organizations have fully offset the need for a twenty-first-century international order and structure. And the effectiveness of these newer organizations is limited by the first of the new Four Horsemen, failed and failing governance in states most vital to and responsible for contributing to international cooperation.

At best, the current international structure is barely sufficient to cope with the dynamic dangers, challenges, and uncertainties of the twenty-first century. Hence, while opportunities for advancing the common good persist in theory, they are marginalized or negated in practice by dramatic changes to the current international system. In particular, the absence, produced by globalization and the diffusion of power, of effective or even partially effective governance is a major danger. Similar limitations and organizational dysfunctions apply domestically: the results of failed and failing government have no geographic limitations and, sadly, seem to be becoming ubiquitous.

WHITE HOUSE PERSPECTIVES: 1914, 1954, AND 2014

In many ways, the first years of the twentieth century were reaffirmation of a golden age and what was then considered an unprecedented era of progress. The Congress of Vienna maintained the peace among the great European powers despite the revolutions of 1848, the Crimean War, the unification of Germany and Italy, and the Franco-Prussian war of 1870–71. Naval arms races and crises between great powers over colonies and possessions were unsettling. But the Spanish-American War of 1898 and the Russo-Japanese War of 1904–1905 had been resolved. And the intermarriages of so many noble European families augured well for peace trumping war.

Technology and trade were transforming the world, as globalization brought states closer. In New York, London, or Paris, the affluent had the world virtually at their immediate disposal, or not far from it. Underwater telegraph cables linked distant continents with news and information in matters of moment, and steamships could cross vast chunks of the Atlantic and Pacific Oceans in days, not weeks, covering more than four hundred nautical miles a day.

Electricity was lighting cities. Railways had taken the industrial revolution to higher levels. Airplanes had crossed the English Channel, and pilots were eying the day when transatlantic flight would be possible. Cars were replacing horses, eliminating what New York's governing fathers had believed in 1880 was the city's major environmental problem—removal of what was politely called "horse pollution." Radio was making its debut, soon to be followed by television and even talking movies. Einstein was conjuring up concepts that would lead to the nuclear age.

Henry Ford, J. P. Morgan, John D. Rockefeller, and Andrew Carnegie led the second and third industrial revolutions, while robber barons made fortunes that would dwarf the richest and most successful hedge-fund managers of today. Steel, electricity, automobiles, oil, and investment banking turned the United States in the early twentieth century into the richest country on earth and established there a large, comfortable, and well-paid middle class. Interestingly, both Carnegie and Rockefeller spent the latter parts of their lives giving away their fortunes. Warren Buffet and Bill Gates have taken notice, and perhaps Jeff Bezos, Sergey Brin, and Mark Zuckerberg should too!

Globalization was real and the subject of conferences in London and other capitals. Indeed, economic interdependence in Europe, along with intermarriages among royal ruling families, led to the publication of Nobel laureate Sir Norman Angell's *The Great Illusion*. Angell argued that because war was so costly as to be unaffordable, conflicts in Europe would be settled short of sending armies and navies into battle.

But by June 1914 the golden age was crumbling. Europe seemed bent on a war no one wanted. Up to that point, senior diplomats in Paris had regarded the unfolding crises in the Balkans as "serious but not yet desperate." In Berlin, the view was more cynical—conditions were described as "desperate but not fully serious." The assassination of Archduke Ferdinand in Sarajevo in June ignited the gathering explosive forces in Europe. Whether or not an "invisible" bullet fired by a modern-day Gavrilo Princip, the archduke's assassin, can strike with commensurate, if not necessarily as swift, effect remains to be seen.

The reasons why World War I was tragically unavoidable are well known. Close ties among the European ruling royal families through blood or marriage were common. Intense and unhealthy competition had flourished over colonies, as well as naval arms races and the pursuit of power and influence. Great rivalries among the powers had been sealed through secret treaties and alliances. These treaties made war inevitable through promises of military responses to thwart attack against or invasion of a signatory.

The rapid victory of Prussia over France in 1871 was made possible by the leading technologies of the day (including railways to speed troops to the front, machine guns and breach-loading artillery, and later combustion engines). That led to a dangerous and wrong military conclusion, that mobilization was the key to victory. He who mobilized first, given the lessons of the 1870–71 war, almost certainly was going to defeat and even rout the enemy. Thus, European armies planned on mobilizing rapidly and on employing the advantage of striking first—a lesson the Japanese learned as well.

Germany produced the Schlieffen Plan that would be the basis for waging war against France. This was a powerful right hook by the Wehrmacht through Belgium and France. To ensure victory, the general for whom the plan was named demanded that the German soldier on the far right wing of the assault brush his sleeve in the English Channel. General Helmuth von Moltke, Schlieffen's successor, modified the plan to strike south. France responded with Plan XVII, envisaging a swift attack directly into Germany through Lorraine. But victory hinged on mobilizing and striking first—exactly the wrong lessons drawn from 1871.

Illusions of swift victory turned into the horrors of trench war. Tens of thousands of casualties on both sides were common in the first hours of many attacks and counterattacks. Stalemate became a bloody battle of attrition, destroying a generation of European youth. Worse, the subsequent armistice and peace merely deferred the next war for twenty years.

Perhaps World War I could have been avoided. Perhaps the secret treaties and agreements to perpetuate the continuation of the major regimes in Europe could have been more transparent. Perhaps the Congress of Vienna could have lasted another century. Had World War I not occurred, who knows whether Adolph Hitler would have been a forgotten painter or Joseph Stalin a third-rate bank robber? But war destroyed much of Europe and began the dissolution of the Westphalian system. And the forces of globalization and the diffusion of power probably would have persisted with uncertain consequences and perhaps would have accelerated had war not broken out.

Regardless, on June 28, 1914, President Woodrow Wilson was in his second year in office. The nation had recovered from the financial crises of 1907 (precipitated by the precursors of "credit default swaps" [CDSs], which would have even more devastating effects almost a century later and, interestingly, were outlawed because of the 1907 panic). The Aldrich-Vreeland Act, creating the National Currency Commission, passed in 1908 would help stabilize the coming global financial crisis of 1914, which would be caused by the archduke's assassination and mobilization for war.

Women would soon be allowed the vote. The nation's entire GDP for a population of about a hundred million in then-year dollars was $37 billion, or about $848 billion in 2013 dollars. A breakdown of spending then with today reveals profoundly different priorities.

Total federal spending in 1914 dollars was about $1 billion ($23 billion in 2013 dollars), of which defense received $426 million ($9.9 billion in 2013 dollars). Total health-care spending for government and the public was $124 million ($2.8 billion in 2013 dollars); education, $657 million ($15.3 billion in '13 dollars); pensions, $8 million ($186 million in '13 dollars); and welfare, $62 million ($1.4 billion in '13 dollars). And the total national debt was less than 10 percent of GDP, or about $2.9 billion ($67 billion in '13 dollars). All figures have been drawn from the U.S. Treasury and other government records.

News of the assassination of the archduke would have been carried by underwater cable and telegraph and probably delivered to Wilson at the White House in a Model T Ford. The spread of news was not instantaneous; it was limited by technology, as radio and television were in their infancies. Cell phones, the Internet, and satellite communications were beyond the comprehension of even the most creative writers, including H. G. Wells. When news did arrive, the White House was a far different place than it is today.

The concept of the presidency and its importance was far from imperial, as it would later become. Armed guards and security fences and barriers were inconceivable. Access into 1600 Pennsylvania did not require background checks or advanced electronic screening of private data. Nor did legions of reporters vie for access to the president. The building immediately adjacent to the West Wing contained virtually the entire staffs for the State, War, and Navy Departments, with Treasury nearby.

Wilson's "war cabinet" consisted of the secretary of state, the secretaries and military chiefs of the Army and the Navy, and a few trusted advisors. The nation was uninterested in foreign affairs. Despite the power of international economic globalization, for three years Wilson would steer the nation away from war in Europe. Congress played a lesser role in foreign policy, so much so that it was ignored. Wilson would learn that that was a mistake to his great regret after the Versailles Peace conference in 1919 and the Senate's rejection of the peace treaty creating the League of Nations.

The tools Wilson had at his disposal were traditional diplomatic and military policy instruments. The U.S. Army numbered fewer than 100,000 soldiers; the Navy sailed some 127 ships. Intelligence in the form of spying and intrusive surveillance was highly personnel intensive. The tapping of underwater telegraph cables, as well as code breaking, persisted. However, it was thought, as a future secretary of state would remark, that "gentlemen do not read other gentlemen's mail." How quaint that sounds today. Electronic surveillance is routinely conducted by many intelligence-gathering agencies. And the leaks about the massive phone-tapping programs America's National Security Agency (NSA) have threatened U.S.-European relations.

If the events had provoked American entry into the war in 1914, mobilizing sufficient forces would have taken months. True, Teddy Roosevelt had made the "Great White Fleet" into a global navy. However, the Army was hard pressed in 1916 and 1917 to capture and punish bandits and insurgents operating in Mexico and on the U.S. side of the Rio Grande. Despite a one-sided victory against helpless Spain in 1898, the Army and Navy were far from prepared to fight and win a major war in Europe.

THE WHITE HOUSE IN 1954

Forty years later, barely a decade after World War II ended, baby boomers were just reaching their early teens. The sound barrier was regularly broken, and space flight was about to begin. Black-and-white television was soon to be replaced by color. The "box" was transforming American society. Visual images, some in real time, had the power to move or change attitudes and ultimately the nature of politics.

In the United States, women had long been granted the right to vote, and barriers to integration of the races were being dismantled. The major security threat was entirely Westphalian in character. The Soviet Union was the successor to fascism, aided by its junior partner, China. President John F. Kennedy had not yet made the promise to pay any price and bear any burden to support the cause of freedom.

Strategic thought of the time focused on deterring and containing the main communist threats. Ike fashioned a doctrine of "massive retaliation" propounded by his viscerally anti-Soviet secretary of state, John Foster Dulles. Massive retaliation meant that if the Soviets started a war, the nuclear and thermonuclear superiority of the United States would destroy the Soviet Union, killing much of its population. In addition to NATO, created in 1949, Ike would build a series of military alliances beyond Europe, extending through the Middle East to South and Southeast Asia, as a further bulwark against communist aggression.

The Eisenhower years were even then considered "happy days." The Great Depression and World War II were over. Despite the onset of the Cold War, most Americans enjoyed the benefits of a booming economy. Millions bought their first television sets and second cars. Transistor radios were the latest technology. Young people went to drive-in movies or malt shops, wearing the latest fashions— pegged pants for men, poodle skirts for women.

Eisenhower faced important and controversial domestic issues involving critical choices between maintaining prosperity and spending on infrastructure. Civil rights would become an urgent national issue. In 1954, the population was about 162 million.

GDP was $380 billion ($3.3 trillion in 2013 dollars). Total debt was $278 billion ($2.35 trillion in '13 dollars). And federal spending totaled $78 billion ($678 billion in '13 dollars). Defense spending was $52 billion ($452 billion in '13 dollars); pensions, $7 billion ($61 billion in '13 dollars); education and health care, about $1 billion each ($8.7 billion in '13 dollars).

When Winston Churchill visited Eisenhower in Washington, NATO was always high on the agenda. NATO was directed solely against the Soviet military threat. The heart of the alliance was Article 5 of the Washington Treaty, which declared that an attack against one was an attack against all.

In discussions, had the two wartime leaders and friends been asked when Article 5 would first be invoked and where NATO would find itself at war, the answer would have been unequivocal: in response to a Soviet and Warsaw Pact attack on the north German plain. If Churchill and Eisenhower had magically materialized a half-century later in Washington, both would have been stunned. NATO's first ground war would not be in Europe.

Article 5 was invoked for the first time in its history in response to the September 11, 2001, attacks against the World Trade Center buildings in New York. Led by its very able secretary-general, (now Lord) George Robertson, NATO unanimously came to America's aid the very next day. Soon thereafter, NATO forces joining the International Security Assistance Force (ISAF) would be at war in faraway Afghanistan. One suspects Churchill and Eisenhower would have registered utter disbelief over a war so far removed from the NATO Guideline Areas (i.e., Europe) and against a radical religious Taliban-led government. As, or more, staggering to the great men would have been the implosion of the Soviet Union a decade before. Even more bizarre, Kabul is slightly closer to Brussels than Brussels is to Washington, a geographic fact that would have added to the incredibility of NATO fighting its first ground war in Afghanistan.

Before the fast-forward to 2014, the reach of the diffusion of power needs more mention. Technology has been a major driver of the diffusing of power. The revolution in information technology provided instant global communications. These technologies also provided critical means for empowering individuals and nonstate actors. This empowerment has been one of the game changers of the twenty-first century.

That empowerment will grow in large measure because of Moore's law. Gordon E. Moore predicted that computing capacity doubles every eighteen to twenty-four months. That means all prior accumulated knowledge of history doubles in about the same time period. Much of this knowledge may not be usable. However, unlimited access to virtually all known information and knowledge is available to any computer connected to the Internet.

Research that took years to disseminate in prepared papers and other forms now circulates at the speed of light. For those so inclined, knowledge from how to manufacture a nuclear weapon to an improvised explosive device (IED) is a few computer strokes away. That all this knowledge is available and is increasing exponentially in amount is not the issue. Rather, this explosion of knowledge ultimately has empowered individuals and nonstate actors by providing both access and means for advancing and announcing their aims, aspirations, and interests.

The economic diffusion of power has been more visible, incorporating trade, investment, finance, and other forms of mercantile intercourse. Businesses and individuals have become more global and indeed more dependent on the global economy. President Barack Obama's strategic pivot to Asia, analyzed later, reflected the growing economic strength of Pacific states and, in particular, China and India. Ironically, and in many ways, Norman Angell's argument of a century ago about economic interdependence constraining the likelihood of major war may prove valid today.

Political diffusion of power is occurring at all levels. The Arab Awakening and the overthrow of authoritarian governments are examples. In Ukraine at the time of writing, intense reaction against President Viktor Yanukovych's decision to turn to Russia rather than move closer to the European Union shows the impact of the diffusion of political power. Indeed, it is quite bizarre to see on television thousands of Ukrainians wrapped with European Union rather than Ukrainian flags.

The diffusion of military power is another interesting phenomenon. Throughout history, the spread of weapons and the role of "merchants of death" who sold everything from bayonets to battleships to the highest bidder were commonplace. World War I and the interwar years were high-water marks in bringing public attention on the arms trade.

In the twenty-first century, a major collective international aim has been preventing the spread of weapons of mass destruction (WMD) and containing so-called rogue governments that have been branded as the new "merchants of death" in this field. Fear of WMD proliferation is real and understandable. But fear of WMD has possibly been exaggerated, and the term itself is misleading.

WMD include chemical, biological, and nuclear weapons. Chemical weapons are more limited in scope, because damage and death can be caused only by direct contact. No matter how horrible, chemical weapons are no worse than being burned to ashes by white phosphorous or napalm or being blown to bits by high explosives. And the physical area in which chemical weapons kill or maim is not necessarily any greater than the damage-imposing capacity of conventional munitions. Biological weapons are profoundly different, however.

The equivalents of biological weapons obviously exist in nature. Throughout history, plagues and epidemics have killed millions or even billions. The Spanish flu killed approximately fifty million. More recently the Asian flu and other diseases have easily spread from continent to continent, carried by unsuspecting, infected air travelers and in some cases by wildlife. Thus, as in nature, man-made biological agents are indeed potential weapons of mass destruction.

The most destructive WMD are nuclear. Firebombs and conventional explosives killed more Japanese during World War II on a given night than did the nuclear attacks on Hiroshima and Nagasaki. But the former required hundreds of bombers and thousands of bombs, the latter a single airplane and bomb. Those nuclear weapons were measured in the range of kilotons of explosives—around the equivalent of 15,000 tons of high explosive for each atom bomb.

For half a century, however, thermonuclear weapons have existed with explosive forces equivalent to mega- (millions of) tons of TNT. Thermonuclear weapons have existential potential capable of destroying society as we know it. And radiation contamination is a devastating legacy, as plutonium's half-life is about 24,000 years.

Counter- and anti-proliferation have become major priorities of most states as antidotes to this form of diffusion of power. More will be said about North Korean and Iranian nuclear intentions. At present, efforts to disarm and destroy Syria's chemical-weapons stockpile and infrastructure appear to be moving ahead.

The spread of conventional weapons continues. The West, meaning the United States and NATO, and their Asian allies will continue to develop conventional weapons that will be the best in the world. China is spending more on defense, largely on personnel costs. Developing capable defense industries comparable with the West will take time for China, even as the West is spending considerably less on defense.

While the prospects for conventional war, including contingencies in Korea or in the Persian Gulf vis-à-vis Iran, or an intervention in the Middle East, cannot be dismissed, adversaries such as al Qaeda and other terrorist organizations will not slacken efforts to obtain both advanced weapons and more destructive technologies. Nuclear weapons are probably beyond their reach, although stealing or buying a device is something intelligence agencies will regard as a critical agenda issue. Car bombs and IEDs continue to show that cheap and readily available materials can be highly destructive and highly cost-effective. Innovative use of cyber as well as new terrorist tactics can be developed using off-the-shelf technology. Access to small arms and explosives can never be prevented. Drone technology can never be kept out of the hands of adversaries or terrorist organizations. Over time, the hope that terrorists will not employ drone technology will prove false.

As a result, globalization and the diffusion of power are dual edged. Industrialization and modernization have enhanced standards of living in many less-developed and even primitive states. But industrialization has increased pollution. Factories require energy sources, and energy sources ultimately pour trillions of tons of carbon dioxide and other pollutants into the atmosphere, with obviously deleterious and dangerous consequences.

The all-purpose and ubiquitous cell phone and Internet introduced and connected billions of people to global affairs; distance and hostile terrain no longer blocked access to the wider world. Videos and pictures of even the most primitive of countries, cities, and their citizens are filled with images of satellite dishes mounted on roofs and people constantly on cell phones. All of these factors make 2014 a far more complicated and complex time for governments.

THE WHITE HOUSE IN 2014

Today, the president governs, if that is a fair description, a nation of about 320 million citizens. GDP is about $17 trillion, compared with about $900 billion (in current dollars) in 1914, a real increase of about twenty times. Government spending is about $3.7 trillion. Of that, national security and defense receive about $850 billion; pensions (Social Security), $878 billion; health care, $880 billion; education, $96 billion; and welfare, $430 billion. Total national debt is about $17 trillion. Comparisons with 1914 in magnitude and percentages—noticeably declines in education and increases in all other categories—make the point about how much the structure and priorities of American society have changed.

Suppose the equivalent of the archduke's assassination took place today. That would be an important but not necessarily even a pressing headline in the president's morning intelligence brief. Events such as the civil war in Syria, even as Syrian chemical weapons are being destroyed and dismantled, which continues to kill thousands and threatens to unravel the region, get top billing. Libya is unsettled, and violence in Africa has hastened the deployment of U.S. Special Forces.

Negotiations with Iran to limit it from obtaining nuclear weapons remain in a fragile state. The Senate threatened to pass a bill mandating sanctions should negotiations fail, which would have limited the president's negotiating flexibility. Huge Republican opposition at home continued against granting any slack to Tehran in advance of its unilaterally foregoing weapons ambitions.

Violence in Iraq ravages that country. President Hamid Karzai of Afghanistan was unwilling to sign the Basic Security Agreement (BSA). Hence, planning for allied follow-on forces post-2014 was needlessly complicated. Turning security over to Afghan forces did not offer an answer as to who would pay their annual $5 billion bill.

Tensions over tiny specks of land in the South and East China Seas flare among China, Japan, Taiwan, and South Korea. North Korea's leader, Kim Jong-un, executed his uncle—possibly after a failed coup attempt. Southern Sudan is in flames. Egypt is incapable of fully restoring democracy, as insurgencies grow in the Sinai and the former ruling Muslim Brotherhood is designated a terrorist organization. And Russian absorption of Crimea did not help.

Beyond the daily intelligence briefing, a bevy of domestic crises flood the president's desk. In late 2013, the disastrous rollout of the Affordable Care Act, the president's major legislative accomplishment, preoccupied the White House. That law was the battleground in a continuing fight with Republican attempts to repeal. While the economy showed signs of improvement, growth was fragile and disparities between rich and poor widened. And the 2014 election loomed large, as Democrats fought to keep the Senate and Republicans battled to win both houses of Congress.

Welcome to the world of 2014!

Returning to the postulated assassination—if immediate action were required, President Obama would have the capacity to move military forces and use other tools at his disposal within minutes. Under most circumstances, the president could have real-time information on that event. Conceivably, any onlooker possessing a cell phone could stream live video and see it "go viral." Tens of millions of global citizens could see the killing in real time. Obama's advisors would span a government that was orders of magnitude larger, more complicated, and in many ways far less coordinated and more dysfunctional than in 1914 and even 1954. Further, the media and especially Congress would play more influential and intrusive roles.

Were it necessary, the president could rely on overhead surveillance from spy satellites, electronic surveillance systems, and drones relaying in real time gigabytes of information and images directly to the White House Situation Room. And the military and paramilitary forces available to the president are as different from and more capable than those of 1914 as Wilson's army was with respect to Roman phalanxes.

Today's military budget is about the same size, unadjusted for inflation, as Wilson's entire federal budget. With about 1.3 million active-duty personnel and another million in National Guard and reserve forces, the U.S. military is some twenty-five-fold bigger than the Army of 1914. Today's military has capabilities unthinkable even a few decades, let alone a century, ago.

Supersonic stealthy aircraft, nuclear submarines, satellite communications and surveillance, and precision strikes are among these capabilities. America's professional military is highly experienced. Despite the effects of budget cuts and sequestration, which will be discussed, that military remains the most capable in the world. President Obama also has allies and organizations, such as the UN and NATO, with whom to work that were unavailable to Wilson. Instantaneous video teleconferencing means the president could talk to and see other leaders in capitals thousands of miles away. And the "bully pulpit" Teddy Roosevelt loved to climb today confronts the double-edged sword of television and worldwide coverage, as well as minute inspection and dissection.

Despite these order-of-magnitude technological advances, instantaneous communications bring limitations. Global media are actively engaged and enjoy good access; they often have reporters and cameras on the ground in advance of governments. Congress plays a critical and far more active and intimate role. Obama must work within the confines of the War Powers Act and limits on presidential power that neither Wilson nor Ike faced until Wilson's proposed League of Nation was rejected by a Senate he had purposely ignored.

The Internet would immediately generate countless blogs, bloggers, and stories, many barely of rumor quality. Yet, rumors often gain credence simply by being posted online. Social media from Twitter to Facebook connect millions and one day billions to comment and pontificate on any event. Disinformation and outright deception by individuals, where those devices had once been the sole domain of states, confuse and confound interpretation and analysis of what courses of action can or should not be undertaken.

Wilson and Eisenhower understood the threat of likely retaliation in international politics. Wilson did not have to deal with threat of societal annihilation in a thermonuclear war, the prospect that underwrote deterrence during the Cold War. Ike did. And Obama does not.

Today, globalization offers a greater range of policy tools than were available in 1914 or 1954. Economies are dependent on the free flow of goods, services, and money. Because of globalization, policy tools and options such as sanctions are likely to be more effective. For example, if Iran does agree to forego nuclear weapons, the painful effects of economic sanctions will have been a major factor in that decision.

Cyber and globalization are intimately related and pose issues that neither Wilson nor Ike had to address. Concerning national security, cyber provokes exquisitely intractable questions over the meaning of "war" when or if networks and operating systems are attacked. As will be argued, predictions of potential "cyber Pearl Harbors" and other catastrophic scenarios (such as destruction or impairment of power grids, banks, and other institutions vital to advanced societies) sit better in fiction and Hollywood action movies than in reality. Still, cyber has implications for national security that are far from resolved and that underscore the separation between 1914 and 2014.

Governing was never easy. Wilson's crises and problems then probably seemed as challenging as Obama's do today. Eisenhower enjoyed a smoother journey. But the sheer number, complexity, intractability, and relentless nature of today's issues are truly daunting. Comparing GDPs in 1914 with 2014 suggests the magnitude of today's complexities. Relating a dollar then with a dollar today is imperfect. Yet the difference is about twenty-fold—nearly $900 billion versus about $17 trillion in current dollars.

In terms of national security and international politics, three major transformations are clear, however. Societies in 1914 faced existential threats only when physically occupied by enemy armies (or overwhelmed by an environmental calamity). In 1954, the existential threat was thermonuclear devastation. In 2014, with the end of the Cold War and the Soviet Union, the threat of societal annihilation through man-made means has been replaced with the danger of major disruption. To use Cold War jargon, the threat of mass destruction has become one of mass disruption.

Second, because of globalization, the relative power of any single state has been curtailed. In 1914, power was balanced among the strongest countries, limiting what any one state could do alone. After World War II, the United States was the world's dominant power, possibly ever. That status has changed, perhaps dramatically. The United States remains the world's strongest military and economic power. Yet in the last decade China, India, and myriad other states have closed the economic gap.

Militarily, a third and quite unexpected situation, one that did not exist in 1914 or 1954, has emerged. Despite its military superiority, the United States has been unable to win the wars in Iraq and Afghanistan. Globalization and the diffusion of power have empowered individuals, often checkmating military force.

Military power is most effective when used against an adversary's military power. When the adversary uses ideas or narratives as its major weapons and applies them through acts of terror and violence, the cost-exchange ratio is grotesquely in favor of the enemy. This was a lesson that President Eisenhower understood and the French in Indochina did not. The United States had two opportunities to learn from Vietnam and did not. Ho Chi Minh understood that the strategic center of gravity for victory was in living and dining rooms, first in France in 1954, two decades later in middle America—not the rice paddies and jungles in South Vietnam.

The enemies in Iraq and Afghanistan also won their cost-exchange battle. It cost the United States orders of magnitude more money than the enemy had or would allocate to fighting America and its allies. The United States spent about $2 trillion on the wars in Iraq, Afghanistan, and against terror, let alone spilled blood.

In the battle to defeat IEDs the United States spent in excess of $70 billion. Added together, how much have all the explosive devices used against U.S. and coalition forces cost the enemy? That figure is at best in the millions. A billion is a thousand million. So who won that cost-exchange war?

A principal reason for these dramatic transformations has been the empowerment of nonstate actors and individuals. Gavrilo Princip could change the course of history. However, the empowerment of potentially unlimited numbers of people and nonstate actors is a profound game changer. Combined with growing numbers of regional ticking time bombs and hot spots, far more than a handful of bullets threaten stability now than in 1914.

Without firing a shot or committing an act of violence, two entirely obscure Americans have damaged American foreign policy and are doing potentially irreversible harm to American credibility. Bradley (and now Ms. Chelsea) Manning was a twenty-three-year-old Army private first class who leaked to the press, through an organization called Wikileaks, vast amounts of highly classified and sensitive material, including candid diplomatic cables with full detail of events, interviews, and other data meant only for very limited distribution.

Edward Snowden was then a thirty-year-old employee for the consulting firm Booz-Allen working under contract to the National Security Agency. Snowden leaked information about a massive government surveillance program that collected literally billions of phone and other records. Worse from a political perspective, the leaks revealed that the NSA had been tapping the phones of several leaders of governments friendly to the United States, in particular German chancellor Angela Merkel.

The reactions to and outbursts over both leaks were monumental. American credibility and trustworthiness were impeached. Virtually all governments conduct commercial espionage and surveillance of friends and allies as well as of potential adversaries. But the extent of American intrusion was a very unwelcome revelation. The Transatlantic Trade and Investment Partnership (TTIP), central to the Obama administration's economic agenda to create an Atlantic free-trade area, has fallen victim to these revelations. Chancellor Merkel, one of the original advocates of TTIP, is now less supportive because of America's tapping of her phone.

How many future Mannings or Snowdens are lurking is unknowable. Nor is the extent predictable to which cyber is and will be a principal vehicle for empowering individuals to commit acts of massive disruption. While a "cyber Pearl Harbor" may be exaggerated, through the Internet and social media, individuals are able to exercise influence for good or ill.

Al Qaeda and terrorist affiliates lack armies, navies, and air forces. True, many of their members are fighting as insurgents in Yemen, the Horn of Africa, Syria, Iraq, and other inhospitable locales. But it is not military strength that empowers them. And beware the ten-year-old hacker who is able to disrupt or take down significant parts of the Internet or infrastructure and the ability to conduct business!

Korea, India, Pakistan, Iran, the China seas, and the Middle East surely are potential grounds for further conflict. Wildcard and "black swan" events cannot be discounted or ignored. Russia's grab of Crimea raised critical concerns about the start of a new cold war as President Vladimir Putin defied international law and prior agreements (the Budapest Convention of 1994, which guaranteed non-interference in Ukraine in exchange for dismantling nuclear missiles). Whether Mr. Putin goes farther or not, certainly Eastern European states are concerned as to how Russia may act regarding their indigenous Russian populations. However, even given Crimea, the Westphalian state-centric system of politics no longer cleanly fits the range of contingencies and crises to be avoided or mitigated.

The largest and most important geostrategic distinctions between the worlds of Presidents Wilson, Eisenhower, and Obama are not the technological revolutions or the events that have reshaped history. The differences are, first, the challenges to the Westphalian state-centric system of politics and, second, the new horsemen. Threats that were once confined to states are now far more diffuse. Unless these dramatic differences are understood and incorporated into a mind-set for the twenty-first century, today's challenges to humanity and individual well-being will not be satisfactorily addressed. However, the intellectual and organizational foundations for this mind-set are not in place.

Will Americans listen to and heed this warning? Will America exercise its considerable brainpower and ingenuity to *think*, rather than attempt to spend, the nation out of danger, as has been its habit? And who then will emerge to lead, irrespective of whether anyone listens?

2

The New Four Horsemen

The New Testament is not entirely clear about the origins of the original Four Horsemen of the Apocalypse. The four riders were "white," "red," "black," and "pale." The first was linked to conquest and victory (although the evangelist Billy Graham believed this rider to be the Antichrist); the second with war and slaughter, hence the color of blood; the third with pestilence; and the last with death. Today, because of globalization and the diffusion of all forms of power, the biblical Four Horsemen have been transformed and replaced by new and possibly even more dangerous riders.

In my view, the most challenging dangers and threats to the collective well-being of mankind are represented by the first horseman, failed and failing government. Examples loom from Afghanistan to Zimbabwe, with Brussels (as the capital of the European Union) and Washington (as the seat of power for America) in between. Throughout history, states have ruled with varying degrees of competence. The inability of governments to govern has always been a critical issue.

Today, many governments, whether in the first or fourth worlds, are increasingly incapable of governing. Some are unable to provide their publics with basic needs—from safety, food, shelter, hygiene, and education to a sense of dignity. Others, such as the United States, have become dysfunctional and broken. Globalization and the diffusion of power, collectively the deus ex machina of the twenty-first century, are largely responsible. And as the Declaration of Independence so stunningly states, "whenever any Form of Government becomes destructive . . . it is the Right of the People to alter or abolish it, and to institute a new Government"—that is not a sentiment limited to the nineteenth century.

The second horseman comprises economic despair, disparity, and dislocation. Whether in the United States or the most backward states in the world, economic despair, disparity, and dislocation are powerful political forces. The current political debate in the United States over the economy is stalemated over whether to focus on income inequality or job creation. But as Rome figuratively burns, the American middle and underclasses find their standards of living in decline while the wealth of the top few continues to grow. How this impasse will be resolved is far from clear. But it is unlikely that the status quo will continue indefinitely, opening the prospect for many gloomy scenarios.

The third and fourth worlds (that is, respectively, developing states and populations effectively excluded from industrial society) are largely in dire economic shape. Consider Egypt. The World Bank observes that tens of millions of Egyptians live on less than two dollars a day. Even the most effective government would find addressing that stunning figure and moving so many Egyptians out of poverty impossible without the necessary resources. In Afghanistan, the absence of business law and property rights makes widespread economic development virtually impossible. Thus, Afghan peasant and tenant farmers turn to poppy, either to make their livings or on orders from warlords and criminals, refusal of whose orders could mean death—a threat most find persuasive.

The third horseman embraces radical ideologies, principally impelled by religious extremism. Islamic extremism is the most visible of these ideological threats as perceived by the West and by peaceful Muslims. But extremism has many faces. A radical Jew killed Israeli prime minister Yitzhak Rabin. And neo-Nazi and far-right-wing parties are becoming more commonplace in Europe.

Radical Islam has many faces. And it is difficult to define without giving insult, on one hand, or elevating extremism, on the other. The term *jihadi,* for example, is seen as a label of virtue to many in Islam and one of a terrorist by the West. The Shia-Sunni conflict is exacerbated by the Saudi-Iranian rivalry and by Salafism and Wahhabism, brands of extremism that the Saudis deny cultivating or exporting. Bin Laden's al Qaeda declared a holy war against infidels and false believers, including Shia, and perverted Islam to attract and motivate hundreds or thousands of Muslims to the cause of jihad. For many who have been excluded from a better life and a chance for dignity, or who have become motivated by desperation, the lure of jihad is seductive. As the Japanese regarded suicide as the ultimate sacrifice for the godlike emperor, al Qaeda promises that martyrdom is the path to virtue and heaven, arguments that take hold easily among people who are indeed desperate or wish to follow a cause.

The last rider represents environmental calamity and climate change. Acts of nature—tsunamis, hurricanes, earthquakes, famine, drought, disease, and other disasters—have had calamitous consequences. The Spanish flu of 1918 killed an estimated 50 million. Floods and droughts have claimed the lives of many millions. Katrina, "Super Sandy," the British Petroleum oil spill, earthquakes in China and Pakistan, and the tsunami and earthquake that obliterated much of Fukushima, Japan, unleashing radioactive contamination, are examples of current disasters. Another is the typhoon, with winds in excess of 240 miles per hour, that laid waste to a good part of the Philippines in late 2013.

The wildcard is climate change. Debate has focused on and politicized the issue of whether or not global warming is man-made. Facts count. Global temperatures are rising, with both a few positive and many negative, even catastrophic, effects. Obviously, greater global warming will mean reductions in the polar ice caps, increases in sea levels, and further creation of greenhouse gases.

On the other hand, a few regions that are arid could become more fertile. However, a provocative analogy is that of having the most comfortable cabin on board the *Titanic*. Climate change and global warming possess the potential to put the entire planet and its inhabitants in grave jeopardy, irrespective of cause. That possibility, no matter how remote, should—and the operative word is should—demand a rigorous analytical study to assess probabilities, consequences, and corrective actions. Tragically, such an effort will be virtually impossible under any government that is failing or has failed.

Failed and failing government remains the greatest danger and most widespread threat to mankind. The reasons flow in part from the effects of globalization and the diffusion of all forms of power, and they apply to almost all states, from the first (highly developed) to the fourth world. In essence, the complicated and complex nature of governing and governance has outstripped the ability of governments to keep pace. Their failure is exacerbated by interdependence, interconnectivity, and the porous nature (or disappearance) of virtually all borders. All political systems, from monarchies and autocratic regimes to democracies and meritocracies, have fundamental flaws and contradictions. Recognizing and reconciling these flaws has proven inordinately difficult, especially as the world grows more complex and interdependent. The United States is a case study in this regard.

Public understanding of the words "failed" and "failing" usually has been limited to third- and fourth-world states, ranging from Afghanistan to Zimbabwe. However, even the most advanced states suffer from failed or failing government. The United States is a prime and ironic example of how the most powerful and wealthiest state in the world can fall prey to this condition, and its situation is worsening. More follows on other failed and failing states. Because this book focuses on the United States, in order to propose solutions and policy prescriptions, it is imperative first to understand why and how the U.S. political system has become so dysfunctional and in many ways so broken.

The fundamental flaws and contradictions in the U.S. political system arise from its greatest strength—the constitutional mandates of divided and representative government and the balance of power, by which no branch alone has the authority to dominate the other two on a permanent basis. The aim of the Founding Fathers was to minimize the effectiveness and power of government in order to protect and maximize the freedom of individuals, a most noble aspiration of the late eighteenth century.

These inherent flaws and contradictions were understood by the founders. The solution, the way to contain these centrifugal effects, was compromise and ultimately the attraction of centrist politics to overcome political factionalism and divisive government. That the Constitution does not mention political parties is not accidental.

Article I belongs to the legislative, not the executive, branch, showing which arm of government the Founding Fathers meant to be first among equals. Legislative prominence worked at first, because of the splendid isolation afforded by two huge oceans. America was kept out of European wars and was able to pursue the unfettered exploitation of virtually unlimited natural resources. The original United States doubled and then tripled in size through brilliant territorial purchases and expansion westward. But the major constitutional contradictions— concerning states rights and the authority of the federal government—which could only be deferred, not resolved, in 1789 led to a civil war in 1861.

By the start of the twentieth century the United States would begin losing the advantage of that splendid isolation. As America became increasingly dependent on foreign trade and investment (and the explosive growth of the U.S. economy in the latter decades of the nineteenth century was largely financed by British and European banks), globalization would make it an international leader with growing responsibilities. World War I provided the first opportunity for America to undertake that role, after Teddy Roosevelt's earlier attempt to put the country on the world stage.

Following the Great War, the United States turned inward, in keeping with its history of conforming to President Washington's warning to steer clear of permanent alliances. The "Roaring Twenties" and the prosperity of the immediate postwar years, along with indifference to the turmoil in Europe and Asia, reinforced the preference for isolation. Interestingly, for much of the interwar period U.S. war plans were centered on Britain as the future enemy, suggesting a willing suspension of disbelief about what was transpiring in Germany, Japan, and Italy. The election of Franklin D. Roosevelt in 1932 and the looming crises in Europe occasioned by Hitler and in Asia by Japanese expansionism and militarism would end American isolationism and neutrality. On December 7, 1941, Japan's surprise attacks on U.S. forces in Hawaii and the Philippines forced America into the war.

World War II made the United States not merely a global superpower. America was the uncontested dominant global power by 1945 and perhaps the most dominant in history. Fortunately, America's better angels took hold, and in acts of supreme magnanimity and foresight, America began the rebuilding of Europe and Japan, allies and enemies alike, with the Marshall Plan. Isolationism was in remission, but isolationist strains persisted.

The United States went about shifting the vast economic and industrial war engine to peacetime pursuits. The GI Bill educated and would provide homes for millions of young Americans who had served in the war, generating intellectual capital that would last for a half-century and a housing boom to stimulate the postwar economy. In many ways, government was not as idyllic as often portrayed. But despite uneven economic growth and crises over race and later gender, the United States enjoyed an international reputation as a beacon of hope and opportunity and as the "leader of the free world."

The emergence of the new Four Horsemen would not come into better focus until well after the Cold War had ended. Similarly, the disintegration of the U.S. government and its political process has been a slow and painful process. World War II and the start of the Cold War began a period of so-called bipartisan foreign policy. Partisanship stopped, it was alleged, at the water's edge. In fact, this was a lovely myth. Republicans and Democrats took strong and often antithetical positions on foreign policy.

Republicans assailed President Harry Truman for not expanding the war in Korea after the People's Republic of China poured hundreds of thousands of its troops across the Yalu to halt the allied advance into North Korea in November 1950. The subsequent firing of General of the Army Douglas MacArthur over his failure to obey Truman's orders and his insistence on trying to involve the Nationalist Chinese (who had been driven to Formosa/Taiwan) in the war had significant political ramifications. Many Republicans pleaded with MacArthur to run for the presidency against Truman. The anticommunist paranoia of Senator "Tail Gunner" Joseph McCarthy of Wisconsin further divided the nation.

Eisenhower was among those to bend to McCarthyism. In seeking the Republican nomination for president in 1952, Ike chose not to defend General George Marshall, his wartime superior and mentor, from the senator's spurious and scandalous attacks. Sadly, Ike's political decision reflected the pernicious political atmosphere created by paranoia over communism and reluctance to invoke criticism prior to winning the nomination.

In 1960, presidential candidate Jack Kennedy used foreign policy to attack the Eisenhower administration as "soft" on communism. These allegations were based on ideological and emotional grounds rather than informed by fact and analysis, and they were used to differentiate the young and charismatic senator from his Republican opponent, Richard Nixon. Unfortunately, Kennedy's decision in his first days in office to challenge the Soviets and spark an arms race through huge increases in American military and nuclear might have possibly extended the Cold War by a decade or more. These and other examples challenge the conventional notion of a "bipartisan" foreign policy.

Between elections in the 1950s and 1960s, Congress and the president worked in less hostile, divisive, polarized, and zero-sum environments. One needed not be either "for us or against us." Republicans and Democrats in Congress regularly and socially intermingled. Democratic senator Lyndon Johnson's closest friend and colleague in the Senate was Republican Everett Dirksen. There were many examples of members of Congress reaching across the aisle to support the election of colleagues of the other party.

The Vietnam War began the disintegration of American politics and the dissolution of public belief in the credibility and honesty of government. The war bitterly divided the country. The leak of the Pentagon Papers and constant negative media coverage of the war convincingly demolished the optimistic assessments of both Democratic and Republican administrations. Respect for and trust in government fell.

The nation had to absorb Watergate and the resignations first of Vice President Spiro Agnew and then President Richard Nixon, followed by withdrawal from Vietnam and the first-time loss of a war. The exposure in the 1970s of Central Intelligence Agency (CIA) abuses by the Senate hearings chaired by Frank Church of Idaho (and by Otis Pike in the House) sent public trust in government to its lowest point since the Great Depression.

In Congress, younger Democrats rebelled against the "old bulls" who controlled the House, ending the seniority system. Experience mattered less in appointments to committee chairmanships, further loosening the grip of the party elders. Jimmy Carter defeated President Gerald Ford largely because of the Watergate debacle and Ford's presidential pardon of Nixon. Those and other failures of government to tell the truth led Carter to promise, "I will never lie to you."

Like JFK, Carter was unprepared for the presidency. Hit by double-digit inflation and interest rates, which collectively became known as the "misery index," the economy sputtered. Despite a strong national-security team, with Harold Brown as secretary of defense and Zbigniew Brzezinski as national security advisor, Carter was perceived as weak on foreign policy.

Carter was stunned by the Soviet invasion of Afghanistan in 1979 and said so publicly. He was made to look impotent by the seizure of the U.S. embassy in Tehran following the fall of the shah and the installation of the Ayatollah Khomeini as supreme leader. The much-publicized comment that Carter learned a lot about nuclear proliferation from a discussion with his very young daughter Amy did not help his image either. As a result, disdain and disrespect for government and the presidency that had arisen in the Nixon and post-Vietnam years were not diminished by and probably grew because of Carter's projection of moral superiority.

Meanwhile, the liabilities of FDR's New Deal and Social Security and of Lyndon Johnson's Great Society were accumulating. Life expectancies and the number of entitlement recipients rose. Social Security faced a funding crisis in the 1980s. President Ronald Reagan and Speaker of the House Tip O'Neill collaborated to create a commission that addressed and mitigated the looming problem for the short term. But entitlements would return with a vengeance with the turn of the millennium.

The Reagan and George H. W. Bush presidencies did not overcome partisanship. However, the demise of the Soviet Union, the battlefield success of the first

Gulf War, and economic policies (including tax hikes) that were producing prosperity tempered the fundamental tensions of a divided government. Unfortunately, Bill Clinton's administration would reopen partisan wounds and start the descent toward what would become truly broken government.

Few presidents have assumed office under such auspicious circumstances as Clinton enjoyed. George Bush had brilliantly overseen the dismantlement of the Soviet Union and had begun the process of creating a Europe "whole and free." His economic policies—despite his "read my lips, no new taxes"—were beginning to take hold, and the economy was on a fast upward trajectory. The U.S. military had distinguished itself and shed the memory of the Vietnam quagmire, smashing the fourth-largest army in the world in a hundred hours in the deserts of Kuwait and southern Iraq.

The 1990s were becoming the best of times for America. Unfortunately, Republican hostility toward Clinton was visceral. Clinton, who was portrayed as a womanizing, draft-dodging, pot-smoking candidate, had defeated a war hero and an effective president. In fact, third-party candidate Ross Perot had brought Bush down by taking away 19 percent of the vote. Clinton won with a plurality, not a majority, of the popular vote.

The attacks were vicious. During FDR's four terms, the president had been vilified as much as loved. Truman's popularity ratings had been among the lowest of any president. Adversaries had portrayed Ike as disengaged and not in charge. Had Kennedy lived, no doubt his image would have been tarnished, either by foreign-policy miscues or his reckless personal behavior. Yet the onset of the Clinton administration greatly and sadly accelerated the polarization of government and the breaking of the political process.

Bill Clinton's presidency initially soared; he entered office holding the proverbial royal flush. Much of that luck and goodwill were squandered in unsuccessful pursuit of his immediate priority, changing medical care, in an effort chaired by his wife, Hillary. In Clinton's second term, it took seventy-eight days and NATO's first miniwar to force Serbian president Slobodan Milosevic to withdraw his forces from Kosovo and stop his ethnic killing. That it took so long reflected an abdication of will and strategic competence. Sadly, Clinton's affair with a young White House intern stained his presidency. After impeachment by the partisan, Republican-controlled House of Representatives and a disgracefully embarrassing trial in the Senate, Clinton escaped conviction on a party-line vote.

George W. Bush (known as "Bush 43," to distinguish him from his father, who had been the forty-first president) entered office elected not by the public but by the Supreme Court. In the highly contested 2000 election, victory rested on who had won Florida. Although Vice President Al Gore had received more popular votes nationally, the court found in Bush's favor, awarding him the electoral votes that won him the presidency. That election further fueled and exacerbated the political divide; Bush was the legal winner, but the legitimacy of the election was far from settled.

Despite or because of the electoral crisis, Bush had a very rocky first few months as president. He abrogated unilaterally a major foundation of relations with Russia—the Anti-Ballistic Missile (ABM) Treaty. Then a minicrisis broke out after a U.S. Navy P-3 Orion antisubmarine aircraft was rammed by a Chinese interceptor and forced to crash-land on Hainan Island. The P-3 crisis was resolved, and the aircraft and crew were returned, though only after the Chinese had carefully examined the onboard systems and electronics. However, the Bush administration continued to stumble, and criticism of its shambolic performance mounted.

Then, in the seventh month of his presidency, the attacks of September 11 changed the world, at least for the United States. Those attacks, the declaration of a global war on terror, military assaults into Afghanistan and Iraq, and a financial crisis that would occur six years later were to consume the Bush presidency. These events and decisions would expose the president's weaknesses and inexperience, along with the failure of government to offset the president's shortcomings.

In many ways, September 11 is the single most dramatic example of the legacies of 1914, the erosion of the Westphalian system and the dangers posed by the four riders. Who was the enemy? Osama bin Laden was a disgruntled, angry, and obscure Saudi princeling wannabee. Armed himself with little more than AK-47s, he sent his few foreign legionaries into battle in America armed with box cutters. Highjacked airliners were turned into an air force. Bin Laden had become the twenty-first century's Gavrilo Princip.

In a dramatic response, Bush declared a global war on terror. Afghanistan and then Iraq would be attacked and invaded. Congress would unhesitatingly support those wars with unlimited funding and the USA PATRIOT Act, giving government extraordinary power, unprecedented since World War II, to defend the nation. Tragically, the waging and failures of these wars would prove major contributors to the breaking of government.

Bush's promise to alter the "geostrategic landscape" of the Middle East was honored—but not in the way the president intended. The wars in Iraq and Afghanistan cost the nation dearly. Iraq was arguably the greatest foreign policy blunder in U.S. history.

Because of the wars and the huge tax cuts that preceded them, the U.S. balance sheet became overloaded with debt. Budget deficits were projected for as far as anyone could see. And the explosion in entitlements, combined with an aging population, put in train intractable problems that would test even the most effective of governments.

By the time Bush 43 left office, globalization and the diffusion of power had cut the relative power and advantages of the United States with respect to all other states. The end of the Soviet Union, as its last leader, Mikhail Gorbachev, would joke, had "deprived America of an enemy." That condition would taunt and challenge the United States.

Different policies were essential in an age in which the clear and present danger was radical Islam and terror. But religious extremism resisted precise definition. Worse, because the U.S. Constitution protects the practice of religion and free speech, the threat of Islamic extremism would exacerbate and exploit fundamental tensions between privacy and security, between free speech and search and seizure, and between the protection of the nation from further attack and the application of due process to enemy combatants, especially those with American citizenship.

Barack Obama was the unluckiest of recent presidents when he assumed office. Obama was confronting a still-unresolved 2008 financial crisis and two disastrous wars started by Bush 43. Obama had vowed to end the war in Iraq and win in Afghanistan. He would end the first and in the process leave behind an Iraq in chaos. Although Afghanistan is far from over, it will not be won in any sense except that U.S. and foreign troops will no longer be engaged in combat. Partisanship continued to worsen, as polarization widened the divide between the two parties.

As a result of this polarization, the extreme right and left wings increasingly dominated their respective political parties. Amendment of the filibuster rule in the Senate (requiring only sixty votes for cloture) and the insistence of Republicans in the Republican-dominated House that a majority of the majority is needed to support a bill have turned Congress into a parliamentary and not a representative institution, and the nation into a parliamentary republic. The "tea party's" rigid views personified the ideological hardening of politics.

Middle-of-the-roaders in Congress were made vulnerable to the threat of being "primary'ed," meaning that although a particular district was safe in the general election for a given party, a more extreme challenger from the left or right would defeat the incumbent in the primary. Through Supreme Court decisions, particularly *Citizens United v. Federal Election Commission,* campaign-financing restrictions were loosened. Political action and other surrogate committees could receive virtually unlimited contributions. In 2014, a large number of the more experienced members of Congress retired or chose not to run, most citing the poisonous political atmosphere in Washington and the inability to get anything done.

As a consequence the U.S. government has been correctly described as "broken," "dysfunctional," "in gridlock," and "not working." The litany of evidence supporting these claims fills books, bookshelves, and libraries. The absence of civility and the general unpleasantness on both ends of Pennsylvania Avenue are freely discussed and unarguable but sorry states for a political process. Moving to a three-day congressional workweek in order to spend more time in home constituencies and raise campaign funds also eliminated the opportunity for social interaction among members.

In football, offering further evidence of the brokenness of government would be called "piling on." Yet, a last example brings the story up to date. The colossal failure to implement the rollout of the Affordable Care Act in 2013 was matched by deadlock in Congress and failure to address the most basic of governance issues, from spending to controlling huge debts and deficits. The gross and derelict strategic mismanagement, spanning Republican and Democratic administrations, of the wars in Afghanistan, Iraq, and against terror confirms the conclusion that the U.S. government is surely broken. The costs of war, running into the trillions, have contributed to a badly unbalanced budget and a national debt that will only continue to grow.

There are several consequences (which are also causes) of the failure of the U.S. government. The first is that successive presidents, Republican and Democrat alike, have not been prepared for or capable of dealing with the challenge of governance when entering office. Bill Clinton, George W. Bush, and Barack Obama each lacked the experience and even the judgment to lead the nation certainly for goodly parts of their administrations. Of course, experience and judgment are not constitutional requirements for the office: being thirty-five years of age, being native born, having lived at least ten years in the United States, and winning a majority in the Electoral College (we still do not directly elect a president) are the only four requirements.

The second consequence relates to the organization and structure of the U.S. government. That structure is still based on the National Security Act, which created a Department of Defense and a National Security Council (NSC) structure, as well as the CIA. The act was first written in 1947, when the threat was a traditional state enemy. That threat has been gone for two and a half decades. While changes and amendments have been made, principally to establish a director of national intelligence, a Department of Homeland Security, and a separate Special Forces Command, both the National Security Act and NSC structure need fundamental reform and change. Many fine books and articles have made this argument, which need not be repeated. But the chances of major reforms happening are not good.

The third consequence is the shift from the strategic paradigm of assured destruction to one of assured disruption. More will follow on this and other consequences.

Examination of the failed and failing character of other governments follows in Part Two. Every government or political process has flaws and contradictions. The most important conclusion on the influence of the first horseman is that globalization and the diffusion of power have acted as centrifugal and divisive forces widening the inherent defects.

In conditions of failed and failing government, the symptoms of instability, inequality, and inequity are heightened. In some regions, such as Afghanistan and the Horn of Africa, failed government has led to the breeding of and training grounds for terror. In Syria, a civil war threatens to claim hundreds of thousands of lives and possibly inflame the region. And failed government in Ukraine in large measure caused the Russian occupation of Crimea.

In advanced states, particularly in Europe and Asia, failed and failing government has not been able to cope with economic and social issues. China, for example, with a total population of about 1.4 billion, has an underclass numbering hundreds of millions. That underclass fires the government's overriding paranoia about rebellion and the need for "stability," and it is the greatest vulnerability the Communist Party faces. The EU has remained a largely monetary union, with self-evident liabilities. The issue of political union remains the major flaw in this construct. It will not work. Sovereignty has been challenged by globalization and pressure for political union. And the well-off (i.e., northern Europe) are unwilling to underwrite the less well-off (i.e., southern Europe).

The second horseman comprises economic despair, disparity, and dislocation. The evaporation of borders means that few do not have global access or do not know how many around the world live. Even in so-called backward and distant corners of the world, satellite dishes and cell phones are omnipresent, a direct effect of the information revolution. People want dignity and better lives. Exclusion reinforces despair. The example of a majority of Egyptians subsisting on a few dollars a day has had and will have profound consequences, consequences that have already toppled both an authoritarian and an elected government. What follows next in Egypt is uncertain.

In a larger sense, globalization and the economic diffusion of power are closing some of the poverty gaps between and among states. But, alternatively, in many states, including the United States and the EU, income disparity between the very well-off and the others is growing. This phenomenon is spreading to such advancing states as China and India, although the political effects may take time to register.

Whether economic despair and disparity will lead to change, possibly even violence or revolution, is no longer a purely academic question. The "Occupy Wall Street" movement and environmental terrorism may be fads. Or they could be precursors. As governments fail to provide economic advantage to their citizens, internal pressures will grow for change, reform, and an end to the status quo.

The third horseman is ideological radicalism propelled by religious extremism. In the twentieth century, the dangers to the West were in the form of political "isms": fascism, communism, and, for some, socialism. Capitalism was also the enemy to the East, not merely for the Soviet Union. Nonaligned and Arab states often resented capitalism and its precursor, colonialism.

Today, though the debate between socialism and capitalism continues, radical ideology in the form of religious extremism is the newest danger. A definition of the term is elusive. But the emergence of radical Islam, with its fundamental hostility to infidels and between Sunni and Shia, has created a challenge and anger that test the limits of any government, because this extremism attacks the basis for religious freedom and the very nature of open societies. The dangers posed by this horseman are profound and extensive.

Where in open societies are lines drawn between religious freedom and religious extremism? As now widely reported in the media, the NSA and the British government's security and intelligence organization, GCHQ, have been conducting highly intrusive surveillance to counter Islamic and al Qaeda threats. That surveillance raises often unanswerable and unresolvable issues between privacy and security, thus doing great damage to government and the rule of law.

Why should a state allow a person to enter its borders with a covered face, and thus no means of establishing identity, on the grounds of religious freedom? Given the clashes between Israel and the Arab and Muslim worlds and between Hindu India and Muslim Pakistan that exacerbate religious differences and offer points of great leverage for radicals, are there any solutions for corralling this horseman? Or, as with many movements, will Islamic radicalism run its course and at some future point dissipate?

The vast majority of the some 1.3 billion Muslims are peaceful and opposed to violence. But even one-tenth of 1 percent using terror and considering radicalism and indeed extreme application of Sharia law and the Quran as virtues is still over one million people. Restraining and countering this radicalism, given other grievances and conflicts, remains an overriding challenge.

The fourth rider is environmental calamity and, with it, climate change. Scientific evidence is conclusive that temperatures are rising and that the polar ice caps are shrinking. The legitimate political debate is largely over cause, although the overwhelming evidence is that man-made greenhouse gases are the largest contributors to global warning. As noted, climate change is not zero-sum. But as states industrialize; as billions of new cars, trucks, trains, and airliners are built; and as more energy is exploited, the production of greenhouse gases will increase dramatically, and the depletion of natural resources will accelerate.

Yet, the international organizations and agreements in place to cope with environmental issues lack the authority to impose stringent conditions to relieve the fundamental contradiction between already industrialized states that seek to deal with climate issues and advancing states that need far more energy to continue modernization.

Failed and failing governance; economic despair, disparity, and dislocation; and radical ideologies—all these, however challenging, could be overwhelmed by an environmental catastrophe. A global pandemic, widespread droughts, or further global warming, a rise of several degrees, could be natural calamities. The microbe-carrying psyllid bug threatens to destroy Florida's entire citrus industry by infecting orange groves. No matter how low the probability, catastrophic environmental issues could prove to be wildcards and the most dangerous of the new horsemen.

3

Three Crucial Consequences

September 11 will prove to be a historical inflection point for the United States and for global politics. Concurrently, and surely related, the erosion of the Westphalian system and the emergence of the new Four Horsemen have led to three crucial consequences for how the United States provides for its general welfare and the common defense. Along with the relative decline in U.S. power and influence, these consequences must be incorporated into a twenty-first-century mind-set if America is to remain an effective global leader and not merely a hapless giant adrift in a chaotic world.

First, if the last twenty-two years matter, regardless of how able advisors and subordinates may have been, newly elected presidents are unprepared for and lack experience demanded by the rigors of the presidency. In some cases, that condition persists well into their presidencies, magnifying the failures in governing. Second, the U.S. political system and the organization of its government (along with that of international institutions in general) have not kept pace with the demands of governing at a time of more complex and complicated challenges and choices. Third, the strategic paradigm on which a new mind-set must be based has migrated from the threat of massive destruction to one of massive disruption.

Unfortunately, while the first two consequences are generally and intuitively appreciated, the third has not been recognized. As long as the so-called war on terror associates radical Islam's intent with achieving mass destruction and not with disruption, that war will be lost, if only for that reason alone.

The combined impact of these three consequences helped produce the gross and often derelict mismanagement of the wars in Iraq and Afghanistan and against global terror. Since September 11, two administrations have failed in waging these wars. By successive actions and mistakes, the chances of achieving peace and stability in Afghanistan and Iraq have been made more remote.

Despite the Obama administration's bold decision (which is to its credit) to launch the daring Abbottabad raid that brought bin Laden to justice, the war on terror, no matter what it is called, has been extended possibly indefinitely. The use of drones and NSA surveillance programs, however valuable, continue the battle against terror without offering any chance of ending it.

In a rational world, correcting the absence of presidential qualifications and experience among nominees would seem a critical, lofty, and sensible goal. The nation may be fortunate enough again to elect a president as well prepared for high office as George H. W. Bush was. But for reasons noted below, the likelihood that future presidents will enter office with sufficient experience, knowledge, and preparation is not high. This issue is a problem not only for the United States. As analyzed in part two, failed and failing governments on a global basis suffer from similar problems of inexperience and lack of qualifications.

Even before September 11, dynamic changes in international politics and the increasingly dysfunctional and partisan atmosphere were overtaking the ability of both the political system and the organization of the U.S. government to keep pace. Today, the system of checks and balances and of divided government works only if one party has an absolute majority in both houses of Congress, controls the presidency, and has the guaranteed vote of five Supreme Court justices, *or* when the spirit of compromise and/or a massive crisis overcomes the centrifugal forces of divided government. Any management expert looking at the organization of the U.S. government would be astounded that it works—sometimes. Prior chapters dissected these organizational failings. Parts two and three provide recommended solutions to bring government in line with the twenty-first century and to adopt a new mind-set.

In the old strategic paradigm, mutual destruction was a centerpiece of Cold War deterrence. With the dissolution of the Soviet Union and the elimination of many thousands of nuclear and thermonuclear weapons, the threat of societal annihilation was lifted. September 11 transformed the strategic paradigm to one based on the threat of massive disruption. The Cold War's "mutual assured destruction" and its MAD acronym should become "massive assured disruption," a condition that can be induced by acts of man to include economic or financial crises, cyber attack, and events of nature such as pandemics, earthquakes, and extreme weather.

September 11 was the poster child for the new MAD. Osama bin Laden must have been stunned by the results of the attack and, of course, by the American reactions. First, bin Laden wanted the Twin Towers to remain in situ as smoldering monuments to his cause. The towers collapsed the same day. Second, bin Laden did not anticipate the retaliation the attack would provoke, or its consequences. Third and most important, according to his own diary, bin Laden did not anticipate the enormous disruption that followed. The instantaneous loss of trillions of dollars in stock markets across the world and how much more odious airport security screening made air travel are two examples of September 11's disruptive effects.

Finally, bin Laden was the twenty-first century's first Gavrilo Princip, something he never contemplated before he was killed in Abbottabad. September 11 became the twenty-first-century June 28.

Hillary Clinton notwithstanding, why is the United States likely to face a near-permanent condition of electing unprepared and inexperienced presidents? National politics in the United States now is fixated on campaigning and winning elections, not governing. Because negative campaigning has proved more effective at winning elections than has positive campaigning, politics have become more sordid and demeaning. Because of the Internet, social media, and millions of blogs, "truth" is a casualty and often an unnecessary encumbrance. Candidates should be entitled to their own opinions but not their own facts. Today, candidates manufacture their own facts to support their opinions!

The diffusion of power and the information revolution have accelerated these phenomena. Both parties have become polarized around the more extreme views of left and right in order to attract both funding and support from politically engaged, well-heeled individuals who represent these extremes. Few politicians receive much notoriety by running from and for the center. As a result, the majority of Americans, who are basically centrist, have become disenfranchised. And this poisonous atmosphere has paralyzed or contaminated the prospects for genuine bipartisanship and nonpartisanship taking hold.

In 2001, George W. Bush had what was by any measure an extraordinary group of highly experienced and accomplished advisors. The new president had chosen to serve in the Air National Guard rather than in combat in Vietnam.

But as the son of a vice president and president, Bush had had unique access to the White House, in Ronald Reagan's two terms and his father's four years. Bush should have seen that no matter how able subordinates and staff are, success and failure rest at the very top.

Vice President Dick Cheney too had avoided service in Vietnam. At a young age, in 1969, Cheney had been part of Nixon's inner team working for Donald Rumsfeld during the Vietnam years. President Gerald Ford made Cheney his chief of staff when he succeeded Nixon in 1974. Cheney later won election from his home state of Wyoming to the House of Representatives. In 1989, George H. W. Bush chose Cheney as his secretary of defense, a position he held for four years and during the first Gulf War in 1991.

Gen. Colin Powell served two combat tours in Vietnam. He was Ronald Reagan's national security advisor. Promoted to chairman of the Joint Chiefs of Staff by Bush 41 in 1989, Powell helped lead Operation Desert Storm. His term as chairman extended briefly into the Clinton presidency. In 2001, Bush 43 appointed Powell secretary of state. Few administrations had been endowed with such experience and competence. Yet that administration failed, largely because of the inexperience of the president, the ideological magnetism of faith-based thinking, and a powerful but flawed vice president.

Bush was, by his own proud admission, a born-again Christian. He also publicly expressed faith in a "greater father," meaning God. The September 11 attack was an epiphany for Bush and the opportunity to rally and unify his stumbling presidency. Bush became fixated on the proposition that he now could create a new "geostrategic landscape" in the Middle East by spreading democracy.

A democratic Iraq in this aspiration would not only guarantee Israel's future security. A democratic Iraq would spread democracy throughout the Arab world, forcing positive change. Reassured by the overwhelming and lightning-fast rout of the Afghan Taliban in late 2001, Bush became convinced of the validity of, and quite possibly obsessed with, the vision of a democratic Middle East. Vice President Dick Cheney was already aggressively supporting an Iraq invasion and the overthrow of Saddam Hussein. Bush earnestly believed a military campaign against Iraq was the surest way to establish a new landscape of democracies in the Middle East. Allegations of weapons of mass destruction became the convenient fact used to justify this opinion and predilection.

On the basis of the rapid defeat of the Taliban in Afghanistan and certain that once Saddam was gone Iraq would make a speedy transition to a democratic government, the administration failed to ask the "what next" question. That omission was fatal. Iraq would descend into violence and insurgency that the 2006 "surge" could only temporarily arrest. Today, a divided, violent , and unstable Iraq is a reality. When coalition forces leave Afghanistan in 2014, that country too is likely headed for instability, perhaps some form of partition along tribal, ethnic, or regional lines, or even civil war.

Military force routed the Taliban and eliminated Saddam's army. But military force could not resolve the larger political, economic, social, and ideological issues that engulfed Iraq and Afghanistan. Nor had the other nonmilitary, developmental arms of government been provided sufficient resources or capacity to "nation build" and create democracies from the ashes of chaos and conflict.

The absence of postconflict capacity, called for by NATO in its "comprehensive approach" to security, was a fatal flaw. Two other, interrelated flaws would also guarantee failure. Without an understanding of the culture and history of Afghanistan and Iraq, achieving postwar stability would be a virtually impossible task. Imposing a democratic style of government on societies that had no experience with or preference for that system could not work. Iraq and Afghanistan also lacked any working governing institutions. The outcomes and consequences were foreordained. But Presidents Bush and Obama seemed oblivious to these realities.

In Iraq and Afghanistan (and, of course, Vietnam), "winning" by force of arms alone was impossible. Especially against adversaries who lack military forces and rely on terror, violence, and ideology to coerce or rally followers, that lesson must be learned and relearned. The messages conveyed by these adversaries and their means of broadcasting them should be the strategic centers of gravity in what are inherently geostrategic and political, not military, struggles. Unfortunately, while military force can kill people and destroy things, it is impotent and thus ineffective against messages and ideologies.

This lesson is not unique to the twenty-first century. The American revolutionaries defeated the vastly superior British military primarily because the main enemy for London was France. The colonies, fortunately for the Americans, were a sideshow.

Two hundred years later, the U.S. military could have defeated the North Vietnamese army had it been allowed to do so. However, both President Johnson and President Nixon exercised restraint, in favor of gradual escalation. Johnson feared provoking Chinese intervention, as in Korea in November 1950. Nixon was secretly courting China to counter the Soviet Union. But Hanoi and Ho Chi Minh understood that the strategic center of gravity of the war was in American homes, that it was in front of television sets where North Vietnam would win or lose that struggle.

Too often, despite promises and pledges of new administrations to learn from the past, rhetoric and not reason wins out. Had the United States learned anything in Vietnam, perhaps, with so many officials of that conflict in senior positions in the Bush 43 administration, the wars in Iraq and Afghanistan and against terror might have been waged differently, if at all. The lessons were not learned. When U.S. forces intervened in Afghanistan in the fall of 2001 in concert with the Northern Alliance, the Taliban was quickly routed. Unfortunately, the ensuing Bonn conference in early 2002 did not put in place the foundation and resources for rebuilding Afghanistan into a functioning state.

The Bush administration soon ignored Afghanistan and turned its attention to Iraq, Saddam Hussein, and plans for a war to remove the dictator and to find and destroy Iraq's supposed massive WMD arsenal. The war began in March 2003. The first Gulf War in 1991 and the continued arms embargoes, no-fly zones, and bombing raids had eviscerated Iraq's military capacity, even as Saddam had been dismantling his WMD. The United States, supported by its coalition allies, fielded even more capable forces than in the first war. Iraq's military was overwhelmed and crushed. In no time the Iraqi army collapsed, Saddam was on the run and in hiding, and coalition forces occupied the country.

A great failure of intelligence was the conclusion that Saddam had possessed and hidden WMD. Iraqi WMD did not exist. A greater failure was the White House's not anticipating the peace once Iraq's army was smashed. "Groupthink," in which one opinion becomes collective wisdom, was later blamed for this failure. In fact, incompetence, dereliction, and ideological rigidity were the culprits. Indeed, during the very short combat phase of the war, virtually every competent outside observer was repeating that the tough part would begin once hostilities ended. The White House refused to listen.

One of the reasons for this failure to ask the "what next" question was President Bush's inability to resolve the competing and contradictory views inside his government, a further sign of inexperience. Memoirs and minutes of NSC meetings revealed that Vice President Cheney believed (or was led to believe) that with Saddam's fall, an Iraqi opposition would quickly fill the void and establish a friendly and democratic successor government. Ahmed Chalabi and the Iraqi National Congress were the leaders chosen for this role by the vice president and his staff. Hence, the war plans, code-named Operation Polo Step, were predicated on the assumption that most U.S. combat forces would be withdrawn from Iraq by the end of 2003.

At the Pentagon, Donald Rumsfeld, who held the twin distinctions of being the youngest and oldest secretary of defense, wanted to use the war to showcase the transformation of the military to a more agile, versatile, lighter, and precision force. Hence, the smaller the force and its "footprint"—that is, the size of the logistical tail and supporting infrastructure—the sooner and easier that force could be withdrawn. This "in and out" theory conformed to the vice president's prediction that Iraqis would greet the Americans as liberators, with "candy and flowers," a statement publicly reiterated by Deputy Secretary of Defense Paul Wolfowitz.

At the State Department, Colin Powell and his staff understood that occupation was never a short-term matter, as was reported by the media at the time. Although World War II had ended nearly sixty years before, the United States in 2003 still deployed and stationed hundreds of thousands of soldiers, airmen, and Marines in Germany and Japan, the former enemies. Further, State had developed elaborate plans for the reconstruction of Iraq once fighting had ended.

George W. Bush had gone to war for the reason of "changing the geostrategic landscape of the region" and on the pretext that Saddam had been secretly maintaining WMD. The overwhelming victory in Afghanistan, routing the Taliban, and then a similarly one-sided outcome in Iraq went a long way in removing any presidential questions or doubts about the what-next question. Despite the administration's certainty about and promise of finding these weapons in Iraq, when it became clear that none existed, American credibility, legitimacy, and influence were dealt a powerful setback.

As security conditions worsened in Afghanistan, more coalition forces would be needed. NATO ultimately assumed command of ISAF. Despite the presence of nongovernmental aid organizations and the UN, the bulk of reconstruction, by default, was relegated to the military. ISAF forces applied huge efforts to these tasks. But nation building was not a principal military task, and no one else was up to the job.

In Iraq, reconstruction was begun under the Coalition Provisional Authority (CPA), headed by Ambassador L. Paul (Jerry) Bremer and headquartered in the "Green Zone," in one of Saddam's presidential palaces. Bremer was unqualified and unready for the assignment, lacking any background in the region or in nation building. One of the less-noted reasons why President Bush may have selected Bremer as administrator is that both shared "born again" religious experiences.

Bremer was in charge in Iraq as effectively a proconsul. In charge of him was the Defense Department. Because of animosities and personal frictions between and among the secretaries of state and defense and the vice president, and Bush's inability to resolve those differences, State was largely excluded from the reconstruction effort.

Former *Washington Post* reporter Tom Ricks' book on the war, titled *Fiasco,* is both appropriately named and a devastating critique of the failure of the postwar period in Iraq. In the fall of 2006, as the insurgency threatened to overwhelm Iraq, Bush asked for Rumsfeld's resignation, replacing him with former CIA director Robert Gates. The "surge" of forces began as the Sunni insurgencies threatened civil war. The history and documentation of the many mistakes and fundamental misjudgments in Iraq and Afghanistan are well known. "Failure" is not too strong a characterization. And this sad story is also a case study of the failure of American government to deal with the demands of war and peace.

When Barack Obama entered the White House, he too was unprepared and unready for the demands of his office. He had been a community organizer, a law professor, a member of the Illinois Senate and then (for four years) of the U.S. Senate—none of that experience was sufficient for the presidency. Obama retained Robert Gates as secretary of defense. Senator Hillary Clinton was appointed secretary of state, and Gen. James Jones, retired Marine commandant and former Supreme Allied Commander Europe (SACEUR), was hired as national security advisor. Adm. Mike Mullen stayed as chairman of the Joint Chiefs. In its own way, this team was a match for Bush's. And Vice President Joe Biden had served in the Senate, chairing both the Judiciary and Foreign Relations Committees, accumulating a wealth of experience.

Obama ran for president promising to end the (wrong) war in Iraq and concentrate on the (good) war in Afghanistan. Unfortunately, the Bush administration had been unable to convince the Iraqi government to sign a status-of-forces agreement immunizing U.S. troops from Iraqi law and allowing long-term stationing of American military in-country. The approved strategic framework called for removing all U.S. troops by the end of 2011. The Obama administration could not reverse that decision. In any event, Obama had been elected on the promise to end that war. American withdrawal from Iraq began.

In early 2009, Obama's first major strategic planning effort was the "Afghanistan-Pakistan" study (AfPaK), meant to provide a roadmap for success in Afghanistan. One of the reasons Obama had selected Jones as his national security advisor was that Jones' last military assignment had been as the NATO commander, SACEUR, overseeing Afghanistan. While still in the Senate Obama had read an Atlantic Council study chaired by Jones published in early 2008. The report began, "Make no mistake: NATO is losing in Afghanistan." (That phrase was later softened to read: "The West is not winning in Afghanistan.") Clearly, Jones was an ideal choice if Afghanistan was to be the right war and if Obama needed a national-security expert in his inner council.

The AfPaK study, however, did not work out as desired. Flawed in its assumptions, the study focused too much on the kinetic, or military, options in Afghanistan and failed to address basic socioeconomic-political issues. Essentials for success included reconstructing the agrarian sector, which had been the backbone of the economy for decades; instituting property rights and laws; and not imposing a centralized government on a highly conservative and tribe-based culture. Last, the study failed because its priorities were reversed. Before success could be achieved in Afghanistan, Pakistan had to be stabilized.

One result was a further "surge" of forces, well above what Obama had authorized before the study had been completed but at troop levels lower than recommended by the military commander. This force increase repeated the Iraq experience. Worse, the nonmilitary actions vital to nation building—to reform or create new educational, legal, and penal structures and build or rebuild the economy, transportation, and other infrastructure—were stillborn or kept on starvation diets. The most trenchant critique of Afghanistan can been found in the answers to three direct questions posed in 2013 by me to Marine general John Allen, outgoing ISAF commander, upon his return home, answers based on observations of the state of the war going back to 2003. Had Afghan property laws been put in place? Had the desertion and absentee rates of the Afghan National Security forces dropped below a third? Were girls being educated beyond the third grade? The answers were all no. At the time of writing, in 2014, it is unclear whether coalition forces will remain past year's end, or if so, how many.

In early 2013, the Obama administration delivered new strategic guidance to the Pentagon—a "strategic pivot to Asia." Unfortunately, this guidance was announced in a manner that managed to offend, frighten, or disturb friends, allies, and others around the world. European and Middle Eastern allies saw this as an abandonment of U.S. leadership and interests in their regions. Adversaries in the Persian Gulf, particularly Saudi Arabia and resource-rich Qatar, regarded this pivot as a retreat and further proof of American preference to "lead from behind."

China took issue with the pivot as directed against it and threatened military responses to prevent possible American encirclement. China later declared an "air defense identification zone," covering hundreds of square miles of international waters surrounding contested islands, as a psychological means of countering this pivot. Other Asian allies worried that this shift would exacerbate, not heal, tensions and long-standing territorial disputes among regional powers. The Pentagon scurried to minimize the fallout by renaming the pivot as a "rebalancing."

The White House's rationale for the pivot was based on the economic growth of Asia and an assumption that the importance of a region was proportional to GDP. The messaging of the pivot was clumsy and confrontational. Announcing that a larger percentage of the U.S. Navy would be assigned to the Pacific strengthened the perception that the pivot was a military threat to China. Unfortunately, the Navy's long-term shipbuilding plans are in contradiction to the short-term directive to swing forces to the Pacific, making that a poor measure for demonstrating commitment. But the political damage was done.

Well before the pivot was announced, the Air Force and Navy were developing a concept called the Air-Sea Battle for air and maritime forces. That concept quickly was interpreted as aimed at China. No sooner was the declaratory pivot to Asia firmly in place, however, than the civil war in Syria, turmoil in Libya and Egypt, and Iran's nuclear intentions rightly focused the administration on the Middle East. This attention on the Middle East raised questions about the seriousness of the pivot and the thinking behind it. The Obama administration again looked confused and vacillating.

Specific recommendations for correcting the organization and failings of government and the national-security decision-making process follow. These failings and shortcomings are further exacerbated by a world more complex and complicated than perhaps at any other time in history. International rules, regulations, and restrictions impinge on domestic politics, making governance even more difficult. And crises do not always happen at convenient or predictable times. Simultaneous crises tax or exceed the ability of a national-security system that that at best can cope with a single major event at a time.

Consider the 1914, 1954, and 2014 White Houses again, as measures of the changing complexities and complicated challenges facing government. In 1914, because bureaucracies were smaller and fewer members or committees of Congress were engaged in such issues, decision making was simplified although not necessarily simpler. In those days, the United States possessed insurance and insulation against policy missteps, in the form of two oceans and American economic and resource superiority and independence.

Even in 1954, Eisenhower's federal budget was relatively short and uncomplicated. The Great Society had not been invented, and Social Security recipients were relatively few in number. The defense budget, which accounted for the lion's share of federal spending, was measured in dozens of pages, and only a few committees in Congress had oversight of it.

Donald Rumsfeld echoed the metastasis in regulatory and legislative growth. In 1975, the defense budget was fewer than a hundred pages long and nearly three million troops were in uniform. A quarter of a century later, when Rumsfeld returned to the Pentagon, the force had been cut almost in half but the length of the defense authorization bill had grown more than eightfold.

On inauguration day, Barack Obama had the misfortune of inheriting the most overly regulated government in American history. The growth in governmental intrusion into everyday life and its overhead had been spectacular. That growth had inspired even greater mal-organization of government both domestically and in foreign policy.

In 2012, the *Federal Register,* which publishes proposed new rules and final changes to existing rules, numbered just under 79,000 pages. The *Code of Federal Regulations,* which contains general and permanent rules and regulations, filled nearly 175,000 pages, with more than one million individual regulatory restrictions. The 2010 Dodd-Frank Wall Street Reform and Consumer Protection Act, which no member of Congress read in its entirety, so far contains about 14,000 pages of rules. (It is only about two-fifths complete, even though the specific regulatory additions were to be finished last summer.) Similarly, not a single member of Congress read the Affordable Care Act, about 2,000 pages long, in its entirety.

Regulations are drowning Americans, as well as citizens of most other countries, in complexity and confusion. Has anyone read and understood his or her income tax form sent to the Internal Revenue Service? The answer is usually no. The point is that both government and everyday life are becoming far more complicated. This phenomenon arises from the information revolution, which computerizes even the more mundane and routine aspects of life, from shopping to renewing driver's licenses and passports.

Returning to the Pentagon, the conduct of warfare has become one of "lawfare." Lawfare means the direct engagement of lawyers and judge advocates in operational decisions on the employment of military force, determining what is legal or not. A discouraging anecdote of the incursion of super-rules and regulations into mundane or social issues makes this point. I invited a good friend of mine who is a four-star general to dinner. I have no contractual or other relationship with this general officer. But dinner had to be cleared by his judge advocate's office to ensure that no conflict of interest was in play.

The last and perhaps most interesting consequence is the shift from a strategic paradigm of massive assured destruction to one of massive assured disruption. In the past, the casualties and destruction wrought by war required vast amounts of troops and firepower. Great battles in Europe and Asia cast tactical armies numbering hundreds of thousands into direct combat, with horrendous results. Later, nuclear and then thermonuclear weapons magnified this destructive calculus by orders of magnitude, with the potential to destroy society at large.

Thermonuclear war would have instantly killed hundreds of millions. No one could have predicted the catastrophic aftermath of a thermonuclear war or what might have become a "nuclear winter." A one-megaton weapon was sixty times more powerful than the Hiroshima and Nagasaki weapons and left a crater at least a mile in diameter. And the Soviets had a *fifty*-megaton bomb!

From 1945 until the fall of the Soviet Union four and a half decades later, mutual destruction was the guaranteed outcome if war escalated to a strategic exchange of nuclear weapons. Both East and West had and deployed tens of thousands of tactical battlefield weapons. The United States believed tactical nuclear weapons could potentially serve as escalation controls, deterring society-threatening strategic nuclear exchanges. Had war broken out, however, it is difficult to see how, if not inconceivable that, conflict could have been contained at conventional levels, certainly if one side was winning.

By luck or skill, the era of mutual destruction as the abiding strategic calculus is over, barring some bizarre and unpredictable reversion to a new cold war. The United States and Russia are self-limited to no more than 1,550 warheads each. China has a modest arsenal and shows little sign of making dramatic increases. Numbers of nuclear weapons have been dramatically reduced. While a Pakistan-India nuclear war or a conflict on the Korean Peninsula cannot be ignored (or a nuclear arms race in the Persian Gulf should Iran actually field weapons), massive destruction is no longer a viable or useful strategic framework.

Instead, the diffusion of power and the empowerment of individuals have created a new and in many ways more complex and difficult set of realities. The danger to the West is now one of massive disruption not merely of its way of life but of its economic viability. The destruction of the Twin Towers was the first example of the extent to which massive disruption has become the weapon of choice of adversaries. The cyber world exposes this vulnerability every day, with hacks and attacks even by cranks or sociopaths wishing to impose their will on society.

Beyond man-made disruptive weapons, nature itself disrupts and destroys. Climate change and environmental calamities have become more significant, testing the limits of government, as discussed later. Government's intrusions—from airport security to millions of installed closed-circuit television cameras to intercepts of cell phone and internet conversations—on the grounds of protecting and defending the nation against terrorist attacks are physically less destructive. Yet the disruption is substantial and indeed can prove destructive to individual rights and liberties so important to free people everywhere. Edward Snowden's NSA revelations leave few illusions that the Internet or phone conversations are secure.

The age and threat of mass disruption, for better or worse, have a new paradigm that should form a strategic framework to condition our responses. Yet assimilating and applying this transformation to any political system, less a failing one, will not be easy.

PART TWO

Many Archdukes, Many Bullets

Pre–World War I Britain was not an isle of harmony or an oasis of plenty. Riots, dissent, and socially motivated violence were commonplace well before the archduke and his wife visited Sarajevo. Nor was the world peaceful and free of violence. The worst excesses of colonialism existed in Africa and South America. China had been divided among the great powers into spheres of influence.

Despite the "gilded age" of the last three decades of the nineteenth century, even in the United States, where industry and banking had created a growing and prosperous middle class, women, labor, and other groups were clamoring for greater rights. Race remained very much unfinished business. Assimilation of refugee populations still discriminated against Germans, Jews, the Irish, and many other immigrants.

Societies have always had volatile pressures that could explode into revolution or panic. Just after World War I ended, a handful of terrorist bombings against Supreme Court justices, cabinet officers, and the J. P. Morgan bank in New York in 1919 and 1920 killed only an unlucky night watchman. These attacks induced nationwide panic but virtually no public outrage, as September 11 would. Attorney General Mitchell Palmer led a crusade to apprehend the perpetrators, first identified as Italian anarchists. While thousands of Americans were arrested without due process and several hundred émigrés were exiled, no convictions took place, and the culprits were never brought to justice.

Over the past century, few periods were relatively stable and crisis free. The 1930s contended with the Great Depression and the rise of Nazism in Germany, Fascism in Italy, and militarism in Japan. The first half of the 1940s was consumed with a world war, the second half with the start of the Cold War and the war in Korea.

In the early 1950s, the Cold War dominated foreign policy. The Eisenhower administration was active in overthrowing the Iranian government in 1953 and Guatemala's in 1954. That same year Dien Bien Phu fell to the Viet Minh, ending French control and dividing Indochina into North and South Vietnam. China bombarded the offshore islands of Quemoy and Matsu. Egypt would turn to the Soviet Union for aid, and the U.S. government would view Arab nationalism as coincident with the spread of Marxism.

In 1956, Britain, France, and Israel briefly seized the Suez Canal in a second Arab-Israeli war. Within days, the Soviets ruthlessly repressed the uprisings in Hungary, less ruthlessly in Poland. The next year Russia launched Sputnik, fueling American paranoia about losing the space race. In 1958, after the coup in Iraq and instability in Lebanon, Ike ordered Marines ashore to guarantee the peace in Lebanon. 1960 brought the Congo crisis. Prime Minister Patrice Lumumba, first head of that nation's newly independent government, was driven from office and murdered by Congolese opposition. In part, this plot was contrived by the United States to block possible Soviet influence in the region after the United States and the West refused aid to Lumumba, who then looked to Moscow.

Kennedy authorized the disastrous Bay of Pigs invasion, in which 1,400 exiled Cubans waded ashore to be overwhelmed by Castro's forces in April 1961. That summer, Khrushchev upped the ante over Berlin and built the wall that would last for nearly thirty years. The next year, the Cuban missile crisis arguably brought the two superpowers closer to the brink of war than any crisis before or since.

The most recent crises, including September 11 and the 2008 financial meltdown, are still relatively fresh in most Americans' minds. But the twenty-first century and 2014 are different from the past in one fundamental way. Crises of the last century took place in the context of Westphalian politics, with states responsible for success or failure. The Cold War and the bilateral U.S.-Soviet superpower conflict was the strategic context against which major crises played out for four and a half decades. In 2014, many hot spots and ticking time bombs fall outside the state-centric system. The common denominator and linkage among these potential time bombs reside in the third horseman and religious fanaticism.

Radical ideologies motivated by religious extremism, particularly violent Islamism, link many potential crises from the eastern Mediterranean to the Bay of Bengal. Further, a single crisis is no longer, and cannot automatically be kept, isolated from others. Perhaps this phenomenon of linked crises started after the October 1973 Arab-Israeli War and the Arab oil blockade the war provoked.

The interactions between and among the Four Horsemen explain most if not all the current and lurking regional crises and potentially explosive events. As of this writing, crises in the Central African Republic and South Sudan directly flow from the first three horsemen and are exacerbated by the fourth. The February 2014 Winter Olympics held in Sochi, Russia, were threatened by religiously and nationalistically driven extremists.

The emergence of the Islamic State of Iraq and Syria (ISIS) portends only ill, especially if various regional al Qaeda subsidiaries rally under this banner. Not only will the Shia-Sunni tensions and conflict worsen, but the specter of terrorism will likewise metastasize within the Middle East, the Persian Gulf, and South Asia. This third horseman could prove to be the most dangerous of all.

Unfortunately, because the third horseman represents an idea and a narrative, traditional means to defeat or neutralize it are unlikely to work. This rider is so far stateless. During the Cold War, that the Soviet Union was a state eased the task of containing and deterring it. The West could employ separate political, economic, military, and ideological strategies against that adversary. But the dilemma now is finding a proper strategy for countering an idea and ideology that has no tangible economic or military base. This dilemma has been and remains a continuing struggle and weakness for the United States and the other foes of religious extremism.

4

Regional Crises and
Ticking Time Bombs

Where to start identifying the ticking time bombs of today and tomorrow is a good question. When Herman Wouk's best-selling novel *The Caine Mutiny* was published in 1952, a senior admiral at the time complained that while he had observed each of *Caine's* fictional officers in real life, never had he seen so many bad apples together in a single wardroom. Crises are as old as humanity. Yet, 2014 has its fill.

The interaction of failed and failing government; of economic despair, disruption, and disparity; of ideological extremism fueled by radical religion; and of climate change and environmental catastrophe is at the root of the potential crises and ticking time bombs from Afghanistan to Zimbabwe. Whether in Libya or China or North Korea (or indeed in Ukraine and other European states with large Russian populations), failed or failing government is a main cause of discontent, instability, and violence. The uncertainty is what it will take to trigger a crisis or conflict, how to predict events in which the surfeit of powder kegs and abundance of matches seem to grow.

Despite the Obama administration's pivot to Asia and whatever the so-called emergence of China presages, the Middle East, the Persian Gulf, and South Asia remain the most dangerous regions in the world. Paradoxically, Europe may well remain the most important region to the geostrategic, political, and economic interests of the United States. In this swath of Middle East and Gulf instability, failed government, economic disparity, al Qaeda, and Islamic jihad compete atop the world's major depositories of oil and natural gas. Prioritizing which of these crises is the most immediate or explosive or which of the first three horsemen is the greatest culprit is difficult. Each exercises hugely negative influence, with often catastrophic consequences, defined in terms of human suffering and loss of life.

63

Within this nearly three-thousand-mile slice of geography, the Arab-Israeli-Palestinian conflict; Iran's nuclear ambitions; the Shia-Sunni confrontation playing out in Syria, the Gulf, Iraq, and between Saudi Arabia and Iran; the Afghan-Pakistani-Indian triangle; and the new and old versions of al Qaeda—all have potential for provoking greater crises and regional war. In many ways, while the ingredients for these crises have been long in place, the catalyst to bring them to the surface largely can be identified as American interventions in Afghanistan in 2001 and in Iraq in 2003. The consuming ambition to change the "geostrategic landscape of the Middle East" through the imposition of democracy paradoxically was a mission accomplished—but not in the way intended by the Bush 43 administration. Instead, the wars focused and magnified the deep-seated elements of violence and conflict between and among states and causes.

Twenty years ago, Harvard professor Samuel Huntington produced his thesis of a "clash of civilizations," in which he argued that the Muslim and Western worlds were on a collision course, with antecedents predating the Ottoman Empire. Huntington was prescient, and in ways he could not predict. The postwar policies of the United States are a good starting point to confirm and modify Huntington's thesis.

The history is unambiguous. After the end of World War II, the decision to recognize a Jewish state in Palestine put in the middle of the Arab and Muslim worlds an entity that would attract almost limitless enmity and hostility. President Harry Truman overrode the recommendation of the secretary of state, Gen. George Marshall, against recognizing Israel. In 1948, Israel was born and had to fight and win the first of four major wars to ensure its survival.

The Arab world was divided and largely under the thrall of colonial occupation. Oil had not yet made Saudi Arabia rich. The coming Cold War would make an "us against them" mentality prevail in the effort to contain what the West feared were dangerous Soviet ambitions. It is often forgotten that the U.S. and Israeli governments did not begin their intimate relationship until well into the 1960s, after the June 1967 Six-Day War.

In waging the Cold War, gathering allies was far more important to U.S. administrations than the nature of regimes in charge. Latin America was not the only region in which anticommunist promises outweighed democracy and human rights. The Eisenhower administration and its anti-Soviet secretary of state, John Foster Dulles, joined by his brother Allen, who was CIA director, conspired to overthrow the government of Mohammed Mossadegh in 1953. The next year, Guatemala's leftist-leaning president Jacobo Arbenz was removed through a clandestine, CIA-run operation.

The encirclement of the Soviet Union continued with the creation of the Southeast Asia Treaty Organization (SEATO) in 1954, consisting of the United States, the United Kingdom, France, Australia, New Zealand, Thailand, the Philippines, and Pakistan, and in 1955 of the Central Treaty Organization (CENTO), with the United States, the United Kingdom, Turkey, Iraq, Iran, and Pakistan as members. In fact, many of today's difficulties with Pakistan stem from these alliances. Both failed, in that they created in the Pakistani psyche the notion that Pakistan was so important to American security that it could write its own ticket. This gross misperception was magnified when after September 11, 2001, Pakistan was named a major, non-NATO ally and enlisted to fight in the war on terror.

With Mossadegh gone, the shah of Iran became a key ally against the Soviet Union. Preventing the Russians from moving south to grab the famous "warm water" ports the West mistakenly thought so vital to them, along with the major sources of Iran's oil, became a mutual interest and reason for close relations. Iran became a major purchaser of U.S. arms and later one of Richard Nixon's two security pillars in the Persian Gulf.

The Eisenhower administration found it could neither work with nor overthrow Egypt's ruler, Gamal Abdul Nasser, confusing Arab nationalism with de facto support of communism and socialism. The result was to drive Egypt into the Soviet camp for arms, aid, and for the loans with which the Aswan Dam was built, warts and all. Following the 1973 war and the 1978 Camp David peace accords, under Egypt's courageous president Anwar Sadat, who took office after Nasser's assassination in 1970, Egypt would become a U.S. ally. In return, Egypt became the second-largest recipient of U.S. military assistance, in payment for the peace. Israel would retain the title as the largest beneficiary of U.S. military munificence.

In the Persian Gulf, the Nixon administration crafted a two-pillar policy resting on Saudi Arabia and Iran as staunch allies. The threat of the Soviet Union drew the rivals together and served as a counterbalance to mitigate the Sunni-Shia rift dating back to the seventh century—a split largely unrecognized by the West then. The simplicity of the Cold War, matched by the catastrophic possibility of thermonuclear war that would have killed hundreds of millions, held in check many of the region's powerful religious, nationalistic, and human forces for a better life and greater political enfranchisement. For the United States, Wilsonian idealism persisted in advancing human rights, democracy, and liberty, although invariably subordinated to the necessity of winning (or not losing) the Cold War against the Soviets.

Despite failure to pay any price or bear any burden to secure liberty in Vietnam, American idealism still had some attraction. In the Cold War, pursuit of human rights and dignity was used to pound the Soviets. When Ronald Reagan dared Mr. Gorbachev "to tear down this wall," the power of the argument rested on human rights. When the wall came down, democratization and human rights emerged as parts of the fabric of American policy, now unrestrained by cold war.

But human rights are a twin-edged sword. Allies such as Saudi Arabia and other autocratic states will not be forced to change their forms of government short of a revolution. In Iran, revolutions did not always work well for the United States and the West (or for that matter Iran). Oil and strategic alliances trumped democracy and civil rights as priorities. Hence, U.S. policy could easily be seen as hypocritical, which it was.

Because human-rights excesses in the areas of race, gender, and sexual preference still existed in America, the hypocrisy tag was easy to apply. During the second Iraq War, U.S. mistreatment of Iraqi prisoners of war in Abu Ghraib; "black" secret interrogation facilities that used waterboarding techniques regarded as torture; targeted assassinations; and, of course, the Guantanamo Bay facility for incarcerating terrorists detained without due process—all these were cited as evidence of American hypocrisy. Furthermore, support of Israel at the perceived expense of the Palestinians has deepened hostility against America in the Arab and Muslim worlds.

Moving west to east, all these ticking time bombs can be easily identified. In Libya in 2011, after the intervention of NATO in Operation Unified Protector on the side of Libyan rebels (made more notorious by the Obama administration's proud declaration it was "leading from behind"), Muramar Qaddafi was overthrown and killed. Subsequently, Libya has been incapable of establishing effective governance. Much of its eastern half is ungovernable and dangerous.

The killing of the U.S. ambassador, Christopher Stevens, and three American security officers in 2012 in Benghazi brought on a firestorm of blame provoked by Republicans alleging "cover-up" that has not ceased. Meanwhile, al Qaeda and other terror groups operate freely in Libya. Thus far, the government has been incapable of exerting control of or exploiting the export of the country's vast oil reserves.

Conceivably a coup, led by radicals, and chronic violence are possible, fomenting further instability in the region.

Egypt is back in the hands of the military. Following the coup that ousted longtime president Hosni Mubarak and set in place temporary military control, Mohammed Morsi and the Muslim Brotherhood won power and the presidency through elections. Morsi's regime was incompetent at best, and in 2013 the generals ousted him and his administration. In early 2014, the Muslim Brotherhood was declared a terrorist organization by the ruling army and made illegal again. Morsi was imprisoned.

Morsi's overthrow posed profound contradictions for the United States and for the region, underscoring the complexity of these challenges. Many in the United States declared the regime change a coup and demanded an immediate halt of all U.S. aid, as required by law. There was a missed irony present. As noted earlier, the second paragraph of the Declaration of Independence explains that when government became destructive, it was the right of the people to alter or abolish it and establish a new one. Clearly, Morsi's government had not yet been destructive enough.

The new regime promised to stand by the peace agreement with Israel. Meanwhile, Sinai roils with insurgencies that the government is unable to control. No government in Egypt can cure the economic maladies of an economy lacking natural resources or a manufacturing sector and having only two potential means of attracting foreign exchange—passage through the Suez Canal and tourism— thus the causes of the protests and unrest that triggered the original massive rallies in Tahrir Square that undid Mubarak remain. And Egypt remains unstable and another potential time bomb.

Israel is a source of great concern. At some time in the future, the Arab population in Israel could place Jews in the minority. Occupation of Gaza and the West Bank continues to precipitate violence and strengthen Palestinian resistance. The government of Benyamin Netanyahu seems inflexible as to permitting a "two-state solution." And the question of Iran's nuclear ambitions is a red warning flag.

Obama's second secretary of state, John Kerry, argued that if a peace agreement could not be reached by the end of 2014, it would be decades before another opportunity arose. That was one reason why the secretary made and is making such prodigious effort as a mediator and peacemaker between Israel and Palestine. Little is unconnected in this region. Events in Syria, Egypt, and Lebanon will have impact on any peace. The wildcard is Iran.

Perhaps by the time this book is in print the Iranian nuclear issue will have been resolved one way or the other. The preliminary agreement signed by the P-5 Plus One (the five permanent members of the UN Security Council, Germany, and the European Union) and the Iranian government held great promise. The temporary agreement halted Iranian production of fissile material and stopped construction on a nuclear reactor capable of producing plutonium, along with the promise to ease economic sanctions that were crippling the country.

The agreement if fulfilled would be a game changer, defusing an obvious ticking time bomb. However, as 2014 proceeds, if there is slippage in the agreement or refusal by Iran to honor it—or actions are taken by the U.S. Congress to impose even greater sanctions that might induce Iran to change its mind—the alternative is a military strike to delay and disrupt Iran's nuclear capacity. Netanyahu has threatened an attack. However, unless Israel were to use nuclear weapons, it lacks the military capacity to do more than inflict temporary damage. Israel would risk severe retaliation from Iran, from Hezbollah, and from other terrorist groups. Iran could retaliate in the Gulf as well as against Bahrain and other Gulf states in reprisal. And the threat of or an actual Israeli attack could preempt or force American participation.

Without question, this contingency is among the most dangerous and possibly catastrophic crises confronting much of the world. Iran would threaten mining the Strait of Hormuz and the global supply of oil from the Gulf, precipitating a huge spike in oil prices and possibly a global economic recession. Iran could strike U.S. allies in the Gulf. Despite Grand Ayatollah and Supreme Leader Khamenei's rejection of all weapons of mass destruction, an attack almost certainly would cause Iran to reconsider nuclear weapons as a deterrent.

The geopolitical ramifications are equally stunning. An Iranian nuclear bomb, some argue, would force Saudi Arabia to build or buy several weapons from Pakistan. A nuclear arms race might follow, with unpredictable outcomes. And even more sinister scenarios have been suggested.

In my view, an attack against Iran to destroy, disrupt, or delay building a nuclear weapon would be catastrophic. An attack could be the best example of a twenty-first-century variant of the precipitation in June 1914 of a global crisis. Unfortunately, history is often forgotten.

In 1949, the Soviet Union exploded its first nuclear weapon. Many in the United States called for a preemptive strike against the USSR to remove that threat once and for all. In 1964, China exploded its first nuclear weapon. Again, some advocated a preemptive strike, reflecting often evangelical-like anticommunist hysteria.

Despite the furor that would follow Iran's obtaining a nuclear weapon, common sense and a brains-based approach to strategy provide a far better alternative than an unnecessary and potentially disastrous war. Compared with the USSR and China, Iran is a minimal threat. Containment and deterrence worked against an adversary possessing tens of thousands of weapons. And as for those who argue that Iran's Shia-led clerics are irrational and hence unstable, similar arguments were asserted against "godless" communist leaders.

Should Iran abandon the negotiation process and pursue nuclear weapons, establishing a deterrence and containment regime in the region would be essential. Russia has a keen interest in limiting neighboring Iran's nuclear ambitions and might play a role. The United States could guarantee protection of Saudi Arabia and the Gulf states under its nuclear umbrella. An attack, conventional or otherwise, would immediately generate an American response. The United States also maintains a sizable military presence in the region. At least one *Ohio*-class Trident submarine could be assigned to target Iran permanently. Hence, a robust U.S. and Gulf containment and deterrence posture could be maintained.

Additionally, the joint Central Command operations center located in Doha, Qatar, for integrating Gulf air defenses could be expanded. U.S. antiballistic missiles could be deployed to appropriate land bases in the region. And U.S. Navy ships with antimissile systems could be sent to the region as further backup.

Syria continues to deteriorate. Well over 150,000 Syrians have been killed so far. The opposition, no matter how legitimate, risks metastasizing or being coopted into an arm of radical Islam or branches of al Qaeda. This will be no accident. Small, well-organized radical groups have had the organization, discipline, and ruthlessness to win control of revolutions, as the Bolsheviks, Nazis, and Mao Tsetung's Chinese communists did.

Unfortunately, Russian president Vladimir Putin may be correct. A radicalized opposition winning control of Syria could be a greater danger to the world than the current Bashar al Assad regime, no matter how despicable and brutal. The reason is that such an extremist regime could actively threaten its neighbors and spill Islamist terror across borders.

In dealing with Syria President Obama strengthened the case about his unpreparedness and inexperience. In 2012, Obama declared a "red line" around the use of chemical weapons and demanded that Assad leave office. In 2013, after the UN incontrovertibly found Assad's regime guilty of using nerve gas against civilian populations, the president made two decisions. First, the United States would use force to degrade and destroy Syrian WMD. Second, Obama would seek the approval of Congress before taking military action.

After "leading from behind" in the 2011 Libyan campaign that removed Qaddafi, the president seemed weak and uncertain. Obama now also suffered the same fate that befell British prime minister David Cameron, who sought parliamentary approval for British military action against Syria. The motion was decisively rejected, removing the prospect of British participation in any American strike. So, lacking British support Obama decided to go to Congress.

Congress would have decisively rejected any resolution approving military force, as had the Commons. Hence, Obama was forced to reverse course. In a carefully arranged political maneuver, Secretary Kerry let fall a seemingly throwaway line in a London press conference, wondering why Assad might not be persuaded to give up his WMD. Almost immediately, Russian foreign minister Sergei Lavrov seconded the idea, and a process instantly materialized that, if successful, would destroy or remove all of Syria's WMD capability.

The resulting predicament left the Obama administration in limbo. It was urged to supply arms and nonlethal aid to the rebels. But the increasing influence of radical groups among the opposition raised a basic question. Would these weapons and this training find their way to the most dangerous parties? Because that prospect is not de minimis, the decision to supply arms and training has been deferred. If Assad's chemical weapons are indeed removed, what then is the impetus to force him to leave office? Without a strategy, there is none.

Hence, the slaughter will continue. The conflict between the Alawite minority (a Shia sect) in control and a Sunni majority means that if the regime collapses and the rebels take charge, a further bloodbath is likely. This is a no-win situation. An alternative strategy is offered in part three.

Violence in Iraq continues. The winner is Iran, whose influence among the Shia majority grows. Iraq supports Assad, while the Saudis and Qataris have poured millions of dollars into the opposition. Hezbollah, with Russian arms, remains one reason why Assad has an advantage over the opposition. Meanwhile Jordan, Turkey, and Lebanon are being placed under great stress by the Syrian civil war, the flow of many millions of refugees, and, of course, the machinations of al Qaeda and radical Islam.

Were it not so serious, the situation could be described as a parody. The United States invaded Iraq to remove a dictator and to impose a democracy friendly to the West as a bulwark against Iran. Saudi Arabia and the Gulf states were allies. Today, the United States is negotiating with Iran, moving it possibly from the category of enemy to merely adversary or someday even partner. Iraq opposes the United States in Syria. The Saudis and Gulf states have turned against the United States over perceived weaknesses in Syrian policy and for attempting a rapprochement with Iran.

Prime Minister Netanyahu demeans and ignores President Obama. Some in Congress call for an Israeli strike against Iran, which would require U.S. support for success—a bizarre situation like June 1914, when the decision to declare war was taken automatically once mobilization began. In essence, an Israeli attack would force a de facto U.S. commitment to use force—tantamount to declaring war against Iran.

To the east, conditions in Afghanistan deteriorate. Whether NATO and ISAF will leave behind any combat or support troops after 2014 if President Hamid Karzai refuses to sign a status-of-forces agreement is uncertain. A national intelligence estimate published in late 2013 predicted that without longer-term ISAF presence the Afghan government will not be able to secure the country. Some, including me, argue that no matter the size of a residual stay-behind force, the tribal and decentralized culture of Afghanistan will make it impossible for any government to keep control of the country outside of a few major cities and a limited number of other areas. One reason is that crucial to Afghanistan's future is Pakistan. And Pakistan is far from politically stable.

Pakistan is the larger danger, but for reasons that differ from conventional wisdom. Since the Bush 43 administration, Pakistan has been regarded in many Washington circles as the most dangerous country in the world. That fear is rooted in the growth of indigenous radical Islam and fundamentalism and the country's possession of some hundred nuclear warheads. The prediction is that in the wrong hands these weapons will become an Islamic or jihadi bomb. That Pakistan is fielding tactical or battlefield nuclear weapons as a counter to India's "Cold Start" strategy—that is, a no-warning conventional attack—does not diminish the arguments of those who worry about the security of Pakistani nuclear weapons.

In fact, based on the record—and given the imbalance in numbers, this may not be a fair comparison—Pakistan has a better security record vis-à-vis the safety and control of its nuclear armaments than the United States (see chapter eleven). It is not a secret yet was not fully understood by the United States until 2010 or 2011 that Pakistan has a "three key" system for controlling its nuclear weapons. The future concern, however, is when Pakistan develops battlefield weapons, how and where will they be secured, because, to be effective, weapons need to be positioned in proximity to the intended point of combat. And that is a legitimate worry.

The larger dangers in Pakistan are inherent in its society. Over a third of the 180 million Pakistanis are twenty-five or under and have poor prospects. Uneducated (except for the many who attend one of some 20,000 madrassas, which require memorization of the Koran and preach fundamentalist views of Islam), unemployed, and moving to the city, this cohort is fodder for radicalism. Government is failing, still corrupt, incompetent, and controlled by a handful of families that have run Pakistan since its formation in 1947. These ruling elites include the Sharifs—Nawaz is now prime minister for the third time; the Bhutto-Zardaris—Asif Ali Zardari stepped down as president in 2013; the army—which plays a powerful role; and the Choudhrys—one of whom retired as chief judge in late 2013. Given the incompetence of the Sharif regime and its intention to work a deal with the Taliban, another army-led coup in the distant future is not out of the question.

The economy is weak. Taxes are rarely collected, especially from the well-to-do, many of whom own "farms" that under the law provide generous tax breaks. Electrical-power outages are a way of life. The cause is not a shortage of generating capacity but so-called circular debt and failure to pay bills, forcing power companies to shut off power. Water is in scarce supply. Worse, insurgencies are intensifying, with both foreign Taliban and homegrown terrorists operating against India in Kashmir. Lashkar-e-Taibi (LeT) was responsible for the terrorist attacks in Mumbai in 2008 that almost provoked war between the two countries.

Many of Pakistan's political difficulties reside in the civil-military divide, in which the army and its chief of staff are always key power brokers. For about half of its existence, Pakistan was ruled by the army, which took power through coups against what it saw as incompetent government. Zardari was the first president to complete a full term; the election of Nawaz Sharif as prime minister marked the first time a peaceful and legitimate transition of government had occurred in Pakistan's history.

Further, the army's jewel in the crown is Inter-Services Intelligence (ISI). Combining domestic and foreign surveillance, spying, and covert actions under a single agency, ISI is a combination of the CIA, the NSA, and the Federal Bureau of Investigation into one organization. For much of its history, ISI's target was India, the strategic enemy.

Insurgent groups such as LeT were created to harass India in Kashmir. In the event of war, LeT and others were to operate inside India, much as the U.S. Special Forces were originally designed to operate in Eastern Europe in the event of war against the Soviet Union. Unfortunately, with the war in Afghanistan and the evolution of many domestic terrorist groups into Pakistani Taliban, along with criminal families such as the Haqqani, and other networks, ISI's creations turned into Frankensteins, threatening not India but Pakistan. These Frankensteins are becoming more dangerous.

Sadly, the United States never fully understood Pakistani motivations. The love-hate relationship between Pakistan and the United States led to a transactional relationship rather than a genuine partnership. Indeed, George W. Bush's designation of Pakistan as a major, non-NATO U.S. ally turned out to be rhetoric.

The divisive factor was that Pakistan always believed the United States needed Pakistan more than Pakistan needed the United States. An even larger problem was that successive White Houses never fully understood the culture or structure of Pakistani society. Indeed, in my own visits to the White House to discuss Pakistan, I was shocked by the absence of knowledge and by the superficiality of how key Pakistani leaders were regarded and important issues understood.

By the end of 2013, Pakistan's president, chief judge, and army chief of staff had all retired or left office. General Raheel Sharif, no relation to the prime minister, replaced Ashraf Pervez Kayani as army chief. Although Sharif had ample operational experience commanding brigades, a division, and a corps, the initial reaction in Washington to the appointment was that the new chief would be compliant with the political leadership. If history counts, Prime Minister Zulfikar ali Bhutto had named his former military secretary, General Mohammed Zia ul Haq, as army chief, and Nawaz had done the same with Pervez Musharraf. Neither chief was particularly compliant and both carried out coups. Unlike Bhutto, Nawaz was sentenced to exile, not death.

The often-denied reality is that Afghanistan will never be secure as long as Pakistan is unstable. For many reasons—including the stationing of U.S. drones in Pakistan; targeted assassinations killing innocent Pakistanis; and the disgraceful Raymond Davis case, where a CIA operative gunned down two Pakistanis in

Lahore (a third was killed when a U.S. rescue vehicle from the consulate drove down a one-way street in the wrong direction, hitting a cyclist, after which the White House demanded and got the release of the agent, which rightly enraged the Pakistani public)—America is viewed as the largest threat to Pakistani sovereignty. As NATO withdraws from Afghanistan, the most inexpensive way to move the millions of tons of material is through the Khyber Pass and then south through Pakistan. Transit requires the assent of the Pakistani government and no doubt huge tolls as well.

India may be regarded as the world's largest democracy, but it too has many problems. India perhaps has as many ongoing insurgencies as any country in the world. Although a democracy, its reputation has been sullied by its attitude toward women; a notorious toleration of gang rape; and a recent court decision that makes homosexuality illegal. The growing middle class, the world's largest, requires economic growth to sustain that status. And the corruption of its government has been clearly exposed. Beneath the surface, rather than being a role model for developing states, India faces many problems.

While India and Pakistan have managed to avoid another major war despite terrorist attacks and exchanges of fire in disputed Kashmir, the fragility of the relationship continues. LeT or some other terrorist group could provoke a crisis. As long as India maintains a large army—in fairness, because it does border China—and pursues a strategy of Cold Start, the prospect for another Indo-Pak confrontation must never be ignored.

China's future intentions remain largely unknown. China's remarkable economic growth is the most plausible argument for the administration's pivot to Asia. Along with the realities of geography and population, China's GDP, its political influence and reach have grown to impressive levels. An indicator has been the modernization of its military and the increase in its defense spending, alarming many in the region and beyond. China's cyber intrusion and penetration of public and private enterprises worldwide have not contributed to relieving anxieties.

Both the British *Economist* and *Financial Times* ran editorials in early 2014 marking the hundredth anniversary of the start of World War I and linking that event with the prospect of today's multi-crises exploding into global conflict. The United States was in the role of Britain, the leading but declining power. China was portrayed as a twenty-first-century Wilhelmine Germany whose ambitions and power could lead to crisis. Japan was cast as the current-day France, caught in the middle. Neither paper speculated about the Koreas or whether Kim Jong-un might be a latter-day archduke or a Gavrilo Princip in precipitating war with his neighbors.

About China, four facts are critical in considering the future. For millennia, the overriding concern of Chinese emperors, presidents, and heads of the Communist Party has been perpetuating the regime and guarding against revolutions and uprisings. Communist Party leadership has consistently set as its highest priority maintaining stability. Translated into English, "stability" means keeping power and preventing widespread unrest that could turn into revolution. Central to a preventative strategy is competence of government in sustaining economic growth. To sustain substantial economic growth, China has relied on debt-based financing and easy credit. Managing the internal debt problem is a huge, ticking time bomb for the government.

Second, and this relates to the second horseman, upward of four or five hundred million Chinese live at or below the poverty line. Most, or many, have cell phones, Internet, or satellite television. Thus, even the most humble and impoverished have access to the outside world and see how other people live.

The consequence for the government is the critical need for aggressive economic growth to deal with improving the lives of a cohort larger than the population of the United States or Europe. The risk of economic failure is an uprising. Largely unreported are the astonishing numbers of riots and protests throughout China. Tens of thousands or more Chinese have protested government corruption and incompetence while demanding improvements in standards of living and economic well-being.

Exacerbating this problem is pending environmental catastrophe. Pollution is already choking China. As China develops its industrial base, it is dependent on electrical power produced largely from coal-fired electrical generators, creating even more greenhouse gases. China will also build and import hundreds of millions of cars, trucks, and other vehicles that contribute to pollution. This is a major crisis and one that tends to keep the Chinese leadership focused at home.

Third, outside its proximate borders, which include Taiwan, China has never been particularly aggressive in territorial expansion. Disputes in the various China seas over specks of land and resources are different and represent long-term disagreements over sovereignty, disputes dating back to the empress dowager and the Japanese Meiji restoration well over a century ago.

Fourth, in order to sustain economic growth and access to resources, China has established a very aggressive mercantile policy of overseas investment, particularly where long-term access to important resources is ensured. The Chinese communities working in Africa and Latin America number in the millions. China owns over a trillion dollars in U.S. debt, with nearly the same amount invested in U.S. public companies.

The consequence of these factors leads to a picture of a China with far too many internal problems to solve rather than a state bent on territorial or hegemonic ambitions. Others will argue that as with Nazi Germany, external expansion is vital to alleviate domestic pressures or, as with Soviet Russia, necessary to extend the defensive perimeter. Neither analogy is likely to prove valid. China will grow in influence as its economic power and interests grow. But as China sees military force as a defensive tool—and Mao's dictum that a few atom bombs are enough still applies—unless the West provokes a different reaction, military confrontation can be avoided.

Unfortunately, past U.S. policies have often been based on profound misjudgments and poor intelligence. The United States continuously misassessed and often exaggerated the Soviet military threat. During the Kennedy presidency, the first decisions were to increase defense spending, double the size of the nuclear force, shift to a strategy of flexible response (meaning confronting the Soviets at all levels of unconventional, conventional, and nuclear war), and proceed with the ill-fated Bay of Pigs invasion. The result forced the Soviets to reverse Secretary General Nikita Khrushchev's defense cuts and so perpetuated the Cold War. Vietnam was another example of failed intelligence. The United States likewise failed in the second Iraq War and Iraq's nonexistent WMDs. Failure to understand the other side can be fatal, and it jeopardizes favorable outcomes with China.

In that regard, the U.S. Navy and Air Force concept of the Air-Sea Battle is seen by China as a direct threat. The aim of the concept is to project air and sea power ashore. Who else but China would be the target?

Iran may have been a more appropriate contingency. However, China's strong rhetorical response was predictable and perhaps avoidable if the concept had been limited to the Gulf. Meanwhile as part of the pivot eastward, the U.S. Army is attempting to strengthen its Pacific presence and its flexibility to deploy forces. Given the size of the People's Liberation Army (PLA), U.S. forces are drops in the bucket. Yet perceptions count sometimes far more than reality.

Japan too could be at an inflection point. Prime Minister Shinzo Abe is committed to strengthening Japan's defenses. His visits to the Yasukuni war memorial shrine have raised criticisms from neighbors, given Japan's rapacious appetite during World War II and its wars on the Eurasian continent. The disputes with China over the Senkaka-rhetto/Diaoyu Islands and China's declaration of an air-defense identification zone covering thousands of square miles of international waters have heightened tensions. Taiwan, the Philippines, and South Korea also have territorial claims of sovereignty. Japan still wants Russia to return the northern part of the Kuriles, seized in 1945 after the war ended.

Conflict over these barren rocks requires further explanation. Their resources, in the form of fish and minerals and hydrocarbons, and strategic locations are not insignificant. However, historical animosity among China, Japan, Korea, and Taiwan is a root cause of this conflict. About 90 percent of the public in each country has a negative opinion of the other country. History matters. Japan is still seen by its neighbors as an aggressor, dating back to the 1894–95 war with China and continuing through World War II. Japanese aggression against Korea and China is far from forgiven.

An incident at the end of 2013 is illustrative of the chances of a time bomb exploding. Inside this new air-defense zone, a Chinese coast guard vessel (and not a PLA Navy warship) tried to cut off a U.S. Navy destroyer. Had there been a collision or even the use of force, obviously the incident could have escalated. This was not lost on the other states in the region with far smaller navies.

The incident also brought back memories of the Cold War and "shouldering" maneuvers by the Red Banner Fleets to force U.S. warships to turn away. In 1972, the U.S. and Soviet navies signed an incidents-at-sea agreement to reduce the dangers of these encounters' getting out of hand. Perhaps a similar agreement might prove a long-term solution in the western Pacific.

The Koreas remain clearly worrisome. The North's young and untested leader Kim Jong-un is unpredictable and still an unknown quantity. At the end of 2013 Kim had his uncle tried and executed and publicized the death, raising questions about an attempted coup and the long-term resilience of the regime. The North is pursuing its nuclear weapons and missile programs, although whether it has a device or a working bomb is unclear. But make no mistake: Kim could be a twenty-first-century Princip if he so chooses.

Despite unfriendly regimes in Venezuela and Cuba and a shift of governments to the left, Latin America appears reasonably stable, with the exception of growing narco-terrorism and related crime. Recognizing Cuba, were it not for fear of alienating and losing Florida's twenty-nine electoral votes, would be a strategic coup. How long the Communist/Castro regime could survive the onslaught of capitalism is a good question. However, major political crises are less likely to come from south of the border than from other regions.

Major problems persist over immigration, drugs, and cartels selling their products to and in North America. As Mexico and Columbia shut down the narco trade, it moved to other Latin American countries and remains a ticking time bomb. While violence persists in Mexico, privatizing the oil industry should aid the economy. But outside drugs and immigration, international crises, fortunately, are likely to arise from different directions.

Africa is a conundrum. In parts, economic growth is booming. In the north, terror and instability reign. The middle is wracked with violence, specifically in Nigeria, the Central African Republic, and South Sudan. Its "horn," namely, Somalia and Yemen, hosts terrorists and pirates. The wildcard is Nigeria.

Nigeria is oil rich. Bunkering—that is, the theft of oil, usually from pipelines but also from other links in the logistical chain—runs in the many billions of dollars a year. The Muslim north is rife with insurgents. The government of Goodluck Jonathan has been criticized for corruption, as prior administrations have. And Nigeria has never been able to put its oil riches to good public use.

Nigeria's time bomb is the spread of an Islamic insurgency that occupies a good part of the north and threatens the rest. For years, the Gulf of Guinea has been vulnerable to piracy and local interdiction of tankers. While such activities have so far been minor, a few reports suggest that piracy is only in its infancy. In terms of contingency planning, Nigeria and the Gulf of Guinea must be high on the list.

Last and paradoxically, the most important region to the United States geostrategically and economically is Europe, a view with which the Obama administration seems not to agree. The transatlantic link goes far beyond trade, investment, and commercial interests, which for the United States are the largest in dollar amounts of any of its relationships.

History, culture, shared values, and the legacies of two world wars and a cold war have bound both sides of the Atlantic together. The European Union collectively has the world's largest GDP. NATO has been the source of international stability and cooperation for nearly seven decades. But NATO still must grapple with the existential question of maintaining a strong and coherent military alliance when the principal threat for which it was designed is long gone and no obvious threat has taken the place of the former Soviet Union.

Major foreign, domestic, and inter- and intra-Eurozone strains abound. Obama's pivot to Asia has weakened the perception of U.S. leadership and commitment to Europe as American forces were rebalanced out of the continent. The EU was tested to its limits by the euro economic crisis and again by Russia's move into Crimea. The dilemma over monetary union preceding political union for the long haul remains unresolved and possibly unresolvable. Many in central and eastern Europe are neuralgic over Russia's and Putin's intent to reestablish Moscow's influence and authority in the region. Increased Russian defense spending likewise has provoked concerns.

NATO is at yet another crossroads. In its history, NATO has been challenged on many occasions—the rearming of Germany, shifting to flexible response in 1968, the stationing of Pershing and cruise missiles in the early 1980s to counter Soviet systems, and the end of the threat for which it was designed. NATO was and is a military alliance. However, defining a new threat, the Soviet Union having imploded, has proven elusive.

Following the 1991 Gulf War, NATO began to see its role beyond the European boundaries and guideline areas for the alliance. The phrase was "out of area or out of business," meaning that NATO was prepared to look elsewhere to slay monsters. In 1999, it fought the seventy-eight-day campaign against Serbia and Slobodan Milosevic to stop ethnic murder in Kosovo. And on September 12, 2001, for the first time in its history it invoked Article 5 to support the United States after the September 11 attacks.

Thirteen years later, NATO is preparing to withdraw from Afghanistan, its appetite for slaying foreign monsters satiated. It still had the coherence to support the Libyan opposition and overthrow Qaddafi in 2011. However, economic pressures are forcing major cuts in all but a handful of NATO member states and are reducing the size of the alliance's military and its capability. Despite a strategic concept—based on the principles of collective defense, crisis management, and cooperative security—that was approved at the Lisbon Summit of heads of state and government in November 2010, four years later NATO's role and purpose are elusive for many of its members' publics.

Obviously, a resurgent Russia post-Crimea is of concern to NATO's newer partners. The militarily strongest and nuclear-weapons-possessing members—the United States, Britain, and France—still see out-of-area tasks as important. However, nations other than the United States lack the capacity for large-scale operations. The United Kingdom expects to be able to deploy five to ten thousand troops for an extended period. Without U.S. aerial tankers and transports, the French could not have mounted their operation into Mali.

Attempts at using "smart defense" and "connected force initiatives (CFI)" to do more with less money have not worked and will not. The best to be achieved when spending less money is doing "less, less." Last, NATO expansion is a work in progress. Ukraine and Georgia are too hot to handle. With twenty-eight members already, bringing more on board risks an even more cumbersome decision-making process and difficulty in reaching the mandatory consensus for action.

In this scenario, the September 2014 summit at Celtic Manor in Wales, England, could have been an opportunity to refocus and redefine the alliance in light of these political and economic realities. Lacking were big ideas and strong U.S. leadership to bind both sides of the Atlantic closer. While the Afghan drawdown and Ukraine dominated the agenda, the summit proved inconclusive, deferring the tough issues to the future and losing a great opportunity to reshape the alliance for the twenty-first century.

The above scenario reflects the reality that Russia is central to what is happening and will happen in Europe. That Russia and the United States could cooperate in removing chemical weapons from Syria was a potential breakthrough that was lost. Russia is still dependent on its natural gas and oil exports for cash. As U.S. and other natural gas comes on line and making natural gas from shale oil through "fracking" becomes more prevalent, especially in southern Europe, Russia's cash cow will be under attack.

Putin's autocratic controls have not been popular for the long run, and the rise of the kleptocracy and the oligarchs has provoked the middle class. Some analysts, such as Zbigniew Brzezinski, are optimistic that Russia will turn more toward democratic capitalism once Putin goes and after the Crimea episode subsides. But the problem for the United States is emotional and political.

Barack Obama and Vladimir Putin are far from soul mates. Many American Cold Warriors are even more wary of Russia, given Crimea. Few see strategic advantages to be gained from cooperation. John Kerry is the exception. Handled properly and with respect and dignity, Russia could still be, if not an ally, possibly a partner. The Middle East, particularly Syria and Iran, hold common interests for both Moscow and Washington if resolved. A modernized Russia will end its dependence on exporting energy and create new markets. And greater cooperation with NATO could be in the interests of all.

The Balkans, despite relatively tiny populations, are contentious. Georgia, Moldova, and Ukraine are caught even deeper in the East-West divide. But none is likely to be a source of world war or regional conflict as occurred in 1914, because Putin may see no further gain and too much risk in making additional territorial encroachments. Time will tell, however.

As ice melts and the Arctic becomes far more navigable, competition over resources could take place. Fortunately, the Arctic Council and other groups are in discussion now, trying to lay out an agenda and rules of the road for the future. Hence, the Arctic's importance, if all goes well, is to be seen in terms of finding new resources and opening faster shipping lanes between continents.

Concluding that the world is but a bullet away from regional conflict is a bit too pessimistic. However, crises spots and ticking time bombs exist in excess. Civil war in Syria could spread. At this writing, Iraq is facing both civil war and the onslaught of ISIS/ISIL. Should negotiations with Iran on its nuclear programs fail, the use of force becomes far more likely.

Afghanistan is not more secure after its elections. A Mumbai-like terrorist attack could trigger a new Indo-Pak war, the first in which both sides would have nuclear weapons. Or another, unpredictable contingency could bring any of these potential crisis points to a boil.

In these cases, a common link is the third horseman. Radical and violent Islam is spreading. Bin Laden's al Qaeda may have been smashed. Sadly, like the phoenix, many subsets and offshoots have arisen from the ashes. Each is dangerous. And each must be central to the mind-set needed for the twenty-first century.

Beyond that, wildcard or black-swan events, possibly in the form of many archdukes and vast amounts of bullets, could have profound impact. Chapter seven lists thirteen wildcards. But the reader no doubt can invent or imagine many dozens more.

5

Global Financial and Economic Ticking Time Bombs

One means of better understanding the nature of catalytic and catastrophic geostrategic change such as the events triggering World War I is analysis and review of other forms of crises. While no exact parallels exist, financial crises offer a relevant lens for inspection in which long-term and often seemingly unrelated or unconnected events and actions suddenly become explosive. Whether the tulip bubble that burst in 1637 in Europe or the Great Depression of 1929, financial markets can implode with the speed of light; in each case, the causes were long in the making. The financial meltdown of 2008 is a telling case study for demonstrating how excesses of potential archdukes and bullets can be created, purposely or inadvertently, and what dire consequences can result. Interestingly, cousins of the Four Horsemen played large roles in fomenting this financial crisis.

The United States has suffered several recent financial meltdowns. On October 19, 1987, called "Black Monday," the Dow sunk a record 508 points, the largest loss in its history to that point. The savings-and-loan banks imploded during that decade. The "dot-com" bubble burst when too many technology stocks—indeed, many companies with names ending in dot-com—were overvalued and overpriced and imploded.

The 2008 crisis is relevant to understanding the mechanisms that can unleash geostrategic and political crises. In many ways, 2008's roots go back to the 1907 financial crisis in America. Then, "bucket shops" were early forms of casino capitalism, making huge bets on whether the prices of particular stocks would rise or fall. These bets were the precursors of credit default swaps (CDSs) and synthetic derivatives, in which ownership of an asset is not necessary to wager on its future price. Bets then did not require stock ownership, only as little as a 10 percent down payment, retaining the remaining 90 percent on margin—in essence, an IOU that had to be paid on demand.

The Gavrilo Princip of the day was a company called United Copper. An unsuccessful takeover led to its failure, which also bankrupted a number of banks financing the deal. The failure spread to other banks, and panic set in. People began withdrawing cash from banks deemed unsafe and from stock markets.

Margin calls from the bucket shops drained cash from the market, causing a death spiral. Only the intervention of J. P. Morgan and commitment of his capital resolved the crisis. One result was the formation of the Federal Reserve in 1913. The other was the banning of bucket shops and the regulation of most swaps.

In many ways, cousins of the Four Horsemen contributed to the 2008 crisis. Failed government, as we will see, put in place the policies that generated the explosive mixture. Expanding home ownership, keeping interest rates artificially low, deregulating markets, and limiting oversight would provide both the explosive material and the fuses for the crisis.

Economic disparity and the attempt to eliminate racial and income discrimination through the Fair Housing Act of 1968, the Community Re-Investment Act the next decade, and subsequent affordable housing acts would fuel the subprime mortgage debacle.

Radical ideology took the form of belief in the need for massive deregulation of markets and reduction of oversight, advocated and advanced by private and public financial sectors and by certain elites in both political parties.

While environmental calamity was not present per se, the catastrophic collapse of Long Term Capital Management in 1998, which nearly brought down the financial system, and the implosion of the highly regarded energy and trading giant Enron in 2001 were unheeded precursors of and warnings about what would unfold in 2008.

The seeds for the 2008 crisis expanded globally, having originated decades earlier, in 1968, in noble political intentions to extend home ownership to all or most Americans. Forty years later, low interest rates and government mandates for banks to expand loans to low-income owners would overheat and overcharge the subprime mortgage market. As a result, hundreds of thousands of Americans would purchase homes without the assets to ensure future mortgage payments.

The abrogation of the Glass-Steagall Banking Act, passed after the 1929 crash to separate investment from commercial banking with the so-called Chinese Wall, and the deregulation of CDSs, banned or regulated by most states in 1908, a year after the financial crisis of 1907, would become engines of mass financial destruction. Few considered the risks, especially when seduced by huge money-making potential and misplaced belief in perfect economic models that would eliminate chance and bad luck. It was extraordinary that Robert Rubin, himself both cochairman of Goldman-Sachs—perhaps the onetime gold standard of investment banking—and later secretary of the treasury, could later admit that he had never fully understood the full leverage and destructive power of "derivatives." And Rubin was not alone.

The failure of government began with President Lyndon Johnson and the passage of the Fair Housing Act in 1968. The law was meant to eliminate discrimination in home buying. Nine years later, President Jimmy Carter signed into law the Community Reinvestment Act to encourage commercial banks and savings associations to lend to all members of the community, particularly low-income families. In later years, additional affordable housing acts reinforced this intent. Two "government sponsored enterprises" (GSEs), which controlled the secondary mortgage market, would be encouraged to underwrite a number of these mortgages under Presidents Clinton and then Bush.

By the early 1990s, provisions of the Glass-Steagall Act had been interpreted to allow commercial banks and especially their affiliates to expand operations into other securities activities. Glass-Steagall referred to two of the four original provisions of the 1933 Banking Act that had separated commercial and investment banking on the grounds that part of the 1929 collapse had been caused by the merging of the two activities, in essence enabling the investment side to use banking deposits to pursue its business interests.

With Citibank's 1998 merger with Salomon Smith Barney, one of the largest U.S. securities firms, permitted by the generous Federal Reserve interpretation of Glass-Steagall, the law was practically "dead." The lobbying of the great and powerful of Wall Street, supported by President Bill Clinton, led Congress to pass at the end of 1999 the Gramm-Leach-Bliley Act. That law no longer required the separation of commercial from investment banking. What this meant was that these new institutions, no longer separated by a Chinese Wall, could engage in proprietary trading—that is, using funds from the commercial side in investment banking.

A year later and before leaving Congress, Senator Phil Gramm, coauthor of the law ending Glass-Steagall, inserted a key provision into the 2000 Commodity

Futures Modernization Act exempting over-the-counter derivatives like credit default swaps from regulation by the Commodity Futures Trading Commission. In essence, this law ended the ban on CDSs arising from the 1907 crisis. It was no coincidence that Gramm's wife, Wendy, sat on the Enron board of directors, a further sign of the incestuous relations between government and business.

Two other ingredients were critical to this explosive mixture: the Federal National Mortgage Association (Fannie Mae), created in 1938 as part of the New Deal to expand the secondary mortgage market with securitization allowing reinvestment (mortgage-backed securities, or MBSs), and the Federal Home Loan Mortgage Corporation (Freddie Mac), started in 1970 as a GSE (meaning government accepted the liabilities) to expand further the secondary mortgage market by buying back mortgages. Freddie and Fannie were encouraged by government to support home buying by lower-income families. As GSEs, both institutions also had the full faith and credit of the United States behind them. So, what could go wrong?

Through repurchase of mortgages, both institutions were making money hand over fist on commissions. Worse, the boards of directors, who were very well compensated, were filled with political appointees by both parties, in part as rewards for loyalty. Many former politicians were hired as consultants so both Freddie and Fannie could continue to influence Congress. This was not a Ponzi scheme, in the sense of being illegal. However, in terms of conflict of interests and public perceptions, the process was profoundly flawed. As a result, there was no effective oversight of the two most important institutions engaged in the secondary mortgage markets.

Then, Alan Greenspan, chairman of the Federal Reserve, reduced interest rates further. Everything was present for a meltdown. Firing this meltdown was the innovative creation of new derivatives, in the form of credit default swaps pioneered in 1994 by J. P. Morgan, well before it was forced to merge with Chase.

By 2007, sky-high home prices in the United States finally turned sharply downward, despite the assumption that home prices and values would only increase. The contagion quickly spread to the entire U.S. financial sector and then to overseas markets. Damage was not limited to the financial sector, however, as companies that normally relied on credit suffered heavily, from insurance industries to the corner grocery.

How could this happen? Through its actions, government had deregulated banking, ceased oversight of CDSs encouraged Freddie and Fannie to expand so-called subprime loans to lower-income families, and dropped interest rates so that the housing market became the go-to place to make money.

Mortgage companies began making so-called NINJA loans—"no income, no job, no assets"—to borrowers, often not qualified for ordinary home loans. Subprime mortgages carried for a year or two low "teaser" interest rates that later would balloon to double-digit rates. Freddie and Fannie would guarantee many of these loans. Besides, housing prices only went up, or so conventional wisdom hoped.

Mortgage lenders saw value in making even more money by selling loans to Freddie and Fannie in order to raise more cash to make more loans. Many of these subprime mortgages were turned into MBSs that offered cash flow from monthly payments used as collateral. These mortgages would be "sliced and diced" into packages that banking institutions bought for the cash flow, which provided a much higher rate of return, given the Fed's policy of low interest rates. This revolving wheel seemed to be a perpetual moneymaking machine for mortgage companies, home builders, and bankers, as well as a good deal for low-income families.

The scheme did not stop there. The insurance industry heard the *kerchink* of cash registers ringing with the infamous credit default swaps. So they wrote insurance policies. For a fee, the insurers would assume any losses caused by mortgage defaults. It got better. So-called synthetic derivatives, akin to the bucket shops, flourished in which institutions bought swaps on assets they did not hold.

What began in the insurance world as safe bets and well-managed risk, however, turned quickly into speculation. Financial institutions bought or sold credit default swaps on assets that they did not own, on the basis of unfounded assumptions of markets only going up. Collateralized debt obligations (CDOs) became another part of this moneymaking machine. As early as 2003, to a few, it was obvious that this scheme was producing "financial weapons of mass destruction." In 2001, just under a trillion dollars was insured by derivatives. Seven years later, the figure had soared to just over $60 trillion.

All this worked if and only if housing prices went up. But that was not going to happen in perpetuity. As prices began to collapse and the housing industry went into decline, many homeowners found themselves "underwater"—the values of their homes were far less than the sizes of their remaining mortgages. The effect was metastasizing for the financial, mortgage, and insurance industries. As home-owners defaulted on payment, decreasing cash flow made the MBSs drop in value. Worse, because of the slicing and dicing of these instruments, no one knew which assets were sound and which were subprime or junk. As in 1907, panic set in.

Countrywide Financial Corporation, the largest American mortgage lender, was the first to go, bought at a fire-sale price by Bank of America in January 2008. Then in March the venerable Wall Street firm Bear Stearns was rescued from bank-ruptcy by J. P. Morgan Chase, which purchased Bear first at two dollars, then at ten dollars, per share, with the Fed agreeing to underwrite some $30 billion of Bear's debt. Likewise, Fannie and Freddie had to be rescued by Uncle Sam. The Treasury seized control of the two GSEs in September, replaced management, and pledged upward of $100 billion to cover any gaps in the balance sheets.

Lehman Brothers and Merrill Lynch were the next to go. Merrill was bought by Bank of America. And Lehman, after a failed attempt to arrange a Barclay's buyout, declared bankruptcy.

American International Group (AIG), the country's largest insurer, was unable to secure credit through normal channels. Because it insured potentially trillions of dollars in CDSs and other derivatives, its failure could have brought the system down. To save AIG, the federal government bought 80 percent of the company with a total investment of $120 billion. AIG has since repaid the government.

There were many other casualties. Goldman Sachs and other banks were forced to form holding companies in order to receive federal financial help. The Troubled Asset Relief Program, with nearly $800 billion at its disposal, advanced funds to banks to shore up balance sheets. That money too has been repaid, with interest. Seattle-based Washington Mutual (WaMu) and Wachovia Corporation, a giant North Carolina–based bank crippled by the subprime-mortgage fiasco, were bought by J. P. Morgan Chase and California-based Wells Fargo, respectively.

Meanwhile, the American auto industry, itself outpaced by overseas competi-tion and onerous contracts with dealers and labor, faced bankruptcy and pleaded for a federal bailout. By then, banks had stopped making the loans that business needed to maintain cash flows, fearing that companies could not repay. Worldwide share prices plummeted. The Dow Jones Industrial Average lost more than a third of its value in 2008. By year's end, a deep recession had enveloped most of the globe.

As of 2014, although the 2008 crisis did not unravel the global financial system, economic recoveries worldwide have been lackadaisical and slow. But the broader lessons very much apply to international politics. The erosion of the Westphalian system parallels the activities of the U.S. government that produced this financial debacle by encouraging not only unregulated operations of much of the market but incentivizing the urgent creation of more MBSs to make more money for all manner of corporations.

As the state-centric system erodes, the empowerment of individuals at the expense of government fuels centrifugal forces that states can no longer control. It is for the reader to speculate what parallels exist with al Qaeda in terms of the impact of radical ideologies. However, the inflexible assumptions that housing prices will only go upward, that interest rates will remain permanently low, and stocks will only rise are mirrored in a mind-set that is based on the past and in some ways is as rigid and wrong as the perversion of Islam by al Qaeda and other extremist groups.

Regarding the future, three ticking time bombs are making a great deal of noise: debt, more debt, and still more debt. Despite debates over debt-to-GDP ratios, the United States has some $17 trillion of public debt, not including the Fed's balance sheet of about $4 trillion in liabilities. These liabilities have come from purchasing "treasuries" at the rate of $85 billion a month, or almost a trillion dollars a year, through what is called "quantitative easing," to put money back into the economy to stimulate growth.

In the financial crisis described above, the assumption was that housing prices could only increase. Today, two assumptions must raise equal skepticism. Stock markets will not always rise. Stock indices grew by about a third in 2013. That cannot continue. And second, interest rates have been kept artificially low, although they are gradually increasing. What happens when rates go to 4, 5, or, as in the Carter years, to 17 percent? A huge slice of the federal budget will go to interest payments. Four percent of $17 trillion is nearly $700 billion, or the size of recent defense budgets.

While it is true that the annual deficit is falling, from $1.3 trillion in fiscal year (FY) 2011 to just over half that, $700 billion a year is a substantial amount of money. In the out-years, that figure is destined to rise, as more baby boomers retire and if entitlement programs are not constrained. Consider the state of annual deficits, which in these very out-years are projected to stabilize around half a trillion dollars a year.

In then-year dollars, over the past decade annual deficits amounted to: FY 2015(projected), $577 billion; FY 2014, $744 billion; FY 2013, $680 billion; FY 2012, $1,087 billion; FY 2011, $1,300 billion; FY 2010, $1,294 billion; FY 2009, $1,413 billion; FY 2008, $458 billion; FY 2007, $161 billion; FY 2006, $248 billion; and FY 2005, $318 billion.

China too faces great debt and credit problems that could explode if or when the real estate bubble implodes. The resulting ticking time bomb is, what happens if China's remarkable annual economic growth falters? Many economies are dependent on Chinese demand for goods and investment. To some degree, the debt issue still plagues western Europe. Obviously, long-term growth is the best answer. If TTIP and the Transpacific Trade Pact (TTP) are approved over the long term, that will help economic growth. And the increases in U.S. production of oil and natural gas, particularly through "fracking," are likewise good economic news.

Unfortunately, "reforms" to the financial system in the United States and internationally are still incomplete. The Sarbanes Oxley law of 2002 designed to stop corporate wrongdoing, probably imposed more costs for accounting and regulatory oversight than did corporate criminal or illegal behavior. Dodd-Frank is less than half complete in final implementation, as the federal government, responsible for implementation, is that far behind in its assigned preparation of the regulations that flow from the law.

Europe may be over the worst of its recession. However, consider what happens when interest rates go up, in the United States as well as globally, which eventually they will: credit tightens, stock markets peak and decline, quantitative easing slows, and deficit spending continues. As the 2008 crisis showed, the collapse of the housing market and the impact on subprime mortgages became the Gavrilo Princip. And the casino capitalism over CDSs, CDOs, and artificial derivatives became the archduke. The analogy is clear. Assumptions about perpetual stock-market growth and permanently low interest rates will prove wrong. The question is timing. A good bet is that the fall of 2014 could easily bring bad times. We will see.

While not a ticking financial time bomb in one sense, "sequestration" of defense spending—a mandatory ten-year reduction of $450 billion—poses huge challenges for the Pentagon that will be covered later. But the challenge is clear. Even without sequestration, left unchecked the dramatic cost growth for people, health care, retirement, and weapons systems is so great that by decade's end the

Pentagon will face Hobson's choice of cutting the force in half or buying virtually nothing. And that time bomb will explode.

Last, the 2008 crisis was staunched largely by central banks working loosely in tandem, with the U.S. Treasury Department and the Federal Reserve taking the lead. Given the potential weaknesses in the financial system, as well as China's prospects, it is questionable that this time around the organization is in place to deal with a future crisis. The World Bank, Bank for International Settlements, International Monetary Fund (IMF), and Basel agreements are too limited. Hence, one recommendation is the establishment of an international monetary crisis and contingency agency charged with identifying possible weaknesses and proposing potential solutions in advance of the crisis.

6

Cyber

Perhaps no other subject (or technology) has been as supercharged by globalization and the diffusion of power as much as cyber has. Cyber, in the form of the Internet, is the circulatory and nervous system for globalization and a principal mechanism for maintaining and strengthening interdependence and interconnectivity—or eroding it! A century ago, John Maynard Keynes could brag that a proper English gentleman sitting in his London club had at his (not her!) disposal virtually anything the world had to offer. Today, this access applies to anyone with a computer or smart phone. And unlike the Londoner, with Federal Express or UPS that product could arrive overnight even to distant places.

On the other hand, beyond states interested in exploiting or looting the Internet, cyber has empowered individuals and nonstate actors with the ability and access to do great harm as well as good. The proverbial ten-year-old "whiz kid" wishing to disrupt or hack the Internet for sport or malice can do just that. The flow of information from Wikileaks, NSA revelations, and a low-cost, usually secure operational planning outlet for dangerous and disruptive organizations such as al Qaeda would not be possible without cyber and the Internet. Ironically, while state-run militaries and intelligence agencies spend billions on secure communications, the Internet costs al Qaeda and other terrorist groups virtually nothing to transmit operations plans, propaganda, and other vital information—an asymmetric cost-exchange ratio similar to IEDs, one that nonstate actors will exploit.

Cyber sits at the nexus of privacy and security, posing exquisite dilemmas for governments and publics. The NSA-Snowden affair is only one of many examples affecting search, seizure, secrecy, privacy, and due-process issues. No boundaries have been established between privacy and security. This applies to any and all people whose lives, property, and privacy can be accessed by unauthorized parties.

Facebook, Twitter, LinkedIn, and other social media are used by hundreds of millions of people, who in some cases post or expose the most sensitive of personal material. Identity theft is well known and is now the subject of a Hollywood movie. Use of the Internet for credit-card and banking transactions is subject to interception and foul play by hackers, criminals, and others merely interested in finding information on selected individuals.

Particularly sensitive to intrusion are banks, financial institutions, asset managers, and hedge funds, whose accounts and information can be hacked or are vulnerable to intrusion. Most people are unaware of or indifferent to the dangers and liabilities of having private and personal data posted on the Internet. The cyber penetrations of Target and its seventy million customers, of Neiman-Marcus and now E-Bay were vivid reasons for enhancing security to prevent identity theft and wrongful use of private data. Malicious pornography to embarrass or harm a former partner by posting explicit images of what was meant to be private behavior is the latest Internet excess.

That said, defining cyber has been difficult and elusive. What exactly is meant by the term "cyber," and in addition to the benefits, what are the vulnerabilities and weaknesses created by this and associated technologies?

The United States and other countries have had great difficulty in properly describing and even appropriately naming the dangers emanating from Islamic Jihadi terrorists and extremists. The world of cyber and cyberspace has been equally resistant to acceptable and accepted definition. Cyber war, cyber warfare, cyber attack, and cyber terrorism all vie for inclusion in a universal definition. Nor has balance between security and privacy been defined.

Highly unsettled constitutional and legal issues arising over search and seizure, due process, and oversight authorized by the Foreign Intelligence Surveillance Act (FISA) and by the secret intelligence court that oversees FISA remain in legal limbo, awaiting further settlement. One federal judge has ruled that the NSA has acted unconstitutionally in its surveillance programs. A second argues that it has operated within the law and the Constitution. Yet, a definition of cyber, what it means and includes, remains elusive, as do the actual vulnerabilities and weaknesses.

The ubiquity of cyber has raised genuine fears of massive disruption. The doomsday example is a "cyber Pearl Harbor." That phrase is promiscuously applied as the ultimate national-security threat, in which a cyber attack could achieve levels of destruction equal to those of conventional military weaponry. Such an attack is predicted to do massive damage to the nation through disrupting the electrical grid and the banking system or denying Internet services. If massive enough to affect literally millions of sites and users, an attack could arguably and potentially wreck the economy. No definition or understanding exists for determining if or when a cyber attack constitutes an act or war or what the retaliatory options might be, either in law or accepted international norms. Hollywood and fiction writers have dined out on contingencies based on cyber war. Yet, too much about cyber remains fiction, not fact.

A first step in bounding and defining cyber involves the use of history. Analogies can provide useful insights. Cyber is worldwide, operates at the speed of light, and generally but not always entails the Internet, the connecting infrastructure, computers, and the Internet service providers (ISPs), as well as users. Three historical examples are generically relevant to cyber. All share common characteristics, and each offers insights helping to understand better and define a cyber framework: the nautical rules of the road; money and banking systems; and the intellectual construct for nuclear deterrence.

From the earliest days of oars and sails, formulating a series of rules of the road became essential to avoid collisions, keep mariners safe, and standardize operations on the seas and inland waterways. Over time, these rules evolved into international standards that were universally accepted. Hence, a ship sailing into Athens (actually Piraeus), Greece, operates under the same rules as a merchantman entering Accra, Ghana.

An extension of the rules of the road was the 1972 Incidents at Sea Agreement between the U.S. and Soviet navies. The purpose was to reduce the chances of some accidental or unprovoked incident between warships of the two navies sparking a broader conflict. Whether cyber could be fitted into an agreed-upon, international equivalent to the rules of the road is a question to be explored. Whether the Incidents at Sea Agreement too might apply to the world of cyber to limit incidents on the Internet from becoming international crises between or among states is a second question that needs to be answered, especially given the amount of cyber theft that occurs.

Money and banking systems are a second analogy. Barter—that is, some means of nonmonetary exchange—has at best limited value in advanced societies. Money is ubiquitous and crucial to the functioning of society and never more so than in the twenty-first century. Banking, of course, forms the circulatory system for international commerce.

Further, in banking as in cyber, villains, charlatans, con men, incompetents, and thieves who wish to steal, dupe, trick, or otherwise separate people from their money abound. Security, safeguards, and regulations not different in kind from the rules of the road are in place in banks, financial transactions, and international agreements to prevent money laundering or illegal manipulation of funds. Thorough oversight permeates the banking systems from the Federal Reserve, Federal Deposit Insurance Corporation, and Securities and Exchange Commission in the United States to national and international agencies and offices. Money and banks, of course, depend on the ether for transactions, payments, and transfers. The absolute requirement for protection and encryption is self-evident. Thus, the international financial and banking systems provide a second analogy for a cyber framework.

Last is the construct of nuclear deterrence. The detonations of "Fat Boy" and "Little Man" over Hiroshima and Nagasaki in August 1945 began the nuclear age. At first, while the explosive power of these first weapons was measured in the equivalent of thousands of tons of TNT (kilotons, or KT) and ranged from 10 to 15 KT, conventional ordnance could, given sufficient bombers and time, be dropped on targets with equally destructive effect. In fact, the fire bombings of Tokyo, Nagoya, and Haruna claimed more lives in single nights than did the two nuclear bombs. Many in the first years of the atomic age debated also whether nuclear weapons were just extensions of conventional ones in single packages.

Thermonuclear weapons changed that calculus. In 1954, the United States first tested the H-bomb, so named because the explosive power came from the fusion of hydrogen atoms. Measured in the equivalent of millions of tons of TNT, a single thermonuclear bomb could generate all the explosive power used in prior wars. H-bombs were surely society-annihilating weapons.

By 1955, ten years after Hiroshima, a theory of deterrence had been well established. Deterrence was based on the threat of destroying an adversary should a nuclear war start. The bet was that no one would take the risk. The Soviet Union had a different perception—nuclear war would be a fight to the finish, and hence deterrence had to be based on war-fighting principles. Nonetheless, a construct for deterrence was in place.

Cyber has been around for more than a century. But no construct, such as for rules of the road, monetary systems, or nuclear deterrence, has emerged. This is something that demands action as noted below. Even 1914, rudimentary cyber was present. Radio, telegraphy, and telephones were in abundant use. Code breaking was firmly entrenched.

When war broke out that year, both the Allies and the Central Powers tapped into underwater telegraph cables to read the messages and traffic or tried to destroy or neutralize these means of transmission. Some of these efforts were distant relatives and precursors of the Stuxnet virus that would be used to disable Iranian nuclear centrifuges nine decades later.

The ether was used for deception, disinformation, and misdirection. The famous Zimmermann Telegram of 1917 was intercepted by British intelligence. Germany attempted to induce Mexico to enter the war against the United States on Germany's side. The telegram promised as a reward the return of the lost territories in Texas and the U.S. Southwest. Once they had decoded it, the British provided a copy of the telegram to U.S. authorities to inform Washington of Berlin's malign motives. And during the war, propaganda of every type flowed from newspapers, radio, and air-dropped leaflets.

Less remembered was the extensive use of camouflage, especially by the Germans, exploiting the visible spectrum to deceive the Allies. The Germans even perfected a means of tapping into and listening to Allied field-telephone communications connected by wire to higher headquarters. Early versions of what became cyber attack and cyber war were part of World War I.

Since then, cyber has been present in every war through code breaking, deception, surveillance, disinformation, and offensive uses. Jamming of radio signals, homing beacons, and radar has been critical. The famous code-breaking team at Bletchley Park is best known for Ultra, the code name for deciphering Nazi messages encrypted with Enigma machines and Japanese signals in the Purple code. Less known was the prowess at code breaking of the Germans, who generally were better at it than the Allies.

Ministries and departments of defense generally view cyber as the "fifth dimension," or domain, of warfare along with sea (and underwater), air, land, and space. Cyber warfare is waged in the "ether" of electrons, the universe of zeroes and ones, the digital alphabet, and the language of computers. For the purpose of this chapter, the "cyber" incorporates the components of cyber war, attack, and terrorism, to include espionage, sabotage, denial of service, and what is known as "hacktivism"—that is, recreational attempts to penetrate, disrupt, or steal from Internet sites and users.

Despite the inherent difficulties in defining cyber, a broken U.S. government has been unable to resolve this issue. The PATRIOT Act, passed after September 11, granted government the legal authorities to increase its surveillance capacity, among other activities. The release of sensitive NSA secrets by Edward Snowden captured the tension and debate over privacy and security a dozen years later.

The Department of Defense (DoD), supported by the Department of Homeland Security and the CIA, has been the de facto cyber leader. The National Security Agency, part of the DoD, has long been engaged in signals intercept and all forms of electronic surveillance and code breaking. Given the importance of cyber, Cyber Command was created in 2010; Gen. Keith Alexander, U.S. Army, head of the NSA, was given the new assignment. Critics complained of the militarization of cyber.

In the same year, a Protecting Cyberspace as a National Asset Act of 2010 (S. 3488) was introduced in the Senate but never passed. Its purpose was to increase security in cyberspace and prevent disabling infrastructure attacks. The legislation would have also created an Office of Cyberspace Policy and a National Center for Cyber Security and Communications. More important, the bill would have given the president a "kill switch" to shut down the Internet in crisis. Though the bill never passed, it raised many of the issues and tensions that remain unresolved.

Regarding national security, definition of cyber can and must include cyber war and warfare, cyber attack, cyber terrorism, cyber espionage, and cyber crime. Each attempts to exploit the Internet in different ways to obtain or steal proprietary or classified information from corporations, individuals, and governments; to disrupt or deny services; to shut down, incapacitate, or destroy infrastructure; to steal assets, money, or personal information; to deceive and mislead; to terrorize; to organize political movements; to obtain information available on the Internet, such as plans for designing nuclear weapons; and to influence events and opinion.

Ticking time bombs are everywhere. The Department of Defense reports that millions of attempted hacks and intrusions into its computer systems regularly occur. The national electrical-power grid, the vulnerability of which was identified as a looming crisis thirty years ago in a Center for Strategic and International Studies (CSIS) study, has not been made more resistant to or resilient against acts of either nature or man and is considered one bull's-eye for a cyber attack.

Fifteen years ago, I led a study to examine six nightmarish national-security scenarios. One scenario provoked a massive flow of displaced Mexicans fleeing to find secure refuge in the United States after an environmental calamity. Following a Katrina-sized storm or a shattering earthquake that devastated much of Mexico, a cyber attack was launched against Mexico's power grid, disabling it for a considerable period long after the calamity had run its course. The combination of the calamity and the loss of power precipitated panic among hundreds of thousands of Mexicans, homeless and desperately frightened. Regardless of the credibility of the scenario, the shocking revelation was the ease with which the grid could have been disabled.

Perhaps the most publicized cyber attack was the Stuxnet worm that targeted and disabled many of the Siemens controllers on Iran's centrifuges at the Natanz enrichment facility in 2010. Russian cyber attacks against Estonia in 2007 and Georgia in 2008 are also well known. China's attempts at cyber theft of U.S. and other countries' intellectual property have been well reported. For better or worse, the Snowden NSA revelations have not helped the United States in its international efforts to control cyber espionage and theft. The NSA leaks did untoward harm to U.S. credibility and sophistication. Hence, American motives will be questioned and ridiculed, and it will be difficult for the United States to take the lead in creating a cyber framework.

Because the range of potential cyber targets and vulnerabilities is virtually unbounded, one ticking time bomb is the difficulty of government to structure a framework for dealing with these issues. Many efforts across the U.S. government, from protection of the national infrastructure to offices dealing with cyber terror and related issues, are ongoing. However, no comprehensive government-wide program has produced effective and accepted cyber policies.

Here is a proposed memo for the president on how to redress this deficiency. This memo originated from discussions between Frank Kramer, a former senior Department of Defense official and cyber expert, and me and in a prior unsuccessful effort to launch a cyber think tank (although the Commerce Department has been authorized to embark on such a project).

Dear Mr. President;

Perhaps no single issue presents the breadth of challenges, contradictions, uncertainties, and unknowns that cyber does. From seeking a constitutional and legal balance between security and privacy to defining effective policies for ensuring the future functioning, safety, and regulation of cyber, many of these issues are unresolved. Indeed, no satisfactory consensus exists as to when and what level of a cyber attack constitutes an act of war, if any does. And the recent intrusions into Target in which data from some seventy million customers were stolen, as well as into Neiman-Marcus, are warnings as to the seriousness of maintaining cyber security and preventing identity theft.

Further, attempts to recreate in cyber the equivalent of a new Manhattan Project or the program that put Americans on the moon have failed. A principal reason is that such crash projects produce such things as bombs or rockets. Cyber is principally a cognitive and informational matter. Hence, what is needed first is not things but an intellectual framework and construct on the basis of which tangible and physical products can follow.

The purpose of this memo is to recommend a comprehensive and intellectual approach to deal with cyber. We also appreciate the damage done by the release of classified NSA material and documents. American credibility, legitimacy, and reputation regarding cyber have been badly damaged. And the tensions between security and privacy have been exacerbated. However, we believe that the following recommendations, if implemented, can address and resolve many of these issues. As that occurs, credibility and confidence with friends and allies alike will be restored.

Cyber policy, broadly defined to include both conceptual and operational components, lacks an overarching construct to guide and direct both government and private-sector policy. A useful if rough analogy as to the current state of cyber policy is 1946, soon after the first use of nuclear weapons in World War II in 1945. Then, understanding the impact of nuclear weapons and the subsequent invention and development of a deterrent-based policy were in early formative stages.

The absence of an overarching cyber security framework for both private and government sectors limits the setting of effective policies. The consequence has been many narrow and often uncoordinated actions directed at resolving specific and not cross-cutting problems and issues. For example, the very definition of what cyber means has been elusive and diaphanous at best. Specifically, no guidance exists as to what form of a cyber attack might constitute an act of war, although the laws of warfare would be a good starting point. Placing Cyber Command under Pentagon control suggested a degree of militarization that may not be intended and could be counterproductive.

That said, developing a comprehensive framework for cyber security, as was done for nuclear deterrence, is an achievable goal. But producing a comprehensive framework will require significant analytic and technological research and analysis by appropriately experienced and skilled people drawn from both government and the private sector. This memorandum proposes four interrelated initiatives designed to accomplish this goal.

Specifically:

- Establishing a think tank focused on analyzing and identifying over-arching and key cyber issues relating to the strategic, cognitive, and philosophical underpinnings of a broader framework, including the tension between security and privacy.
- Creating as part of this think tank a technological cyber "skunk works" with the mission of developing a significantly more secure cyber structure that includes offense, defense, rules of engagement, a template for assessing when an attack constitutes an act of war, and retaliatory options and proposals for an associated legal and judicial regime to accommodate the challenges and demands of cyber space.
- Developing public-private partnerships, to include personnel proce-dures that will allow highly capable nongovernmental cyber persons to support analysis and technological development on a special-project basis without all the prerequisites normally associated with classified work.
- Starting an international dialogue among a limited number of key countries that would support the foregoing, and also the develop-ment of international deterrent, governance, and law-enforcement arrangements.

Four premises lead to these proposals. First, analysis of key cyber issues and cyber's overall impact on society and security is still in a formative stage. To extend the nuclear comparison, the state of a cyber framework is still "pre–Bernard Brodie," in many ways the earliest pioneer in this field.

Second, cyber technology, including computers and connections, was nei-ther built to be nor meant to be secure. One consequence is the dominance of offense over defense in cyber, reversing Clausewitz' classical axiom that defense has a three-to-one advantage. Effective cyber security demands enhancing defenses and protective measures. That in turn requires a fundamental change in thinking and practice to shift the balance from offense to defense, realizing that, unlike in war, the offense here has an asymmetric advantage over the defense.

Third, much of the human capital needed to conduct this analysis and/ or changes resides in the private sector. Much of this "capital" is unwilling to enter government service, for many reasons. Government bureaucracy, rules and regulations that impose restrictions, and noncompetitive compensation are major deterrents to government service. But under certain conditions that relieve or waive these restrictions, private-sector talent could be induced to participate in a think tank.

Fourth, cyber is ubiquitous. Thus, making one state secure is insufficient to make global cyber secure. Effective security demands international cooperation among key countries to exchange data and intellectual property and to agree to work together. Thus, what is needed is:

- A think tank focused on key cyber issues, either within government or an appropriate outside venue with substantial government guidance dedicated to the development of both doctrine and operational cyber solutions. To be effective, this think tank requires human capital that is skilled in geopolitics, strategic thinking, deterrence theory and related doctrines; that is operationally experienced and knowledgeable; that possesses world-class technical strengths, including understanding of how cyber actually works; and that has legal and international-law backgrounds, intelligence and security experience, and access to current and projected cyber research and development in both private and public sectors.

  No single person possesses all these skill sets. But if a think tank is to work, it is essential that it have human capital spanning all these skills. A cyber mini–Los Alamos or Manhattan Project come to mind as an example.

  The first deliverable would be a "Cyber Capstone" concept, covering the full range of cyber beyond the Departments of Defense, Commerce, Homeland Security, and Treasury, to incorporate the private sector, appropriate international organizations, and selected foreign partner states.

Central to this concept are the key issues of deterrence, defense, offense, and dissuasion; governance, law enforcement, and a cyber legal regime; the balance between security and privacy; the role of the private sector and the public-private interface; protection of critical infrastructure; resilience and recovery; the effective operation of national security capabilities when under attack; and cyber options in response to and in prevention of attacks.

This think tank would conduct its own analyses and become an international repository for analysis, reports, and lessons learned issued from other institutions. The objective of the think tank would be to provide effective operational guidance and solutions, not merely to identify problems and challenges. Based on historical performance, it is doubtful that the current FFRDCs (federally funded research and development centers) and other government or privately funded institutions will be able to fill this role, given their diversity and the realization that what is needed is a single center focused explicitly on cyber if the aims are to be achieved.

- Second, neither computers nor the mechanisms that connect computers were built to be secure, thus giving offensive cyber great advantage over defense and protection. Security, as now provided, is a "bolted-on" effort—and it is not highly effective. Making systems secure that were never designed with that requirement will prove expensive and most likely ineffective, especially when there is an alternative, based on current technological developments. Such technologies are in various stages of development and range from virtualization and multifactor secure authentication to nontamper hardware and software capabilities.

Fundamental design changes will also change the security equation in favor of defense and protection, including use in appropriate circumstances of attack-resistant, single-purpose computers, redesigned key protocols, or redesigned processor machine languages. Process changes, including automatic patching and testing and the review of past applications, would also be highly valuable.

Cyber is a man-made capacity; it has changed greatly over the past fifteen years and will change greatly again. The Internet of tomorrow will be incomparable to today's, as Moore's Law continues to double chip capacity every eighteen to twenty-four months. What must be assimilated—and is the key security solution—is that no systemic or comprehensive effort currently exists to make the necessary changes leading to a securer cyberspace. While much work is ongoing, that effort is generally stovepiped and overly focused on narrow capabilities, and it does not provide quantitative means of accurately measuring the effects and impact of this work on security.

A cyber "skunk works" working within the auspices of government to provide solutions to particular problems could be the centerpiece of a systems approach to cyber security. The skunk works would not have to develop all solutions. But it could be tasked to undertake the key and foundational work critical to a capstone concept. The United States did not undertake either the Manhattan Project or the race to the moon on the basis of market-driven solutions, although neither would have been possible without the private sector.

- Third, and noted above, the private sector has many of the capabilities, including human capital, needed to field effective cyber security. In general, this is individual brainpower. An obvious critical element of cyber security is computer programming, and the private sector has many truly great programmers, as well as many of the hardware, architectural, and testing capabilities that would also be critical. Similarly, on the doctrinal/operational side, critical analytic capabilities are found in the private sector.

However, particularly in the technical arenas, for reasons noted above, government service is neither desirable nor sought. Nonetheless, private-sector human capital capabilities are invaluable. A system to recruit and obtain these talents must be put in place. Age and cultural preferences can also be barriers. The very young may have more talents than the more mature. And the image of a "computer geek" with long hair, tattoos, and other body markings must not discourage or prevent employment.

- Fourth, cyber is ubiquitous and hence international. Collaboration and common approaches will be critical to effective security. For the most part, serious collaboration has just begun and is generally restricted to very trusted intelligence channels. An alternative approach could follow one of two tracks.

Track One would adapt the sharing/collaboration models developed in the counterterror arena to cyber, where much broader collaboration has taken place. Of course, adaptation would be necessary, since some of the states in which cyber attacks and penetrations originate collaborate in the counterterror arena. The precise countries to be included and the level of information and Internet-Protocol sharing need evaluation. So, it would be sensible to start with a limited group.

Track Two would utilize an informal grouping organized under a designated think tank with trusted persons from the private sector and with appropriate informal inclusion of government personnel for freer dialogue and brainstorming. The value of such a dialogue (or dialogues) would depend entirely on whether governments would find it useful.

To conclude: the development of analytic thinking, a commitment to technological change, the establishment of focused governmental efforts, the use of the private sector in creative ways, and the generation of effective international collaboration would be key elements in creating effective cyber security. There would undoubtedly be resistance to the approaches suggested above, and such efforts would have to be undertaken with mature and sensible judgment. The importance of effective cyber security for an information society is sufficiently great to warrant the effort.

The opportunities and challenges relating to cyber are immense. Unlike three historical analogies of international maritime rules of the road, banking, and deterrence, cyber has sprung from the brow of Zeus, like Athena. The other three frameworks took time to develop. Cyber is not only present. Its growth is as exponential as Moore's Law.

Understanding the complexity and many boundaries of cyber reinforces the need for a twenty-first-century strategic mind-set. Shifting from an offense-dominated to a defensive orientation will be difficult as well as anti-Clausewitzian—another small piece of evidence reinforcing the dissipation of the Westphalian system, as states will have far less control.

Above all, a strong intellectual foundation is essential to developing sound policies and practices, including balancing security and privacy concerns. While a Manhattan-style or "man to the moon" level of effort need not be replicated, a brains-based approach is essential. Otherwise, the negative aspects of cyber could overwhelm the positive, leading to a more disruptive and less stable world.

In a further memo, we will suggest certain organizational changes that may be needed. Given the complicated legal issues involved, the Justice Department may be the best location for housing the overall cyber coordinating and integrating efforts across the private and public sectors. Perhaps authorizing a second deputy attorney general for cyber would provide sufficient seniority and clout. And giving the commander of Cyber Command a second hat as the assistant or under deputy secretary is a sound way to ensure that perceptions of overly militarizing cyber are eased. In any case, should this office be created, the cyber think tank could be moved from the White House to Justice.

In conclusion, few areas avail themselves more than this to brains-based analyses and action. Offense will almost certainly overpower defense. Hence, given this disparity, cyber policy needs to rely on clever and even asymmetric options. A framework for cyber and an associated think tank are the starting points for this effort.

7

Wildcards

Looming Archdukes and Lurking Bullets

T he impact of globalization and the diffusion of power were described earlier. The erosion of the Westphalian state-centric system of politics through the empowerment of individuals and nonstate actors at the expense of governments has led to a proliferation of potential crises and a world that is far more complicated, complex, and interrelated. This chapter offers thirteen wildcard scenarios prompted by the Four Horsemen that could redefine the international order for good or ill. Some might consider wildcards as straightforward. However, each needs to be read closely to understand how the thirteen scenarios link surfeits of archdukes with excesses of bullets, along with the often extraordinary interactions between seemingly disparate and unrelated incidents.

Clearly, these wildcards are not fully comprehensive. Territorial and sovereignty disputes in the China seas could lead to greater conflict between or among the claimants. Putin's Russia remains problematic and is viewed with alarm by some, post-Crimea. Turkish politics could unravel the region. Iraq and Syria are wracked by civil wars. Narco-crime has migrated from Colombia and Mexico to other Latin American states, where it is flourishing. Nigeria could face a civil war instigated by jihad and Islamic extremism and separatists. And violence in Africa has not diminished.

Revolutionary technologies are, of course, potential wildcards. If Moore's Law proves valid, the Internet of tomorrow will be unrecognizable from today's. Chips will find myriad applications. Apple and Microsoft are unveiling eyeglass and wristwatch computers. Chips will spread to clothing to monitor bodily functions, and to homes to control everything remotely from sprinkler systems and temperature settings to television, stoves, and microwaves. Futurists are predicting that interoperability between and among smart devices will lead to an explosion of information transfers, many unwanted or not understood, further complicating the tensions between privacy and security. And genetic research will lead to extraordinary possibilities.

That said, below are thirteen wildcards that could match archdukes with bullets and provoke not only more crises but dramatic shocks to the international system.

1. Further erosion and collapse of the Westphalian system
2. Mass disruptions
   - Economic and financial tsunamis caused by rising interest rates, tightening of credit, halting of quantitative easing, slowing of international monetary flows, and compression of China's economy
   - Gigantic earthquake or derecho in Mexico
   - Grave water shortages.
3. Success or failure of nuclear talks between the P-5 Plus One and Iran
4. Success or failure of the Arab-Israeli-Palestinian peace process
5. Establishment of a fundamentalist state such as ISIS in control of a large landmass
6. Afghan civil war
7. Indo-Pak confrontation
8. Coup in North Korea
9. Dissipation or collapse of NATO
10. Permanent gridlock and breakdown of the American political system
11. Nightmare I: Collapse of the Shia empire
12. Nightmare II: The cyber threat against the free market
13. A new cold war or a rejuvenated NATO?

1. FURTHER EROSION AND COLLAPSE OF THE WESTPHALIAN STATE-CENTRIC SYSTEM OF INTERNATIONAL POLITICS

This wildcard will lead to a more Hobbesian and chaotic world with greater sources of potential conflict at substate levels. The driving force for this wildcard is the empowerment of individuals and nonstate actors at the expense of states. And this phenomenon is occurring on both intra- and interstate levels.

In this wildcard, states, including autocracies, lose authority and influence over both their publics and broader events as individuals and nonstate actors gain greater influence and power. The tea party in the United States and the rise of nationalistic and neo-Nazi groups in Europe represent extreme dissatisfaction with failed or failing government and are examples of the shift of power away from government. Even in repressive societies, such as China, Iran, and Saudi Arabia, because of instantaneous communications and the Internet controlling populations is far more difficult. And in the Gulf states, the Sunni-Shia split and the emergence of "al Qaeda 3.0" tests the limits of state control.

Meanwhile, international organizations such as the UN, the EU, and NATO will prove less effective, because each requires consensus to act. A single veto in the Security Council stymies decisions. The requirement for consensus (which usually means unanimity) limits the ability of these organizations to respond to crises or to support policy actions in aid of the greater good, a further sign of the erosion of the state-centric system.

The Libyan intervention to protect and defend civilians against Muramar Qaddafi's forces may be an exception. In this wildcard, civil wars such as in Syria and Iraq will be left to the many warring parties to resolve, not outside intervention. Smaller conflicts, such as in Mali, may be subject to outside intervention but with smaller numbers. For example, the French deployed only a thousand troops to Mali. Al Qaeda–like groups will metastasize and gain control of substantial landmasses, further eroding the state-centric system. Potential conflicts noted in other wildcards will become more likely. And one conflict will spread or provoke other wildcards (see wildcard 11).

A post-Westphalian world will be exceedingly more dangerous and fractious. The prospects for civil war and revolutions—remember the language in the Declaration of Independence on destructive government—will mount. Unfortunately (and as with cyber), no accepted framework or conceptual foundation has been fashioned to deal with this post-Westphalian world, reinforcing the desperate need for a twenty-first-century mind-set.

2. MASSIVE DISRUPTION: THREE SCENARIOS

Financial. Prior to the 2008 financial crisis, the operative assumption was that home prices must always rise. In 2014, the analogous beliefs are that the U.S. stock market will increase in value and that interest rates will remain low. But the Dow Jones and other market indices cannot indefinitely defy the laws of supply and demand. Interest rates cannot be kept permanently low. As federal budget deficits persist in the half-trillion-dollar range or higher, borrowing will not stop. Then, at some point, fiscal gravity must take hold. This is how this wildcard will then play out.

Interest rates will rise to 5, 6, 7 percent, or as in the late 1990s, to double digits. The federal deficit, approaching $20 trillion, will demand interest payments of possibly a trillion dollars a year or higher, consuming a third or more of the federal budget. The impact on government's ability to fund both discretionary and mandatory programs, such as Social Security and health care, will be destructive. Huge cuts will be inevitable. The economy will stall, and the Dow will fall.

The economic consequences will immediately affect the rest of the global economies, as occurred in 2008. Europe, already beset by a fragile economy, will suffer. Asia too will be adversely affected. And there is a second time bomb.

Global growth is dependent on the Chinese economy and its demand for goods, services, and investment. In China, however, a real-estate bubble appears to be forming. As credit tightens, forced by a large internal debt, China's economy will stumble, cutting demand. Less demand will have profoundly negative global repercussions shrinking global GDP. If the U.S. and Chinese economies falter together, the consequence will be a global economic meltdown.

Natural Calamity. A huge Katrina-, Super Sandy–, or tsunami-sized derecho, a colossal earthquake, or a pandemic are the more obvious potential catastrophes that could disrupt large parts of the globe. Climate change that induces droughts, floods, and extreme conditions of hot and cold will likewise have profound effects, beginning with limiting food supplies, creating great scarcities, and upsetting the global economy. Any such act, if severe enough to test the ability of governments to respond, will be a game changer.

This wildcard envisages a massive derecho hitting Mexico of the order of Typhoon Haiyan, which struck the Philippines in late 2013. The destruction in Mexico forces hundreds of thousands and possibly millions to flee north to the safety of the United States. The border is impossible to control, and the attempt overwhelms the resources of the U.S. government. Violence breaks out as many Americans feel threatened by the mass migration. In some cases, gunfire is exchanged. Martial law is declared in Texas, Arizona, and Mexico as the influx drains the resources available to clothe and feed the refugees or to send them back to Mexico.

Freshwater Scarcity. A corollary of this wildcard is already occurring. The most precious and vital resource for mankind is water. And water is in very short supply in parts of the world. The German Marshall Fund released a report last year on what is a "dam building race" in South and Southeast Asia, dramatically affecting and altering the flows of major rivers. At this writing, Pakistan is close to crisis, with only thirty days' worth of water reserves, when it usually has over a thousand. California is close to a water-scarcity crisis too.

Resource scarcity is as old as history. However, in Pakistan's case, the wildcard of scarcity of water will have an enormously disruptive and destructive impact on society. Given the fragility of Pakistan's economy, its continuing circular debt (which produces permanent electrical shortages), a crisis in shortages of heating gas, and a mounting insurgency, a water crisis could implode that country. Immediately, such an implosion would spread to India and wildcard 7. The massive scarcity of water is not limited geographically either. Contamination of water supplies recently led to a critical scarcity in West Virginia, forcing its governor to declare a state of emergency.

Whether armed conflict over water is to come has been a persistent question. The possible linkages between India and Pakistan on this issue suggest another lurking archduke.

3. THE SUCCESS OR FAILURE OF THE P-5 PLUS ONE TALKS WITH IRAN

Interestingly, both outcomes in this wildcard will have highly positive and highly negative consequences. Either way, the impact on the region could, again, be a game changer. If talks succeed and Iran effectively and credibly foregoes its nuclear-weapons ambitions, the outcome will remove from consideration the option of military force and the risk of war. The lifting of economic sanctions and the reintegration of Iran into the community of nations would follow.

Global reintegration almost certainly will jump-start Iran's economy with significant increases in exports of oil. Oil exports will provide a needed influx of capital and generate greater demand for imports of goods and services. The net effect will be a significant positive contribution to the global economy. And it is arguable that economic growth could empower individuals and provide the incentives to the replacement one day of the ruling theocracy with a more open system of government.

Economic growth, however, would release huge domestic pressures and public resentment over the lack of goods and services, strengthening the rule of the ayatollahs. Greater economic growth would allow Iran to build up its security forces, given larger tax revenues that would flow from a rising GDP. Nor would growth necessarily reduce the inherent Shia-Sunni conflict with Saudi Arabia.

As Iran exports more oil and America increases its energy exports, Saudi Arabia would be directly effected as oil and energy prices dropped or stabilized. A decline in oil revenues would make it difficult for the Saudis to dispense as much money as is needed to keep the country's indigenous and foreign populations placated. Greater internal pressure for reform would be a threat to the rule of the royal family. The net result of this wildcard would likely be exacerbation of Saudi-Iranian tensions. Nor would Russia necessarily be pleased, as the economic advantages represented by its energy exports would likewise by challenged.

Obviously, an agreement will be in the greater good, because war in the Gulf could prove as catastrophic as the second Iraq War, or more so. The worst case, of course, is a regional version of June 1914 and major war. However, as the United States never asked the question before invading Afghanistan and Iraq of "What next?" it cannot repeat that blunder in planning for what happens if negotiations fail. Not addressing these questions constitutes another wildcard that reflects the absence of strategic thinking and reinforces the need for a new mind-set.

Should no agreement be reached, the most catastrophic outcome is a military strike by Israel, the United States, or both against Iran's nuclear infrastructure. Such an attack would come from manned and unmanned aircraft and cruise missiles. Most likely, to be as effective as possible, the strikes would last a few days or a week and almost certainly would provoke a regional war that too easily could spread. In this case, the metaphorical excess of bullets would turn the attackers into many Gavrilo Princips. By the time this book is published, the Iran issue may have played out. However, an attack would be an act of war, and Iran would respond in both predictable and unpredictable ways.

Because Iran has marginal power-projection capacity much beyond its littorals, a largely indirect and asymmetric response is likely, with one exception—the threat to close the Strait of Hormuz. Whether or not Iran has the military capacity actually to close the strait for an extended period, the real targets are insurance companies. Threat of closure will initially drive insurance costs beyond shipowners' willingness to pay.

Thus, a spike in oil prices would occur and threaten the global economy. How long that spike would last before tanker traffic reverted back to normal in Hormuz clearly would affect the magnitude of oil shock. But given the fragility of global economies, even a short-term spike would impose considerable harm.

Iran would exercise other, asymmetric options. Iranian-controlled Hezbollah would launch missile and terrorist attacks against Israel. Hezbollah might also seek to destabilize Lebanon and threaten Jordan, putting far greater pressure on Israel through the instability of its neighbors. A massive public-relations campaign would discredit the United States, and Iran would use the UN General Assembly to condemn the attacks. Iran most likely would exploit large Shia populations in the Gulf, especially Bahrain, to foment riots and potential coups. And it would use its access and leverage in Iraq and Syria to inflict whatever damage it could against U.S. and Israeli interests.

Saudi Arabia and possibly other Gulf states would implicitly or explicitly threaten to obtain nuclear weapons to counter a Shia bomb. Conventional wisdom is that Pakistan could provide a few weapons, saving Saudi Arabia the cost of development, and be compensated for the transfer. Pakistani prime minister Nawaz Sharif has close ties with the Saudis dating back to his period of exile following the 1999 coup that deposed him.

Such a contingency must be prevented at all costs, as a nuclear arms race in the Gulf could spiral out of control, as did the naval arms race in Europe a century ago. Pakistan is not a signatory to the Non-Proliferation Treaty (NPT) and thus not legally bound in regard to transferring nonpeaceful nuclear technology. Some of the more extreme Pakistani fundamentalist groups would push for such a transfer, in part to curry favor and receive more money from the Saudis; in part to check Iran and, of course, the Shia; and in part because a Sunni bomb could advance ideologically the more extreme Salafist agenda against infidels and Israel.

More fundamentalist factions in the army and ISI might also support a transfer mistakenly thinking that a Sunni/Saudi bomb would weaken U.S. influence—and many Pakistanis hold lower opinions of the United States than of the Taliban—and provide an added deterrent to India. The lure of Saudi oil wealth providing generous payment cannot be excluded. Within the United States, very vocal anti-Iranian voices might consider such a move important in checking Iran. Hence, while in all likelihood any Pakistani civilian government, including Sharif's, would consider sending nuclear weapons or nuclear technology as foolhardy and against Islamabad's interests, the alternative position is surely possible.

4. THE SUCCESS OR FAILURE OF THE ARAB-ISRAELI-PALESTINIAN PEACE PROCESS

If history applies, the chances for an agreement are remote. That the United Kingdom could end the Northern Ireland–Ireland feud, which was centuries old, suggests that not every seemingly frozen conflict is beyond solution. As Secretary of State John Kerry wisely advises, if a solution in the Middle East is not achieved, it will be decades before another opportunity will arise.

In many ways, the Arab-Israeli-Palestinian conflict remains one of the central geopolitical and geostrategic wildcards—if not *the* central wildcard—confronting global security of the twenty-first century. The conflict has direct links with terror and Islamic radicalism, by which the state of Israel has been continuously threatened with elimination. Saudi Arabia is a crucial player. King Abdullah's 2002 overture suggested that full recognition of Israel by the Arab world could, and the operative word is *could,* be forthcoming. Resolution would engage and aid Egypt, itself confronted with a full insurgency in Sinai. Of course, Iran with its support of Hezbollah in Lebanon and Syria and sworn commitment to destroy the Zionist state, is irreversibly connected to this issue.

The points of conflict, confrontation, and disagreement are altogether too well known. Israeli occupation of the West Bank, Gaza, and the Golan since 1967 and expansion of settlements in the West Bank; the right of return of Palestinians; and the status of Jerusalem—these are among the so-far intractable disputes. Four major wars, aerial attacks into Syria, occupation of southern Lebanon, countless acts of terror by all parties, and the continued repression of the Palestinians in Gaza multiply the animosities, hatreds, and distrust between and among the parties.

Should an agreement be reached, perhaps the most difficult and complicated issue will be ensuring security for all concerned. A reliable third party must be the buffer at security checkpoints and between Palestinians and Israelis to prevent terrorist attacks. The UN would not be acceptable, certainly to Israel, and it is doubtful it could raise a sufficiently capable force for the mission. The ideal force for this mission would be NATO.

It is impossible to exaggerate the benefits an Arab-Israeli peace settlement would bring. Arab recognition of Israel would be central to any agreement in exchange for the creation of a Palestinian state. That recognition alone would have devastating effects on Islamic radicalism. Arab support for continued anti-Israeli and anti-Semitic policies would evaporate, given recognition especially by Saudi Arabia. While instability in Syria and Iraq would continue, the end of the Arab-Israeli conflict would ease containment of those civil wars. And by extension, Saudi Arabia could rely on Israel's nuclear weapons as a further deterrent to Iran.

Not every conflict in the world would cease following a settlement. Al Qaeda and other jihadi groups would still oppose the West and autocratic rule in Saudi Arabia and other Gulf states. However, a major impediment to stability will have been removed. A parallel is that if France and Britain had stopped Hitler far earlier and gone to war before Germany rearmed, the world might have been a far better place. Of course, that did not happen. Still, peace between Arabs and Jews would prove as significant as the end of the Soviet Union, but without a residual Russia in place that could emerge as a new irritant.

Getting NATO to agree might prove as difficult as bringing the feuding parties together in the Middle East, or more. Afghanistan has exhausted the patience and support of NATO publics for intervention. While NATO is actively engaged in the Balkans, the Mediterranean, and the Horn of Africa, stationing substantial ground forces in Israel and on its borders would be very hard to achieve. But the argument could be made, and on the basis of the coalition of the willing, the dependence of a peaceful settlement on NATO engagement would be a powerful case for approval.

A peace settlement would also bring risks, dangers, and uncertainties. Radicals and terrorists could attempt to disrupt the agreement with attacks. Past hatreds could reignite. As Israel became an increasingly Arab-populated state, Jews would fear loss of political control and indeed sovereignty. And the inherent fragility of an agreement, no matter the goodwill and commitment on both sides to succeed, could be shattered.

Failure would perpetuate the grievances and grounds for political instability and, probably, violence, as John Kerry has recently warned. Palestinians and Arabs would conclude that the only way to gain independence is violence. Al Qaeda and other terrorist groups would intensify anti-Israeli propaganda, along with terror attacks, to provoke overreactions and to wear Israel down with the strategic equiva-lent of death by a thousand cuts. Almost certainly, the geopolitical and geostra-tegic situation would worsen. The equivalent of a new cold war in the Middle East would set in. And for the United States, the impossible choice of enhancing or decreasing its engagement and presence in the region, as it was pivoting to Asia, would be exacerbated by this wildcard.

5. ESTABLISHMENT OF A RADICAL FUNDAMENTALIST-CONTROLLED STATE SUCH AS ISIS

This is a most frightening wildcard. Even in Taliban-dominated Afghanistan, the horror of that rule was directed inward. Because of *Pashtunwala,* the code of honor and conduct of the Pashtun tribes for millennia, Osama bin Laden was afforded protection. However, it was he, not the Taliban, who operated beyond the Afghan borders.

Perhaps the aim of the radicals and terrorists in forming the Islamic State of Iraq and Syria (ISIS) will have dissipated later this year. Yet, seizure of control of a landmass by radical Islam with external aspirations raises profoundly worrying possibilities, as did Lenin's defeat of the Mensheviks in Russia and the Nazis' of their opponents in Germany a decade or so later.

Part of a twenty-first-century mind-set must be anticipating such a contingency. Uncontrolled territories in northwest Pakistan, parts of Yemen, and Somalia are precursors. The use of armed drones, Special Forces, special-operations forces, and local police and security forces, along with security assistance and training, have been the principal means of dealing with these ungoverned areas. But establishment of a de facto state raises daunting issues and questions of how to respond. In essence, seizure of substantial territory and a claim of legal status constitute a de facto coup.

For argument's sake, suppose al Qaeda or an affiliate seized a large part of western Iraq and eastern Syria with sufficient strength to defend the territory against attempts by the Syrian and Iraqi governments to retake it. Further suppose that this quasi-state became a magnet for attracting jihadis worldwide and was mounting terrorist attacks well beyond its borders.

The current tools of drones and Special Forces would not be sufficient. Syria is in such a state of chaos that it is ineffective against its insurgents. Iraqi forces could and would be used as surrogates against the new Islamic state. But the Sunni-Shia divide could impede an offensive, especially if locals supported the Islamist Sunnis.

The only effective alternative would be direct outside intervention. But who would be prepared to volunteer? And once the jihadis were routed, who would provide the governance and nation building essential to preventing their return? Iraq and Afghanistan provide the strongest arguments against intervention and nation building.

Thus, an al Qaeda–dominated territory is both catalyst and explosive material for further violence and a wildcard that will indeed transform geopolitics and continue the erosion of the Westphalian system.

6. AFGHAN CIVIL WAR

An Afghan civil war would lead to territories controlled by groups hostile to the West. The sticking point as of early 2014 is Afghan president Hamid Karzai's refusal to sign a basic security agreement. The BSA would grant foreign military personnel immunity from Afghan law, thus allowing U.S. and ISAF forces to remain post-2014. Karzai's reason for the delay was inexplicable, although his likely successor will approve the BSA. The vexing problem for ISAF is that logistical planning, whether for long-term presence or withdrawal, needs substantial lead time. Not knowing whether to stay or to leave at the end of 2014 puts ISAF in an impossible situation. Thus, without agreement, ISAF will begin planning for a drawdown and if one is signed accept the penalties and refocus on post-2014 presence. Irrespective, however, a civil war is very likely.

The reasons are straightforward. Historically, Afghanistan has been ruled by local tribal chiefs, warlords, and strongmen, not by a strong centralized government in Kabul. The past dozen years have not changed that fact of history and have not created the means and infrastructure to contain these centrifugal political forces of decentralization. No property laws exist, so the courts cannot adjudicate claims. In fact, much of the law is interpreted locally and by tribal *maliks*, not Kabul. The irrigation and transportation systems have not been replaced or modernized. And the biggest obstacle—the north-south divide—persists.

The Northern Alliance and the Pashtun-controlled south have been in conflict for centuries. The Northern Alliance, with U.S. airpower and less than 500 Special Forces soldiers and CIA officers, routed the Pashtun Taliban in 102 days. In the south, serious tensions and conflicts continue among tribes, the Taliban, local warlords, and criminal gangs and organizations.

Afghanistan's security forces require a budget of at least five billion dollars a year. Outside the drug trade, ISAF spending, and a small amount of foreign investment, Afghanistan remains an impoverished state. Any idea that it will be able to pay, let alone train and equip, its military, police, and local militias without external funding is absurd. Nor do the security forces have enough mobility, airlift, fire support, medical support, or the logistical and supply infrastructure to remain effective once ISAF and the United States depart.

The question is not whether Afghanistan disintegrates. The question is when. The consequences of this wildcard will have spillover effects for years to come.

In an ironic twist, civil war and the withdrawal of ISAF may benefit Pakistan. Given Pakistan's resentment and animosity toward the United States, withdrawal from Afghanistan lowers the American profile. If the U.S. drone attacks launched from inside Pakistani territory ceased, conceivably that might reduce strong anti-American sentiments. Perceptions of U.S. intrusion on Pakistani national sovereignty would be reduced. And an Afghan civil war could enable ISI to operate more freely in the border regions, as violence will degrade and dilute Afghan control over its security forces.

The precursor to an Afghan civil war is Iraq. The United States was forced to leave because the Bush administration could not convince Prime Minster Maliki to sign a status-of-forces agreement. The Strategic Framework Agreement that was signed did not exempt U.S. forces from Iraqi law. Shia persecution of the Sunnis continued. Dysfunctional government could not exploit oil resources essential to restarting the economy. Iran exerted more influence on Baghdad. The result so far has been an al Qaeda and partially Sunni insurgence in al Anbar Province. A similar litany of failure could lead to the same outcomes in Afghanistan.

7. INDO-PAK CONFRONTATION

This wildcard offers a much different type of confrontation, although the last Indo-Pak war, fought in 1971, provides some interesting parallels regarding escalation and miscalculation. In 1947, Pakistan was created and divided between east and west, with India in between. By early 1971 the west's repression against the east had led to a declaration of independence, in part prompted by a cyclone the year before that had devastated East Pakistan, reportedly killing a million people. The West had not responded.

By December, relations with India had become so frayed that many Pakistanis demanded strong action in the east. President (and General) Yaya Khan ordered preemptive air strikes against Indian air bases, in essence a declaration of war. India responded with a series of ground, air, and sea attacks and moved a large force into East Pakistan to assist the rebels. In a few weeks the war was over. Pakistan surrendered in the east, and Bangladesh emerged.

This wildcard begins with a breakdown of Pakistani society because of the government's failure to provide basic necessities of life. Grave shortages of electricity, water, natural gas, and food finally compel Pakistanis to take to the streets in massive protests. The government responds with a heavy hand, as it did in 1971 in the east.

Pakistani Taliban (TTP) and other insurgent groups see these protests and initial repression as an opportunity to intensify their attacks to overthrow the government. The army, not wanting to use force against countrymen, faces a huge dilemma. The government orders the army to stop the riots and protests. But the army sees the danger from the TTP. ISI also fears another Mumbai-like attack, designed to enrage and engage India, as the air strikes in 1971 had brought India into the Bangladesh conflict.

Pakistan's army is paranoid about India, for many reasons. India's Cold Start strategy, noted earlier, is a direct threat. India's engagement in Afghanistan is another. To counterbalance Cold Start, Pakistan deploys short-range nuclear weapons, raising unsettling issues about miscalculation—World War I began in part due to the theory that he who mobilizes first wins.

Seeing Pakistan disintegrate, the army has no choice but to overthrow the civilian government and impose a state of martial law. LeT, in conjunction with TPP, promises a raid into India, and violence spreads to Kashmir. The Indians mobilize their forces against a terror attack. Fearing this is a cover to hide preparations for mounting Cold Start, the Pakistani army mobilizes and puts its nuclear weapons on a high-alert status.

The insurgency in Pakistan worsens as insurgents gain control of several cities. Indian concern likewise mounts over the threat of a terror attack and the fear of the TTP or other extremist group seizing a Pakistani nuclear weapon. Threats and counterthreats fly. Engagement of the United States, China, and Russia, with Britain, the former colonial power, as the intermediary, cannot ease the tensions.

A border incident in Kashmir provokes between Pakistan and India an artillery duel that lasts for two days. Both sides dust off contingency plans, but the Pakistani army is overstretched and exhausted from battling the insurgents and the many protesters. The corps commanders and general staff realize that if India mounted Cold Start, Pakistan would be defenseless unless it used nuclear weapons.

Then a wise staff officer raises the 1971 war and how miscalculation then forced West Pakistan to make an incredible blunder. Was that about to happen again? Had Gavrilo Princip reappeared in a Pakistani uniform, and would the Indian army become the latest archduke? This is a menacing wildcard indeed.

8. COUP IN NORTH KOREA

North Korea remains a ticking time bomb, with the unpredictable whims and rule of thirty-one-year-old Kim Jong-un. Kim has shored up his leadership with bluster and bluff and by killing his possible enemies, his uncle a case in point. But given Kim's youth, immaturity, and the no doubt many enemies he has made, a coup by the army is not out of the question. The question would be the cause.

Would a coup result from fear of Kim's vindictiveness and willingness to destroy his opponents? (Stalin may have been poisoned, to prevent him from killing his colleagues.) Would a coup arise from policy differences, from his dealing with the south and outside world either too harshly or not harshly enough? Or would Kim's incompetence warrant an overthrow, as the Egyptian military ousted President Morsi?

Each is unknown. However, a North Korean coup is a wildcard with the capacity for profound impact in any direction. A war or conflict could break out. Perhaps unification might be expedited. Or, since a cabal might have strong Chinese backing, would a coup bring North Korea into an even closer relationship with China?

9. DISSOLUTION OR COLLAPSE OF NATO

NATO has been the most successful military alliance in history. It won the Cold War without firing a shot—in Sun Tzu's grading scheme, the highest form of generalship. NATO forced Serbia out of Kosovo in 1999 in seventy-eight days. It forced the fall of Muramar Qaddafi in 2011. And it spent eleven years at war in Afghanistan in what at best will be described as a worthy operation whose failure was not because of military shortcomings. The principal failure was the absence of cultural understanding by the outside powers, abetted by the absence of non-military capacity to rebuild the Afghan nation and provide it sufficient economic wherewithal to sustain itself without enormous foreign aid. But Russia's occupation of Crimea turned NATO into a paper tiger.

In this wildcard, the September 2014 biennial summit of NATO heads of government and state is held at Celtic Manor in Wales, in the United Kingdom. The summit had the promise of setting a new direction. That does not happen. Afghanistan and Ukraine become divisive issues that crowd out other more strategically important considerations, including preserving the alliance in the future. NATO's publics no longer support the war. Austerity and the need to stimulate domestic economies have led to huge spending cuts in defense. And NATO is unable to produce a short, pithy argument to explain to its publics the need for the alliance even after the occupation of Crimea.

The failure of NATO to stand up to Russia after it absorbed Crimea cripples the alliance. An effort is made to rally around Article 5 of the Washington Treaty. However, differences among the twenty-eight member states over how to deal with Russia over Ukraine and with further threats to border states with Russian-speaking populations lead to further division. That NATO has no effective public diplomacy campaign exacerbates the lack of cohesion. Most Americans have no idea what NATO means, mistaking it for an energy drink or new computer "app."

As a result, the alliance becomes less relevant and less vital. Over time, members lose interest in providing it funds and political support. The headquarters and the North Atlantic Council, or NAC, become debating societies, even less useful than the UN. And while interoperability and the links between militaries exist, so that if it came to war or operations some capacity would remain, the alliance gravitates into an insurance policy to be invoked after catastrophe hits.

In many ways, the decline of the alliance parallels the erosion of the Westphalian system. States and alliances become less influential. The United States, with its pivot to Asia and fixation on the Middle East and South Asia, can still call on its allies to form coalitions of the willing. Hence, the dissolution of NATO seems acceptable. That is, of course, until a major crisis sweeps out of the Middle East and into Europe that demands a military response. But that response has long dissipated.

10. PERMANENT GRIDLOCK AND BREAKDOWN OF THE AMERICAN POLITICAL SYSTEM

What a wildcard! Yes, a second government shutdown was avoided in 2013. The debt-ceiling crisis was temporarily relieved. However, the intractable issues of entitlement reform, curbing of spending, creation of jobs, stimulation of economic growth, and provision for a rational common defense went untouched. The gerrymandering of electoral districts has ensured permanent Republican control of the House, and the political fight shifts to the Senate.

Republican heavy-handedness, driven by the tea party in its assaults against government and its insensitive and foolish social policies, pushes the presidency toward near-permanent control by Democrats. Empowered by the support of minorities and women, who find themselves increasingly driven from the Republican Party because of its hostile and rigid ideologies, Democrats keep control of the White House. Given congressional deadlock, the White House makes use of executive orders to bypass the legislature. Massive lawsuits and litigation follow as a result of undue executive orders, further paralyzing government.

Democrats are no better, waging class warfare against the rich and against the growing income inequality. Instead of focusing on the macro and vital issues, politics became even more driven by campaigning to win elections, not to govern. Civility in Washington becomes a lost art, and the hostility on both ends of Pennsylvania Avenue grows even worse. The idea that "you are with me or against me" plays out in every issue; the middle ground and compromise become the no-man's-land of politics.

When the stock market begins its decline, interest rates rise and quantitative easing ends. The government is incapable of responding to a new economic recession, as bad as or worse than in 2008. In foreign policy, the civil wars in Iraq, Syria, and in Afghanistan after the 2014 withdrawal threaten regional war. Terrorism is on the rise, and "al Qaeda 4.0" claims a hundred million followers, with many, many more expected to join.

Instead of finding two experienced and qualified presidential candidates to run in 2016, Republicans choose a relatively young firebrand. Democrats stick with more of the same. Thus, when the president takes the oath of office, experience and qualifications do not count, and thin résumés still elect chief executives.

U.S. infrastructure continues to fail. The electrical power grid cannot meet demands imposed by extreme weather conditions of heat and cold. Increasing numbers of bridges and highways collapse or require major repairs as raging rivers overflow their banks and the effects of snowstorms pothole the nation's roads. Ports are not dredged, in part because of environmental restrictions, so super cargo ships ply their trade in Canadian and Mexican, not American, ports. Education remains a losing proposition. Despite the Affordable Care Act, medical treatment is polarized into a two-tiered system, one for the rich and one for the poor.

Social Security cannot sustain the burgeoning retiree class and the shortage of tax revenues owing to a declining ratio of workers to pensioners. Congress is forced to make major cuts that impoverish many of the elderly. Shale gas and oil offer promise, but the revenues and proceeds go to shareholders and corporations.

Far worse, the nation has to accept diminished expectations for, and great reductions in, standards of living. No longer will future generations, except for the privileged few, live better than their parents and grandparents. The great experiment conceived of and started by the Founding Fathers has run its course. And no alternative is in sight.

11. NIGHTMARE I: COLLAPSE OF THE SHIA EMPIRE

While it would be convenient if the analogy of democratization of the East European–bloc states after the Berlin Wall came down in 1989 fit the Middle East and Persian Gulf, in fact, the dissolution of the key Shia countries in the region would produce more chaos than comfort and far more uncertainty than stability. Perhaps the breakup of Yugoslavia is a more relevant wildcard. How might a collapse of the Shia unfold? This is the next wildcard.

Unraveling starts in Iraq. The central government in Baghdad simply loses control of much over the country. The Kurds declare an independent state, protected by oil wealth and outside interests, and the Sunnis in the west proclaim a Sunnistan. Baghdad is unwilling to risk a major civil war by using the army to regain control and has no choice except to accede to the de facto partition of Iraq into three ministates divided ethnically, politically, economically, and religiously.

The civil war in Syria finally splits that country east and west. A stronger ISIS, largely populated with extremists, wrests control from Damascus and declares an independent free Syrian state in the north and west. Assad and the Alawite community continue to rule the south. And, as in Korea, Vietnam, and Yemen, the geographic divide is perpetuated with cross-border clashes and hit-and-run attacks by each side against the other.

These divisions play heavily in Iran. Discontented Iranians, many resenting Tehran, see an opportunity for quasi-independence. The Kurds, Azeris (who number in the tens of millions), and Shia in the south (who control much of the oil) each declare some form of independence. The army divides along similar lines, and the Republican Guardsmen are insufficient to fight three separate insurgencies against the breakaway quasi-states.

Such dissolution would have profound effects for war, peace, and policy. Jordan, Lebanon, Egypt, and Israel would be swept up in this dissolution. In essence, the worst combination of new archdukes and bullets could be in play. And the only adequate description is a nightmare wildcard.

12. NIGHTMARE II: THE CYBER THREAT AGAINST THE FREE MARKET

In this wildcard scenario, the provocateurs are states, persons, or groups with access to "national technical means" (or the equivalent intrusion and penetration technologies). Concentrating on businesses and public and private companies, intrusion is not merely to steal intellectual property. The rationale is the lure of huge profits through the use of cyber to make hostile corporate raids to acquire companies; alter balance sheets and press releases to affect the price of shares; rig prices to win or lose contracts; and affect the actual flow of funds internationally to affect local and global economies.

Cyber and the Internet would be the new tools for corporate raiders carrying out the old practices of robber barons to manipulate business and make fortunes in the process. For example, depending on whether or not the play is to "short" or go "long" on a stock—that is, betting the share value will rise or fall—the technology exists to penetrate corporate data and balance sheets. Alternatively, if Company A were bidding on a project, not only knowing Company B's costs but being able to change them electronically will produce winners and losers.

The analogy is putting Ponzi schemes and Bernie Madoff scams on the steroid of the Internet. Some of this cyber manipulation is already under way. The nightmare wildcard scenario, using the 1907 crisis as an example, would be creating the equivalent of unlimited bucket shops, each out for its own profit and indifferent to the damage done to the selected targets. And given the power of offense over defense, the cyber robber barons have a huge advantage over unsuspecting companies and businesses.

13. A NEW COLD WAR OR A REJUVENATED NATO?

Clearly, as this book goes to press, Russia's actions in Ukraine have sparked a new confrontation between Moscow and its neighbors in Europe. Should President Putin decide to move into eastern Ukraine or the Transnistria region of Moldova, then the West will have no choice but to react with stronger sanctions and possibly greater defense spending. Given Russia's abrogation of the Conventional Forces Treaty and the Budapest Agreement of 1994, a new form of cold or "cool" war could easily result.

NATO could, of course, use these acts of aggression as a basis for a major revitalization and rejuvenation. Putin's aggression could spur far greater alliance cohesion and cooperation. Indeed, Putin's takeover of Crimea could end up as his

Afghanistan, if an insurgency were to break out. If he moved into Ukraine, almost certainly that would be the case. Under these circumstances, and despite Putin's temporal popularity, permanent occupation of Crimea or beyond could induce a third Russian revolution, as sanctions bit and exclusion of Russia from part of the international system imposed real economic hardships especially as revenues from oil and gas reserves dwindled.

For those who argue that Putin's actions really confirmed the force of the Westphalian system, indeed the cause was failed Ukrainian government, which provoked the crisis Russia was to exploit. And as this plays out, the empowerment of individuals and nonstate actors will certainly be felt in Crimea.

The purpose of this chapter has been to demonstrate how the cumulative effects of the Four Horsemen could induce scenarios to challenge society and government. Politics and governments have always been challenged by scenarios that forecast good or ill. But the twenty-first century poses a unique and different problem set. States have less control of their publics and of broader events. Technology has created great opportunities and great vulnerabilities. The presence of failed and failing government, economic despair and disparity, ideological and religious extremism, and environmental calamity adds new dimensions to these challenges, as well as constraints in resolving them. One solution must be a new mind-set to provide new ideas and means to address the twenty-first century.

PART THREE

A Brains-Based Approach to Strategy:
Corralling the Four Horsemen

For America's first century, survival, expansion, and prosperity rested on the twin fortunes of geography and location. After the winning of independence from Britain in 1783, the geographic fortune of two vast oceans protected the fledgling and vulnerable nation for decades. The good fortune of location provided a virtually unlimited bounty of North America's resources from millions of acres of highly arable land to millions of wild game animals, precious minerals and hydrocarbons, and nearly limitless rivers, streams, and lakes. Climate, although varied, was hospitable. And the original North American inhabitants would not seriously impede the great expansion westward.

By 1914, the United States had all the ingredients required of a global superpower. After the Great War and isolationist American policies in keeping with George Washington's admonition to avoid permanent alliances, Japan's attack on Pearl Harbor did more than awake a sleeping giant. War would supercharge American industry and technology. In building the arsenal of democracy and weapons of war that overwhelmed the Axis enemy, America became seduced by (or addicted to) the ability to commit virtually unlimited resources to the war effort. Spending our way clear of danger would become a viable and effective alternative strategy.

Defense and national security would not always be lavished with resources. But when the nation encountered weighty problems, whether at home or abroad, the checkbook provided many solutions. President Kennedy proclaimed as much in his inaugural address, vowing to "pay any price and bear any burden" to protect democracy and liberty. In the race to send a man to the moon, resources were rarely a limitation.

President Johnson's Great Society never had a strict or capped budget. Medicare, Medicaid, the war on poverty, and a raft of other domestic programs were not resource constrained. The United States would spend billions on Vietnam, deploying at one stage a half-million soldiers. "Guns versus butter" only later became an issue, as Vietnam turned into a quagmire.

The first Gulf War was ultimately paid for by other states, who were prepared to spend money rather than blood to drive Saddam Hussein from Kuwait. But the twenty-first century was to prove financially precarious. The century began with a balanced federal budget and even a small surplus. To stimulate the economy, the Bush 43 administration pushed through tax cuts of more than a trillion dollars. The Afghan intervention beginning in 2001 and the second Iraq War were paid for entirely by Uncle Sam and cost over two trillion dollars. And the demographics of an aging population would stress the ability to pay the skyrocketing costs of Social Security and health care.

Regardless of its fiscal condition, the United States has considerable wealth and capital to provide for both the general welfare and the common defense if those resources are used wisely. Therein rests another ticking time bomb. The nation simply has not adopted a mind-set or approach to strategy in which careful thought and reason drive policy solutions—lack of which are the ultimate reward of failing government.

If the United States is to deal effectively with the greatest threats and dangers to the nation and to mankind, a new mind-set is essential. Part three of the book proposes both a mind-set for strategic thinking and a plan of action to deal with each of the Four Horsemen. Although principally focused on the United States, the findings and proposals can be applied more broadly and globally. The starting point must be corralling the most dangerous of these riders: failed and failing government. And that begins at both ends of Pennsylvania Avenue.

8

Failed and Failing
Governments

The Irish bon vivant Oscar Wilde wickedly observed that the reason the politics of academic life were so sharp was because the stakes were so small. In America today, politics are growing even sharper and nastier—but because the stakes are so large. The United States is at a dangerous inflection point. And the trajectory is not good.

How America arrived at this juncture is less important than what can be done to reverse this direction. Unless this trajectory is changed, two outcomes are predictable. Future American expectations will be dramatically curtailed. And the collective standard of living will decline, beginning now.

The crucial question is whether or not a political system of checks and balances designed by the best minds of the eighteenth century can tolerate or survive the rigors and pressures of the twenty-first century and a post-Westphalian world. To work, checks and balances demand compromise. Unfortunately, both political parties have sacrificed compromise on the altar of partisan ideology. American politics have turned into zero-sum games in which the objective is to beat the opposition at any cost.

America has faced prior existential political and economic crises. The Civil War and the Great Depression were the most threatening. America survived the first. World War II overcame the second. World War II and forty years of Cold War also constrained many of the divisive, centrifugal political forces that have since led to a dysfunctional and failing government.

Vietnam and Watergate began the current wave of the erosion of government. The last two decades of politics, a fragile economy, growing debt, deficits that appear unending, and two disastrous wars have led to seemingly unbridgeable ideological divides between the two political parties. America's capacity to govern has been crippled. Short-term and Band-Aid fixes are applied to long-term and complex problems. These are at best temporary measures and will not resolve these pressing issues.

The most pressing issues for the United States are economic, financial, and geostrategic—an increasingly perilous international environment best character-ized as June 1914 in slow motion. The rational solution to the economic and finan-cial set of issues comprises reform of the tax code and entitlement programs and establishment of a national infrastructure bank, both for job creation and mod-ernization of the nation's crumbling infrastructure. While both parties recognize the symptoms of America's present condition, no agreement exists on the causes. Worse, gridlock prevents producing workable solutions.

The Obama administration and a majority of Democrats in Congress believe that current steps to reduce the debt and annual deficits are sufficient. Increased taxes on the 1 percent constituting America's richest provide more revenues. The Affordable Care Act will cut medical costs. Unfortunately, entitlement programs are unsustainable. When interest rates go up, the federal budget will burst. So far, government has been unable to take preventive action and is probably incapable of doing so.

Ironically, the president is following a Keynesian course recommended by Dick Cheney. As vice president, Cheney could say, "Deficits don't matter." Democrats assume that the large current annual deficits are necessary for stimulating eco-nomic growth. Reform of entitlements is, for the time being, less important. More cynically, entitlement reform could adversely affect a large number of constituents whose votes are vital for Democrats if they are to retain the presidency and control Congress again.

The Republican Party is in disarray, lacking a leader. The tea party's rigid ideo-logical opposition to new taxes and commitment to large spending cuts puts it irreconcilably in conflict with Democrats. The threat of being "primary'ed"—that is, being challenged in the primaries—has silenced centrist Republicans not want-ing to lose their safe seats. The surprising defeat of House Majority Leader Eric Cantor brought this reality home. Given electoral gerrymandering, unless the 2020 census alters the political map, the House will likely remain in Republican hands and the Senate, less certainly, under Democrats.

Contributing to this political deadlock, President Obama declared in his 2014 State of the Union address that the White House will use executive authority to circumvent Congress. And, if necessary, the White House will reinterpret the law accordingly. Republicans, with some justification, claim that this executive ploy violates the Constitution. The only certain outcome is continued government paralysis.

At the same time, the White House has mobilized its powerful campaign organization to promote the president's political agenda, turning governing into a nonstop process of campaigning. Because the *Citizens United v. Federal Election Commission* Supreme Court decision permits virtually unlimited campaign spending for political purposes, the Republican counterattack is mounted through political action committees, armed with hundreds of millions of dollars. Talk radio, cable television, and thousands of blogs and bloggers on both sides of the political spectrum use those platforms to distort and demean the other side. Facts will be manipulated to conform with opinions, not the other way round.

Concurrently, the international picture is bleak. Chaos and violence are commonplace from the Mediterranean to the China Sea. The Obama administration lacks a coherent foreign policy strategy beyond sound bites and platitudes. Success rests on the ability of the current secretary of state's personal diplomacy, not a cohesive plan. Perhaps these crises will be self-limiting. Perhaps the threat of religious extremism is a temporary phenomenon. But perhaps not.

The president retains a dominant domestic position should he exercise it, despite Republican control of the House and possibly the Senate after November 2014. His many subsequent speeches have been designed to advance his agenda with or without Republican support. Meanwhile, the Republican Party resembles a rudderless ship adrift in heavy seas without a captain, charts, or workable compass.

At some point, debt and deficits will matter. At some point, an international hot spot will explode. If those explosions are severe enough, perhaps some measure of bipartisanship will reemerge. But do not bet the farm on that happening. American politics are in a dangerous downward spiral. And no one is at the controls.

Since the latter part of the 1990s, one of the U.S. government's greatest failings has been in the strategic conduct of war. The 1999 Serbian campaign was a close-run thing. Milosevic should have been forced from Kosovo in hours, not seventy-eight days.

Afghanistan and Iraq (and I believe the second Iraq War was the greatest geopolitical catastrophe in U.S. history since the Civil War) have made the world more dangerous and less stable. The root causes and reasons for these results are not complicated. One is the repeated failure of American administrations to understand divergent cultures and their tendency to concentrate on winning battles, not wars. As time passes, and unless our mind-set changes, the Vietnam-amnesia syndrome will infect memories of Afghan and Iraq.

Second, and since the early 1990s, inexperience and lack of qualifications of newly elected presidents have been crippling. Ideology and overly simplistic views of politics have substituted for strategic thinking. Today's composition of Congress also reflects this trend toward inexperience and declining numbers of members with prior foreign-policy or military service.

Third has been mission creep. Military tasks have been broadened to include nonmilitary objectives of nation building. However enthusiastically the "can-do" military has embraced this role, nation building is not and never has been a core mission of the armed forces. Absent adequate civilian and nonmilitary resources to deal with nation building and political reconstruction, failure has been inevitable.

The lessons are obvious and likely to be forgotten. Despite the rhetoric about American exceptionalism and advancing democracy and human rights, since the end of World War II and the rebuilding of Europe and Japan the United States has had a perfect track record after sizable military interventions and particularly wars it has started. Intervention has not worked.

Germany, Japan, and Italy were unconditionally defeated. They were also physically devastated, and their postwar survival depended on external help. The Allied occupiers had total control and authority over each of the defeated powers. All three had traditions of and experience with democracy, however limited. Each also had an educated and bureaucratic middle class. Through the magnanimous Marshall Plan, resources were available to rebuild and remake those societies into democracies.

U.S. forces occupied South Korea (and Russia the North) in 1945. But it took decades for democracy to evolve. Vietnam was a calamity without geostrategic consequence, and the fiction of a South Vietnamese democracy was short-lived. Bush 41 was clever in not repeating the blunder of further intervention after Saddam was driven from Kuwait in 1991 and wisely did not occupy Iraq. However, neither his son nor President Obama seems to have learned or understood this lesson.

Going to war to protect vital interests should be the single most important determinant for using military force, although "vital" is not easily defined. Going to war to advance democracy, to pay any price, and bear any burden (even to the point of ensuring that Afghan girls receive an education) should be constitutionally banned.

Humanitarian missions to protect and defend are more complicated and perplexing. On one hand, the morality of ending the slaughter of innocent civilians is a strong argument. Many African massacres and genocides, including those in Rwanda and the Congo, are cases in point. Forcing Milosevic to withdraw from Kosovo was noble in intent.

But Qaddafi was toppled in 2011 on humanitarian grounds, and Libya is still wracked with violence. In Syria, with nearly 200,000 dead, the double tragedy is that Assad may be the lesser of two evils, in a choice between the Baathists and the radical sects in the opposition. The latter could take control of the opposition (as the Bolsheviks did a century ago), giving terror a permanent geographic base. And no matter who runs the opposition, if it wins, revenge on the Alawite minority is likely.

If the United States considers future intervention, the first question that must be asked and answered is, "What next?" In most cases, the United States will be ill advised to act unilaterally and without some measure of international legitimacy. Past administrations have failed in that regard; a twenty-first-century mind-set can rectify this glaring weakness.

America's broad strategic objective must be the advancement of peace, prosperity, and stability through partnerships. Practice, and not lip service, must mandate that military force is the last resort. Very few if any vital national-security issues are likely to warrant unilateral action. For over a century, the United States has not waged a foreign war unilaterally (although when asked about Asians who fought alongside the United States in Vietnam, President Johnson bragged that they "were the best allies money can buy!"). Winning the Cold War would have been impossible without allies and NATO.

Because none of the Four Horsemen is fully susceptible to traditional solutions of the Westphalian world, partnerships must become the new centerpiece of policy. The difference from the past century is that partnerships need not and should not be formed explicitly on military relationships. Partnerships are essential to preventing Iran from acquiring nuclear weapons; Tehran and six others are engaged in negotiations.

A dose of humility is also sorely needed. Using military force to offset failed and failing governments or attempting to impose a political system on cultures unprepared for democracy mandates the toughest scrutiny. The United States would also be well served now to focus on fixing its own broken and failing government. That effort demands understanding the causes of failing and failed government.

Contradictions in the U.S. Constitution and the system of checks and balances and divided government are evident, are generally ignored, and produce bad governance. Politics today in the United States no longer values governing as the highest priority. Winning elections and political battles is what counts most. That is a further corruption of the process.

Negative campaigning and discrediting the opposition regardless of fact or truth are contaminating the political system. Permanent campaigning and solicitations for money consume the practice of politics. The impact is a government that is politely described as dysfunctional and in reality is badly broken and in gridlock.

Compromise and civility are essential to divided government. Both have become artifacts and dismissed as anachronistic. The two parties are polarized. Moderation and the political center are not only no-man's-lands. Both are "free fire" zones.

Worse, accountability in government, certainly at the top, is nonexistent. In the disastrous rollout of the Affordable Care Act in 2013, no one in the executive branch was fired. When radical Republicans in Congress forced a shutdown of government, no one lost his or her seat, and many gained additional support from constituents. No senior general was fired over Iraq for other than ethical misconduct. The Director of National Intelligence (DNI) misled Congress without consequence. The list goes on.

To the degree the past twenty-two years of history count, the odds are against electing anyone who has the experience and qualifications needed as president. Bill Clinton was fortunate to inherit the legacies of George H. W. Bush, both economically and geostrategically. George W. Bush was clearly unready for high office and, despite what seemed a superbly experienced team around him, lost two wars, one of which was arguably the greatest strategic disaster in American history. Barack Obama took on a horrendous hand. Yet his inexperience and absence of qualifications resulted in exacerbating, not improving, the strategic situation.

Finally, such cogent themes as deterrence and containment are missing, despite countless national-security strategies and reviews. These documents usually value rhetoric over substance and hence tend to be banal. As General of the Army George Marshall believed in a different era, if one got the objectives right, a lieutenant could write the strategy.

In a post-Westphalian era, getting the objectives right is far more difficult. However, basic principles for a national security strategy can be more instructive guides than rhetoric about protecting national interests; countering terrorism; and keeping Iran from acquiring nuclear weapons. But the focus must be on addressing causes, not symptoms, and on winning wars, not battles.

This condition of failing U.S. government will last for a long time. The consequence will not be the end or the demise of the United States. The United States will still remain the world's strongest military and economic power for a long time to come, China withstanding. Its businesses will be envied. Immigrants will still wish to live here. And no barbarian of real consequence threatens its collective gates.

Left unchecked, however, the decline in the national standard of living will be inexorable. Expectations about future generations doing better than their parents and grandparents will be curtailed. Income inequality will widen, and the middle class will be the bill payer for both richer and poorer. All this will happen unless or until the American people demand action or divine intervention occurs. When that point is reached, if it ever is, repairing failing government will require action across a wide front. Action requires a strategy. Using our brains, we can devise and implement a strategy.

Governors, states, and mayors provide a model. Mayors need to ensure criminals are arrested and the garbage is collected. Governors have to balance budgets. But Washington only needs to talk about issues. As a result, states are generally better run than the federal government.

Most states have balanced-budget amendments (mandating a balanced budget amendment for the federal government would be unwise, in that it limits flexibility in deficit spending). State legislatures are less ideological and more pragmatic. Hence, state governments are less affected by partisanship, ideology, and the inability of the executive and legislatures to work regardless of party.

When George W. Bush governed Texas, he and the Democratic head of the state senate worked well together. Republican governor of New Jersey Chris Christie and the Democratic legislature in a Democratic state are not at loggerheads. Can anything be done to subordinate politicking to governing?

Political polarization, increasing influence of political extremes, campaign financing laws, and public apathy have unbalanced the system of checks and balances. Small, minority, issue-oriented interest groups and individuals have become empowered, much as globalization has wrought internationally. These interest groups have far greater power and influence, worsening the polarization. Teachers' unions, the National Rifle Association, and individuals with great wealth, such as the Koch brothers, often hold as much or greater sway than electoral majorities.

A symptom and cause of broken government is the sorry statistic that only slightly more than half of eligible Americans vote in presidential and congressional elections. Suppose 70, 80, or 90 percent of all eligible Americans voted. How might that dilute the influence of small, powerful interest groups and reduce the political polarization that is crippling government?

If more Americans voted, presumably more would take a stronger interest in government. Second, in nominating candidates, both parties would have to appeal to a broader electoral base. Most Americans prefer the political center. More extreme views would likely be rejected, particularly during the primary process. Of course, within the center, debate over issues persists. But mitigating extreme views should make debate more civil.

One reason that Mitt Romney was defeated in 2012 was a nominating process that doomed his chances, in two ways. To win the nomination and support of minority but highly conservative constituencies, the former governor had to take more extreme positions than he favored. And in the extended numbers of debates the bizarreness of some of his rivals turned the contests into farce. When Romney tacked back to the center for the general election, it was too late. The Republican nominating process had become Obama's secret weapon.

With a much larger voting population, the impact of money would be diluted. To reach and affect this broader base, far more money would be needed. Such an amount could be raised. But the impact is doubtful.

Regardless, campaign finance laws must be reformed. Removing all restrictions on campaign spending is an alternative, provided that full transparency as to donors and amount is mandated and honored. Stiff fines and penalties to ensure transparency would have to be effectively imposed.

Only one way exists to get the vote out: universal voting. Every eligible and able voter would be required by law to be present at polling stations for congressional and presidential elections. No ballot need be cast. However, attendance would be universal and mandatory.

Under these circumstances, perhaps 80 or 90 percent of eligible Americans would vote. That statistic would help change the political system for the better. Universal voting exists in many other nations, including Australia and Switzerland, where it is popular, well received, and effective.

Critics argue that many Americans lack the knowledge or intelligence to be responsible voters. Others claim that a universal voting law is unconstitutional. Some will question that any penalties or punishments levied for not voting would be cruel and unusual. And even if more centrist Americans vote, will that take the politics out of politics?

These questions reflect oldthink. In the twenty-first century, Americans are better connected to the outside world. Most Americans understand that the role of government is to govern. And Americans appreciate that an engaged public is essential to an effective government. Universal voting is the means to reconnect the public with their government.

Regarding accountability, an equivalent of the Sarbanes-Oxley Act is needed for government. That act held public corporations, boards of directors, and key executives accountable and required chief executive officers to certify under penalty of perjury the accuracy of corporate accounts. The president and members of Congress need to be held equally accountable.

Regarding the experience needed to become president, the Constitution specifies only four qualifications: to be native born, to have lived for more than ten years in the United States, to have attained the age of thirty-five, and to win a majority of electoral votes. No other qualifications are noted.

A solution is changing the Twenty-Second Amendment. That amendment limits a president to serving two elected terms. Incumbents should be given the option for a third term. If presidents learn and grow—and the jury is out on President Obama—why should a new and most likely inexperienced replacement automatically take over after two terms? Amending the Constitution is a laborious process. But the Constitution may be the only way to inject experience and qualification into the Oval Office.

Regarding Congress, the overlapping committee and subcommittee structure is absurd. Too many hearings have become show trials. The 113th Congress had an abysmal legislative record. Sadly, none of that will change.

Congress is incapable of imposing major self-reforms, no matter how badly needed. Surrogate actions could force or prompt congressional reforms. Prior to a vote, a Sarbanes-Oxley type law would require each member to acknowledge publicly that he or she has read the bill in its entirety and understands the proposed legislation. Failing to make that pledge would expose each member to public scrutiny and even ridicule. Embarrassment may be the only way to get action.

The terms of House members should be extended to four years. Given the continuous pursuit of campaign funds, a two-year election cycle is too short. Members of both houses are elected to legislate and govern. Solicitation of funds is too much of a diversion.

A four-year term would provide relief to the pressures of fund raising. Beyond the laboriousness of the task of amending the Constitution, opposition will come from sitting senators. Few will welcome a challenge from House members who could still retain their seats there after losing Senate races (although a provision of the amendment could require House members to forfeit their seats if they run for the upper chamber and lose).

While genuine reform of Congress may prove more whimsy than wisdom, the national-security organization must be modernized. The original National Security Act was signed into law in 1947 and formally amended in 1949 and 1958, although changes have continued. The law created the Department of Defense, the Central Intelligence Agency, and the National Security Council. Since then many changes have been made. A Department of Homeland Security and a DNI were established after September 11. And the FBI has shifted its principal duties to include countering terrorism in addition to its crime-fighting functions.

No organization can substitute for the deficiencies of a president, a White House, or a Congress. White Houses have increasingly sought to control all aspects of policy and in particular those relating to foreign policy. Cabinet secretaries have become less advisors and collaborators in policy making and more implementers. Despite coordinating committees and attempts to break the stovepipe organization of the current structure, information sharing is far from perfect.

The Bush 43 decision to invade Iraq and Obama's AfPak strategy and pivot to Asia were profoundly flawed. Changes in organizational structure can minimize (but never prevent) potential flaws and erroneous decision making. The National Security Council is the first place to introduce change.

The NSC and its staff should have a permanent "red team" with the responsibility to identify potential weaknesses, flaws, and the full range of consequences of proposed policy actions. This must be a separate and distinct function. The reason for a red team is that as policy is developed, a consensus emerges around it.

Creators of any policy become proponents and advocates. Hence, "group-think" arises. As the U.S. legal system rests on adversarial proceedings, that is how a red team should operate. Only an adversarial interaction can produce an objective cost-benefit-risk analysis. Such analyses may not change presidents' thinking. But this process does guarantee that presidents will have the opportunity to evaluate contrarian views.

The intelligence community needs further streamlining. The establishment of the Department of Homeland Security and the Office of Director of National Intelligence represented incomplete solutions and added to the bureaucratic layering. The flaws and weaknesses of a large bureaucracy consisting of sixteen (often competing) separate intelligence agencies are organizational and structural, and not the least of them is in ensuring full information sharing—intelligence's greatest strength and weakness.

In terms of funding, the Department of Defense has the largest share of the intelligence budget, including NSA, the Defense Intelligence Agency, the National Geospatial Agency, and the big-ticket item of the National Reconnaissance Office (NRO), responsible for space-based systems. The Pentagon rightly argues that much of this capacity supports military operations that invariably are of a tactical, battlefield nature. But tensions and contradictions permeate this structure.

"Tactical" versus "strategic" thinking is one tension reflecting White House predilections favoring battles over wars. The need for immediate tactical intelligence by military commanders must be balanced with longer-term strategic analysis of threats and dangers to the nation. In cyber, the contradiction is between offense and defense. At the CIA, it is covert operations versus analysis. And throughout the intelligence community, the tensions between security and constitutional issues pertaining to search, seizure, and due process are far from resolved.

Cyber offers a unique opportunity for a new mind-set. The formation of Cyber Command suggests undue militarization. Because cyber is ubiquitous and holds the greatest consequences for civilian and private sectors of society, a new construct must correct that imbalance. The most appropriate place for rebalancing is the Justice Department, because legal issues will prove the most vexing for cyber.

During the Nixon administration, a second deputy secretary of defense was authorized with responsibilities for intelligence. At Justice, the office of a second deputy attorney general for cyber should be created. That office would have oversight and responsibility for a national cyber policy and program. An assistant or deputy position should also be created and filled by the commander of Cyber Command, with dual hats. Further, the NSA should return to a three-star command and remain a component of Cyber Command, with a separate commander.

This proposal creates a cross-government organization for cyber. This office must be given the authority to coordinate and where appropriate change the organization, integration, and funding of government agencies with cyber responsibilities. Congressional oversight can be conducted through the Joint Intelligence Committee, negating the need for another committee or subcommittee. The cyber think tank would report directly to this deputy attorney general.

Finally, how can the level of experience and competence in the U.S. government be elevated? First, the National Defense University (NDU) should become a National Security University (NSU). Currently, NDU offers courses for flag officers. Capstone is for new one-stars; Pinnacle is for three-stars.

NSU would offer courses for assistant secretaries and above in security-related departments either before or shortly after assuming office. The Foreign Service Institute does this for new ambassadors prior to assuming their posts. The practice should be extended across government.

Similarly, military officers promoted to four stars should be given ample preparation time for new assignments. Because of advice and consent and of legal limits on the number of flag and general officers, little or no opportunity for preparation between assignments is allowed for four-star officers. It is unwise for an officer assigned to a position of great responsibility not to be fully prepared for those duties. In fact, it is foolish.

Likewise, the confirmation process is dangerously lengthy. Too many senior positions remain unfilled as new administrations take office or at the start of a second term when old officeholders leave their posts. One solution is to require confirmation only for under-, deputy, and cabinet secretaries, allowing the president to appoint assistant secretaries without Senate approval. To exclude patronage or political expediency from this process, bypassing the assistant-secretary confirmation process would require prequalification.

Prequalification could be done through attending a course taught at NSU and passing an oral or written examination. Potential officeholders could apply as much as a year in advance for this program. The question is what to do about presidents and cabinet officers.

In the past, the outgoing administration and the incoming transition team were responsible for preparing the new president. No set agenda or formal curricula exist in that regard. Congress should authorize the drafting of presidential briefs to be provided to both candidates to assist in preparation. The Congressional

Research Service or other nonpartisan institution could be commissioned for that purpose. The same process would apply for all cabinet officers, including the DNI and Director of Central Intelligence.

While this proposal may not be perfect, more structure is needed to improve the transition and preparation periods for administrations. One addition to reinforce a brains-based approach is to use case studies that dissect decisions, identify assumptions that were sound or flawed, and examine why certain decisions worked and others failed. The analyses offered here critiquing the conduct of the wars in Iraq and Afghanistan and other failures, along with the assessment of the 2008 financial crises, could be useful guides in demonstrating how this process would work.

What would a new mind-set mean for the Department of Defense and for the cornerstone for U.S. security—the capacity and capability of its military forces? A Quadrennial Defense Review (QDR) was completed in 2014. For a number of reasons, that review did not make or propose major changes necessary in response to a far bleaker fiscal outlook and to uncontrollable internal costs for personnel, health care, retirees, and weapons systems. One reason was that debate existed over whether the QDR should or should not be budget constrained. The law says no. Practice says yes. That conundrum was not resolved.

The 2012 Strategic Guidance for the Defense Department issued by the White House remained in force, with its strategic pivot to Asia. The QDR did not amend that. Moreover, the senior military is convinced that Congress will intervene with more money and that while international threats amply exist, no full-blown crisis that the department cannot handle is imminent. Congress did reverse itself and restore retiree benefits to the budget. However, that was relatively minor and will not relieve the huge financial shortfalls facing defense.

For the short term, the budget picture is opaque. The future of sequestration, which cuts nearly a half-trillion dollars from defense over ten years, may or may not be altered, even though the Pentagon received modest relief for 2014. The Obama administration is consumed with the withdrawal from Afghanistan and its options if the BSA is not signed and follow-on forces are not allowed. Major changes or fixes to defense are not on the White House agenda, barring a crisis demanding action.

As argued, the international and domestic environments are undergoing tectonic and possibly revolutionary change as profound as the threat from and then demise of the Soviet Union—potentially more. Driven by globalization in general and all forms of the diffusion of power in particular, these dynamics have altered the nature and the character of the major threats and dangers to global security. As we have seen, this diffusion has empowered individuals (such as Edward Snowden and Bradley Manning) and nonstate actors (such as al Qaeda) at the expense of states. In simple terms, the major threats and dangers to global order and security are no longer state-centric, despite claims about Chinese or Iranian ambitions.

The twenty-first-century Four Horsemen directly affect far more people than did the Cold War and the threat of nuclear war, which fortuitously never occurred. None of these horsemen or the threats each represents is susceptible to a military solution; they require a far broader range of corrective or preventive policy instruments. Unfortunately, policy makers tend to view these issues with a twentieth-century mind-set steeped in Westphalian politics.

Second, defense spending is entering a period of draconian budget cuts far harsher than those of the post-Vietnam period. Even without sequestration cuts over ten years, uncontrollable personnel, health-care, weapons-systems, and pension costs, unchecked, will slash the buying power of the current defense budget by about half before the decade's end. On the current fiscal course, the Department of Defense will have to make cuts equivalent to at least 40–50 percent of a combination of force levels and associated weapons systems.

Compounding the budget problems, when interest rates go up—and they will—a larger share of nondiscretionary spending will mandate even greater cuts to discretionary accounts. Defense will be vulnerable. For the time being, the gravity of this situation has not been fully absorbed on either side of the Potomac.

Third, the international structures for global security and the U.S. national-security decision-making apparatus date back to the end of World War II and the Cold War. Neither has kept up with the changes to order and stability. And Congress too needs organizational reform.

Nor is the grammar and syntax of the twentieth century capable of dealing with twenty-first-century threats. The old strategic calculus of the twentieth century, characterized by the paradigm of mass destruction, has been replaced by one of mass disruption. The attacks of September 11 and the common use of terror more globally seize on the vulnerabilities of societies to disruption. And the preference for White Houses to act on symptoms, not causes, and concentrate on winning battles, not wars, compounds this strategic deficiency.

Fourth, after a dozen years of war, the all-volunteer force has become an extremely expensive (and some say overly pampered and even spoiled) military. For many of the forces engaged in combat, "capture or kill" missions have had devastating impact physically and psychologically. After withdrawing from Afghanistan at the end of 2014 (with possibly a smaller, although as yet undefined, force left behind), the Pentagon will have to transition to missions and operations based on routine peacetime tasks more boring and mundane than the demands of combat. Transitioning the force to a different and less challenging operational environment brings a new set of complications.

A very concerning development for the all-volunteer force is the surge in reports and allegations of ethical lapses and misconduct at all levels of the chain of command. Sexual assaults and abuses, cheating on tests in the nuclear forces, a reported $400 million fraud in recruiting, and a rash of general- and flag-officer investigations raise profound questions about integrity and ethical standards inside the U.S. military. Clearly, with over two million uniformed and civilian members of the Department of Defense, even a tiny percentage guilty of abuses can be a big number. However, as the United States exits a dozen years of combat operations, people remain the preeminent issue and resource and must be so treated—a point that will be emphasized later.

What should condition U.S. strategic responses? Five propositions set the context for specific recommendations. Each is based on the aim of securing peace, prosperity, and stability through partnerships. These propositions are derived from qualitative, and not quantitative, judgments, with acute appreciation that barring a crisis, economic realities and the absence of an existential threat will mandate far lower defense spending.

First, because most major threats are not amendable to military solutions alone, specific military strategies cannot exist in isolation. Instead, in close collaboration with friends, allies, and others, the U.S. military must be ready and able to carry out on short notice as directed by the president a variety of missions that require agility, flexibility, and intellectual innovation. Dealing with the disposal of Syrian chemical weapons was not part of any standard playbook but reflected the need for this dexterity.

Second, given the likely operating environments and threats, future force size and structure, readiness, modernization, and deployments should be based on maintaining a smaller, highly ready, and capable force with global access—although on this point of "smaller," heated debate will follow. Further, resources must go into retaining a reconstitution and regeneration base, so that should a peer threat emerge over the next decades, needed capability can be brought on line.

Third, the future active-duty force will be more dependent on partnerships. Much closer coordination and integration with allies and other partners will be essential. Greater flag-to-flag and general-officer interactions, exercises, and operations and more extensive personnel exchanges with partners will become essential parts of this strategy. Traditional partnerships such as NATO must be qualitatively strengthened and rejuvenated and new partnerships put in place. The quality, and not the quantity, of these interactions will become the critical and determining metric for success. Given the forward-deployed status of naval, ground, and air forces, partnership building is inherently easy to achieve.

Fourth, people are the most vital asset and must be treated as such. Because spending will decline, the military will not be awarded the same generous levels of pay, benefits, and other perquisites that have tacitly become accepted as entitlements. Nor will budgets allow massive spending to meet all operational requirements. New personnel policies are essential to deal with these cutbacks and the more onerous and boring rigors of peacetime in place of the challenges of wartime deployments to dangerous regions. And the ethical and moral issues that have been raised, from sexual abuse to senior-officer misconduct, require immediate attention.

Finally, as Churchill reputedly quipped, "Now that we are out of money, we will have to use our brains to think our way clear of danger." The department can achieve this by embarking on a revolution in military education. This revolution must be based on the goal of achieving greater understanding through a process of continuous learning and knowledge. Instead of a linear progression of education that is based on seniority, learning must become more horizontal.

Knowledge and learning extend beyond professional duties and responsibilities. The impact of globalization and diffusion of power must be integrated in this process. Greater regional, technical, and strategic expertise and understanding are required. To ensure that the capacity for reconstitution and regeneration is maintained, as part of this knowledge and learning requirement the twentieth-century notion of a defense industrial base must be replaced with a twenty-first-century defense intellectual-property and industrial base.

In summary, the pillars of this defense and national security strategy must rest on: partnerships that demand far closer cooperation and coordination with friends, allies, and others, including potential adversaries; identification of people as the number-one priority for the future force; regeneration and reconstitution of forces should new or unexpected threats arise; and establishment of knowledge and learning as central components of the tool kits used by our forces.

Devils and details are incestuous. Obviously, many force structure options exist. The leading criterion for fielding future forces is that readiness and modernization must be kept high, at the expense of numbers.

Today, of an active-duty force of about 1.3 million, the United States plans to keep about 100,000 troops forward deployed in the Pacific; 80,000 (headed down to 68,000) in Europe and the littorals; and after the drawdown in Afghanistan and assuming war with Iran does not break out, perhaps 10,000 in the Persian Gulf and associated regions. Wildcards cannot be discounted, however, from operations in Libya and Mali to what may or may not happen in Syria or with Iran.

Maintaining a ready joint force of 150,000 on each coast to include deployed and deployable units would account for 300,000 active-duty personnel. That number should be sufficient to meet two concurrent contingencies, such as in Korea or the Persian Gulf. A further 300,000 troops would be in rotational training preparing for deployment and serving as a reserve should contingencies demand more forces. The remaining 200,000–300,000 would be in a stand-down status performing routine peacetime duties at home, as well as undergoing training, education, and other assignments, able to return to fully active status in eight to ten months. Clearly, a strategy for regeneration and reconstitution of forces and combat systems is vital to providing for unforeseen contingencies that will require greater numbers and capabilities.

Over time, a total active-duty force of 800,000–900,000, with equivalent reductions in the reserves and National Guard (understanding that, for example, the Navy assigned certain critical skills, such as medical, to these components), would result. One significant change would be to place units in a cadre or "reserve" service, with skeleton manning, as part of a strategy for reconstitution and regeneration to restore numbers. It is pointless to decommission ships, especially aircraft carriers and aviation squadrons and nuclear submarines, that still have service life left when they can be placed in a cadre status for contingencies and other eventualities.

Meanwhile, changes to the all-volunteer force are needed. Suicide rates are symptomatic of certain personnel problems, as are ethical abuses and instances of misconduct. Recruitment and retention will become more difficult in peacetime even without major economic growth. Benefits for pay, compensation, retirement, and health care must be reduced, because each contributes to making personnel costs unaffordable. As the Nixon administration was forced by Vietnam to put in place the all-volunteer force, sometime in this decade the all-volunteer force will likewise be subjected to review.

Germany and Norway have adopted a hybrid force—part volunteer and part draftee. The United States should consider a similar scheme. The size of the draftee cohort need not be large. Perhaps 10–20 percent is enough. And draftees would be afforded opportunities to become regulars along with volunteers. A draft would be restarted, along with full registration under Selective Service of women along with men. Considerable opposition to ending the all-volunteer military will arise from many corners, especially in Congress. That opposition will have to be overcome, and that is not a simple proposition. Aside from relieving the pressures of personnel-cost growth, benefits of a hybrid force would include reintegrating more Americans into service and reducing the isolation of the military from society, as the consolidation of military communities and bases have produced de facto gated communities.

Beyond strategy and people, reorganization of the Pentagon and the Unified Command Plan (UCP) is long overdue. The Pentagon has five sides. The department goes one better, with six centers of power, probably two or three too many. The secretary of defense and his immediate staff; the Office of the Secretary of Defense and various defense agencies; the chairman of the Joint Chiefs and the Joint Staff; the Joint Chiefs of Staff; the military services and secretaries; and the combatant commanders—all are power centers, often with competing or overlapping roles, missions, and responsibilities. As a result, bureaucratic inertia is endemic, and change usually occurs only on the margin, and slowly at best.

Competition is good, provided it yields good results. Too often, however, competition produces waste, inefficiency, and redundancy. With the strategic pivot to Asia, aka rebalancing, the Air Force and Navy have announced the Air-Sea Battle concept to project power onto the littorals. Not to be left behind, the Army has announced plans to increase its adaptability to the Pacific theater, suggesting the emergence of a second Marine Corps, which has always had an Asian focus.

To deal with these overlapping, competing, and often wasteful issues, a military version of the Glass-Steagall Act is needed. The Joint Chiefs of Staff (JCS) should be separated from their responsibilities as service chiefs and separate service chiefs appointed. As their full-time responsibilities, the chairman and new JCS should serve as principal military advisors, with the responsibility for preparing the budgets and the POM (Program Objectives Memorandum) with the secretary of defense. The services would become strictly implementers. This separation would permit taking decisions less tinged with service parochialism.

Second, the UCP needs revision in keeping with twenty-first-century needs. Combining various commands and expanding the composition of remaining staffs to accommodate a whole-of-government approach are important. European and African Commands should be reintegrated into a Western Command. Northern and Southern Command should be integrated into Americas Command. In some cases, as civilian control of the military has worked in Washington, a civilian commander could be appointed in the field, with a four-star deputy responsible for the military component of the command.

The regional commanders would be Western Command, Pacific Command, Central Command, and Americas Command. Each staff should be expanded to provide expertise across the whole of government. In essence, mini-NSC staffs would develop in each command to enhance partnerships with regional states without excessively stressing the military-to-military relationships. Obviously, this concept is not new. Commands have moved in this direction. But this movement needs to be accelerated.

Third, because education in the form of expanding knowledge and learning is so vital, a retired or active-duty four-star officer should be appointed as an undersecretary of defense to oversee and coordinate cross-department education and be given the additional duty of president of the National Defense University (or National Security University), reporting directly to the new JCS. And while wholesale reform of many defense agencies is sorely needed, that effort, given the unsuccessful track record of such attempts, should be deferred until a new president enters office.

Repairing failed or failing American government demands both greater accountability and greater public engagement. America is and will be the wealthiest of states. A majority of its citizens live relatively well. The lengthy and unsuccessful wars in Iraq and Afghanistan and economic recession have not been sufficiently painful to convince most Americans to demand more from their government.

Many Americans are apathetic, reluctant, or unwilling to force or convince govern-ment that reform is essential. Politicians from both parties will continue to seek higher elected office and then become convinced that keeping office is a higher priority than governing well.

Presidential aspirants understand and will accommodate the need to win the primary as an obvious prerequisite for the White House. As such, nominat-ing campaigns will be organized around courting relatively small and divergent constituencies and interest groups, winning 270 electoral votes—not around pro-viding good government for all Americans. Given extreme partisanship, virtually unlimited campaign financing, the pernicious political atmosphere in Washington, the absence of an incumbent running, 2016 could prove to be the nastiest and most demeaning presidential election in the nation's history.

If polls are accurate, the credibility and performance of the U.S government as perceived by its public (and many other countries as well) are at a low point, possibly lower than during the Vietnam War. Perhaps protests are fewer because fewer body bags are coming home from the wars than in those years. Watergate continued the depletion of public confidence in government.

Past failings were correctable. Economic recovery, the demise of the Soviet Union, and the first Gulf War lifted American spirits and confidence. After September 11, the present and future are far different. That event triggered a slow-motion version of June 28, 1914. Recovery, as long as government continues to fail, is far from certain. And failure to understand these new circumstances will make recovery that much harder.

The erosion of the Westphalian system, the empowerment of individuals and nonstate actors, and four dangerous horsemen constitute the realities and chal-lenges of the twenty-first century. Each is largely ignored as the United States rico-chets from crisis to crisis.

Short of a vocal public demanding action or an unprecedented event that shocks and awes both ends of Pennsylvania Avenue into action, failing government will be the greatest threat to America, democracy, and the nation's way of life for much of the twenty-first century.

9

Economic Despair, Disparity, and Disruption

Economic despair, disparity, and disruption are powerful forces. Despair eventually produces deprivation. In the Middle East and South Asia, deprivation of life, liberty, and the pursuit of happiness has driven many to radical Islam. How much economic despair, disparity, and disruption will it take to cause or provoke greater political consequences is uncertain. But social media linking future Tunisian fruit vendors with mass audiences suggests an answer that may not be favorable to ruling governments.

Despite the myriad of international and national organizations dedicated to relieving economic despair and disparity, waging war on poverty may prove an endless task. Resource scarcity due to physical depletion or obstacles to access, such as geography and politics, exacerbate this impoverished condition. Combined with failed and failing governments and despite the promises of breakthrough technologies, a Malthusian view of the future is not out of the question. But relieving these grievances, however difficult, will help corral the third horseman.

Too often, solutions to economic crises come either too late to be preventive or are not sufficiently robust to redress the problems. The Great Depression of 1929 took more than a decade to end and required a world war ultimately to restart the American economy. In 2014, global recovery from the 2008 crisis has been fragile and slow at best.

U.S. and global economies ultimately must deal with the causes, and not symptoms, of economic despair, disparity, and disruption. Creation of demand and of jobs is the most crucially needed cure. To achieve both in the United States, it is vital to establish a national infrastructure bank and over time to migrate this concept to other regions and states. Repair and modernization of infrastructure, to use a Clausewitzian metaphor, constitute the strategic centers of economic gravity.

Second, trade is likewise crucial. John Kennedy's phrase that a rising tide lifts all boats is well known. For that to happen, implementation of TTIP and TTP is essential. Many argue that these pacts will vacuum jobs out of the United States to where production costs are less overseas. In fact, TTIP will generate demand and create jobs, because the labor markets on both sides of the Atlantic are roughly equivalent in cost structure. If properly implemented, TTP over the long term will diminish economic despair, disparity, and dislocation.

Third, the growing middle class is a highly important consideration. The 2013 National Intelligence Council report concluded that the rise of the middle class is one of the game changers of the coming decade. Ensuring that the status of the middle class can be maintained and expanded will be imperative in overcoming the dangers of this horseman.

Last, safeguards and laws that have been put in effect to deal with the prospect of a financial crisis or meltdown must be strengthened.

Economic disparity—that is, the gap between rich and poor—has always been present, and not only in colonies and fourth-world states with permanent upper classes. China, Russia, Europe, and the United States exhibit striking disparities. Disparities are found in virtually every state. President Kennedy's presumption that growing economies lift all boats has one critical catch—how can economies be launched on a trajectory of sustained growth?

In the United States, income disparity is a major political issue in 2014 and will be in 2016. Democrats argue that the bulk of prosperity and wealth rests with the top 1 percent of Americans. Comparing the nation's GDP in 1914 to today's, in real terms, that of 2014 is twenty times larger. On a per capita basis, that increase is only seven times larger. So where did all that wealth go?

Better foundations for dealing with economic despair, dislocation, and disparity would be job creation and stimulation of demand without generating hyper- or excessive inflation, overhaul or creation of national infrastructure, and prevention of global financial crises. Mechanisms for each part of this collective foundation exist individually. The chronic problem is integrating each into a comprehensive economic plan and then implementing that plan.

Given the limitations of regulation and oversight and the inherent vagaries of the market, in the United States the most sensible course of action to offset the dangers posed by this second horseman rests in repair, modernization, and, in some cases, construction of new infrastructure. For the United States, infrastructure modernization is not merely a high, or even the highest, domestic priority. It is also the most effective means of creating jobs and making the country ready and able to compete in the twenty-first century.

To understand the power of this argument, a short assessment of the state of infrastructure is a vital starting point. The quadrennial reviews of the American Society of Civil Engineers (ASCE) provide invaluable and comprehensive analysis. From that point of departure, appreciating what programs and legislation have been proposed and why none so far have been approved yields conclusions for structuring a plan that could work.

ASCE's *Report Card for America's Infrastructure* (*Report Card*) uses grades A to F and eight criteria to evaluate the state of America's infrastructure: capacity, condition, funding, future need, operation and maintenance, public safety, resilience, and innovation. Since 1998, the grades have been near failing, and they average D—a stunning critique of the world's largest economy.

Water and environment: Dams, D; Drinking Water, D; Hazardous Waste, D; Levees, D-; Solid Waste, B-; Wastewater, D

Transportation: Aviation, D; bridges, C+; inland waterways, D-; ports, C; rail, C+; roads, D; transit: D

Public facilities: Public Parks and Recreation, C-; Schools, D

Energy: D+.

The conclusion from the report reads:

Infrastructure is the foundation that connects the nation's businesses, communities, and people, driving our economy and improving our quality of life. For the U.S. economy to be the most competitive in the world, we need a first class infrastructure system—transport systems that move people and goods efficiently and at reasonable cost by land, water, and air; transmission systems that deliver reliable, low-cost power from a wide range of energy sources; and water systems that drive industrial processes as well as the daily functions in our homes. Yet today, our infrastructure systems are failing to keep pace with the current and expanding needs, and investment in infrastructure is faltering.

Since its inception, the U.S. government has always invested in national infrastructure from roads and ports to schools and transportation. In the 1930s, FDR's New Deal built a great deal of the nation's current infrastructure, much of which remains in service seventy or eighty years later. A cross-country drive made as part of army maneuvers in 1919 and then exposure to the German autobahns after World War II made the need for a system of national highways self-evident to Dwight D. Eisenhower. Ike promised and had passed the Federal-Aid Highway Act of 1956, popularly known as the National Interstate and Defense Highways Act (Public Law 84–627), enacted in June 1956.

At that time, the act was the largest public-works project in history. Funded by taxes on gasoline and diesel fuel (the states would contribute 10 percent), nearly 70,000 miles of highway were built in the first ten years. The Highway Trust Fund continues that work today, with more interstate highways under construction.

Proposals for a national infrastructure bank are not new; they were introduced in Congress two decades ago. The more recent BUILD Act of 2011, which would create a nonpolitical national infrastructure bank, was cosponsored by Senators John Kerry, Kaye Bailey Hutchinson, Lindsay Graham, and Mark Warner. The act was supported by U.S. businesses, the AFL-CIO, and the U.S. Chamber of Commerce.

The bill as written failed to pass the Senate in November 2011, on a party-line vote in which the two Republican sponsors voted against it. Their ostensible reasons for rejecting the bill rested on the opposition of conservative and tea-party elements who considered the bank both an unacceptable expansion of government and a new government expenditure that would only add to the deficit. A more important, less visible, and cynical reason was political. With presidential and congressional elections a year away, denying the economic and employment benefits that would accrue to the Obama administration was more important than governing.

Currently, The Partnership to Build America Act (H.R. 2084) of November 20, 2013, proposed by House freshman John K. Delaney and fifty sponsors (split evenly between Republicans and Democrats) is in play. The act would create a national infrastructure bank capitalized at $750 billion and have no public—that is, government—funding. The proposal is as follows, taken in its entirety from Representative Delaney's website:

Investing in Infrastructure

- According to the 2013 Report Card for America's Infrastructure, U.S. Infrastructure has a cumulative grade of "D+" with an estimated $ 3.6 trillion investment needed by 2020.
- The Partnership to Build America Act would finance the rebuilding of our country's transportation, energy, communications, water, and education infrastructure through the creation of an infrastructure fund using repatriated corporate earnings as well as through utilizing public-private partnerships.
- The legislation would create the American Infrastructure Fund (AIF) that would provide loans or guarantees to state or local governments to finance qualified infrastructure projects. The states or local governments would be required to pay back the loan at a market rate determined by the AIF to ensure they have "skin in the game." In addition, the AIF would invest in equity securities for projects in partnership with states or local governments.
- The AIF will be funded by the sale of $50 billion worth of Infra structure Bonds which would have a 50 year term, pay a fixed interest rate of 1 percent, and would not be guaranteed by the U.S. government.

    U.S. corporations would be incentivized to purchase these new Infrastructure Bonds by allowing them to repatriate a certain amount of their overseas earnings tax free for every $1.00 they invest in the bonds. This multiplier will be set by a "reverse Dutch auction" allowing the market to set the rate.

    Assuming a 1:4 ratio, meaning a company repatriates $4.00 tax-free for every $1.00 in Infrastructure Bonds purchased, a company's effective tax rate to repatriate these earnings would be approximately 8 percent and the $4.00 could then be spent by the companies however they chose.
- The AIF would leverage the $50 billion of Infrastructure Bonds at a 15:1 ratio to provide up to $750 billion in loans or guarantees.

- At least 25 percent of the projects financed through the AIF must be Public-Private Partnerships for which at least 20 percent of a project's financing comes from private capital using a public-private partnership model.

Benefits

- Creates a large-scale infrastructure financing capability with zero federal appropriations.
- Creates significant jobs in the short-term and helps U.S. competitiveness in the long-term.
- Allows for repatriation while ensuring U.S. corporations' tax savings are truly invested in the U.S. economy to grow quality jobs.
- Pushes the project selection decisions down to state and local governments who have to have "skin in the game."
- Encourages and creates a framework for growth in public-private partnerships.

Whether or not the Delaney bill passes, a national infrastructure bank is needed now. That bank should be privately run as a corporation—and a private-public partnership is possible—and capitalized at about a trillion dollars to make an economic impact. Funding would come in the form of thirty-to-forty-year debt offerings—that is, bonds sold to the public by the corporation with interest rates 2 to 3 percent above prime as an incentive. These bonds would be insured by the federal government. Interest and final payments, as well as money to cover the costs of insurance, would come from user fees and tolls arising from and generated by the infrastructure programs.

For U.S. companies holding substantial funds overseas to avoid double taxation—and those funds are estimated at one or two trillion dollars—bond offerings could be very attractive if coupled with tax breaks for money repatriated to this bank. That incentive and a good interest rate could raise a large amount of investment.

Prior to beginning operations, a comprehensive infrastructure repair and modernization program would be prepared to recommend priorities and funding targets. The National Academy of Sciences, ASCE, or other nonpartisan organizations could be responsible for undertaking this effort. With a trillion-dollar bank, politics would otherwise dominate determination of where the money would be spent and what infrastructure projects would be selected.

Congress and the White House would be intimately involved. Unfortunately, this is not 1954 and the highways bill. Politics would intrude, and intrude heavily. To minimize the intense political and partisan pressures, a process for selecting and awarding projects similar to the base-closing commission would have to be established and a formula devised to provide some measure of fairness in ensuring each state received an appropriate share. Otherwise, government will not be capable of administering an infrastructure-renewal program.

The bank would focus on the categories used by the ASCE in evaluation of the nation's infrastructure: the power grid, Internet, obsolete and failing bridges and highways, ports and dredging (in particular), education and educational facilities, water, energy, levees and dams, railways, and aviation. The assessment would provide priorities driven by safety, security, and long-term positive impact on economic growth and job creation.

Based on this project in the United States, the concept of infrastructure banks could be exported to any country that could offer collateral. Resources, a form of debt-equity swap, or very high likelihoods that tolls and user fees would be sufficient to repay bonds could serve as collateral. Through repair and modernization of infrastructure, jobs, opportunities, and demand would be generated.

Potentially, the larger and less tractable strategic and political problems arising from economic despair, disparity, and dislocation could be mitigated. By attacking the economic forces of despair that make radical movements attractive to people with no alternative, people who can be convinced that martyrdom is the key to paradise, extremism can be countered and ultimately beaten with jobs and brighter expectations.

Global economic growth rests in passage of TTIP and TTP. The transatlantic economy accounts for over 50 percent of world GDP. Even with the U.S. pivot to Asia, this economy will remain the largest and wealthiest global market. The EU alone accounts for 22 percent of world GDP and more than a quarter of global consumption. The transatlantic economy generates about $5.3 trillion in commercial sales and employs about fifteen million workers.

European investments in the United States are around two trillion dollars. A report commissioned by the European Commission found that TTIP will annually increase the EU economy by about $150 billion and the U.S. and global economies by about $130 billion, as well as increase EU exports by about 6 percent and U.S. exports by 8 percent. Translated into family terms, TTIP will add about $865 annually to a U.S. family of four and about $720 for the same-sized European family. All but five U.S. states export more to Europe than to China.

TTP involves negotiations among twelve nations (the United States, Australia, Brunei, Canada, Chile, Japan, Malaysia, Mexico, New Zealand, Peru, Singapore, and Vietnam) and is more problematic. However, one advantage is not economic. If TTP succeeds and economies grow, the shadow of the second horseman will shrink, possibly dramatically. Critics argue that the United States could lose jobs, ignoring the fact that six of the partners are advanced and high-wage states. However, TTP should be considered in geostrategic as well as economic terms. And both agreements can help the growing middle classes to keep that status while allowing others entrance.

Regarding preventing financial and economic crises, history offers cures. The 1907 financial crisis was fully described earlier. The cures rested in prohibition of speculative betting on stocks in bucket shops and restrictions on and oversight of derivatives, equivalents of CDS and CDO. The establishment of the Federal Reserve was important.

The oscillation of world economies, the crash of October 19, 1987 (when the Dow lost 508 points), and the bankruptcy of Long-Term Capital Management (which came close to causing a financial meltdown) were harbingers of things to come. The 2008 crisis still has not been fully absorbed, and global economies have yet to rebound. But 2008 did put in place certain safeguards, and most corporations and financial institutions have reacted positively in learning from that crisis.

In response to corporate wrongdoing in the early 2000s, with the implosion of Enron as the catalyst, and to Sarbanes-Oxley, American business by and large has become far more efficient. Despite the onerous costs in accounting and legal fees encumbered by public companies, managerial oversight in general has greatly improved. Dodd-Frank has not been fully implemented. However, a de facto return to Glass-Steagall to limit proprietary trading is an important step. Central banks understand better the catastrophic downsides of mismanaging risk and the need to keep capital markets flowing so that ample credit exists.

Financial institutions likewise will now exercise better risk-management oversight. The balance sheets of many public corporations are strong; it is estimated that U.S. firms have nearly two trillion dollars in cash. The problem is that with-holding cash makes greater rates of economic growth difficult if not impossible to sustain.

That said, weaknesses in the global economy and international financial system persist. First, China is problematic. Its real estate market, internal credit and debt, and need to sustain high rates of growth to stimulate both domestic and international demand are challenges for any government, authoritarian or demo-cratic. Presumptions about sustained long-term growth in the U.S. stock markets have the ring of the perpetual high plateau predicted in 1929.

Interest rates cannot stay low indefinitely. Quantitative easing will end. Per-manent deficit spending will not fill the gaps between government revenues, obli-gations, and liabilities arising from entitlement programs. All this suggests that at some stage another recession or economic dislocation is likely. As with any predic-tions, timing is everything, and how much time will pass before these speed brakes take hold is guesswork.

In philosophical terms, humanitarian interests are important both abroad and at home. The United States is the largest provider of foreign aid, assistance, and humanitarian contributions (about $30 billion in 2013). Yet foreign aid, in all its forms and from all its sources, cannot solve many of these regional economic and social problems. The implication is that the United States should consider shifting foreign aid and assistance to economic aid and investment—that is, as the bromide goes, teaching people how to fish rather than giving them fish.

Workers of the world may not necessarily unite. But many may mobilize. From the Arab Awakening and many unreported riots in China to the failed Occupy Wall Street movement, economic despair, dislocation, and disparity will continue to powerful political consequences. Implementing infrastructure banks and ratify-ing TTIP and TTP will not solve all or even a goodly part of economic inequities. However, these actions are a good start. And a new start is sorely needed—another component of a mind-set for the twenty-first century.

10

Ideological Extremism and
Religious Fanaticism

America and many other states, some of whom are not close allies or friends, are engaged in what could be an enduring struggle against ideological extremism propelled by religious fanaticism. Americans could not understand the Japanese embrace of suicidal fanaticism during World War II, with its banzai charges and kamikaze attacks. Islamist extremism that extols suicide in jihad or holy war is likewise a foreign and repugnant construct that defies rational explanation for most people.

Therein rests one reason why winning this struggle is difficult. Understanding the enemy, as Sun Tzu wrote centuries ago, is essential to victory. The United States does not understand this adversary. But that is no surprise.

The United States has not learned yet that the best armies in the world alone cannot defeat enemies who lack a military of any size and rely on terror as the weapon of choice. Because of the appeal and ease of finding tactical solutions in this war on terror, the United States has embarked on attacking symptoms rather than concentrating on the causes that lead people to die willingly for a perverted form of religion.

Islamic or any other type of well-organized extremists hold an asymmetric advantage in the exchange ratio of what it costs them to attack us and what it costs us to defend ourselves and defeat them. And as in the Vietnam War, the enemy does not have to win a single battle to win the larger war. It simply must not lose—George Washington's strategy in the Revolution.

Last, U.S. counterterrorism strategies are predominately defensive, designed to prevent another major attack against the homeland. But to succeed, strategy must be more offensive and proactive. As Sun Tzu recognized, the most efficient means to victory is to defeat the enemy's strategy first, not his army.

Above all, Islamic extremism and terrorism are based on a perversion of Islam and an overarching vision of driving the infidels from the holy lands by any means. Extreme interpretation of Sharia law impels this vision, while posing exquisite constitutional dilemmas for freedom of religion and what is acceptable to the American public. Hence, if Sun Tzu is correct, the path to success rests in defeating this idea. Unfortunately, this simple advice has been overlooked, ignored, or dismissed by the United States.

Ideological extremism in many forms has done incalculable damage throughout history. Whether Islamic extremism is nothing more than a painful ailment or a life-threatening cancer is also far from clear. From the crusades to Nazism and fascism, extremism and violence have too often been synonymous and have threatened the international order. Less violent proponents of extremism are likewise dangerous, distorting and capturing what otherwise could be sound ideas and principles turning them into cynical arguments in support of causes that ultimately prove to be damaging and destructive.

In the United States, extremism applies to social issues as well and has accelerated the failure of government. The extreme wings of the two political parties are irreversibly opposed on issues ranging from the size and role of government to the raising of taxes and the cutting of spending. Obamacare has been a lightning rod for extremists of both persuasions.

The debate over "guns, gays, God, and gestation periods" is another example of how extremism has distorted, vilified, and brought violence to social issues best resolved civilly and with common sense, within the rule of law. Bombing abortion clinics and killing pro-choice practitioners on the grounds of saving the lives of the unborn is akin to insanity and the darkest side of extremism. So too has the debate over gun control and Second Amendment rights descended into a polarized and uncompromising situation, even as the number of shootings in schools and malls rises.

Extremism has tainted and contaminated U.S. foreign policy, and never more so than in the decades after World War II. Adversaries were characterized as new versions of old threats even when the political philosophies we despised were antithetical to National Socialism. The Soviet Union, Red China, and today Islamic extremism fall into the category of new threats disguised as old ones. The irrationality and viciousness of Joe McCarthy may not be as prevalent. But it is present. Iran is one such case.

An Iranian nuclear bomb is seen as so unacceptable as to convince some extremists of the absolute necessity and legitimacy of preventive war. No one wants Iran or anyone else who may have a hostile agenda to acquire nuclear weapons. But war is not the only answer.

The United States has lived with a Soviet bomb, a Chinese bomb, Pakistani and Indian bombs, an Israeli bomb, and most recently a North Korean bomb. No matter how frightening the Iranian mullahs may seem, surely Kim Jong-un is no better. But war has not been declared to prevent the North from obtaining some sort of nuclear device or for that manner anyone else.

In political and policy terms, extremism distorts and defeats rationality and reason in forming conclusions and choosing best courses of action. Worse, in dealing with extremism from groups such as al Qaeda, overreaction in the use of excessive countermeasures is self-destructive and can do as much damage to our political system as enemy attacks. The rendition of "enemy combatants" to long-term imprisonment in Guantanamo without due process became an unintended assault on the Constitution. "Waterboarding" and harsh interrogation techniques to pry information from detainees—torture, to most—were extreme methods viewed by Dick Cheney as essential in defeating extremism.

The use of drones and targeted assassinations against enemies of the United States likewise brings into focus the debate over using extreme means to defeat extremism. Exposure of NSA surveillance has unleashed a tsunami of outrage and anger, much of it from allies. One of the most exquisitely troubling questions is whether a major danger posed by religious extremism is not so much physical damage it inflicts as the destruction it does to the Constitution.

In waging the war on terror—that is, countering extremism—repeated violations of the Constitution have inflicted as much political, moral, and legal harm as any terrorist attack could achieve. The conflicts over security, privacy, and due process are very much unresolved. Without a new mind-set that makes their resolution a high priority, they will remain unsettled for a long time to come.

"Islamic radicalism"—a term that still demands a clear definition—is regarded by many as the most dangerous threat facing the West since Hitler and the Soviet Union. Regardless of what it is called, why has this perversion of religion aroused such reactions? How did this reaction come about? How dangerous is Islamic extremism? What can and should be done in response? And what should not be attempted?

Islamic extremism and the schism between Shia and Sunni date back to 632 AD and Mohammed's death. When the Muslims sought a successor to Mohammed, the Shia believed leaders of the faith had to come from his direct descendants. The Sunni believed leaders should be selected from the most qualified. Ali, a Shia, assumed the fourth caliphate and was later killed by the Sunni. In 661, his son Hussein led a revolt against his father's Sunni assassins. Hussein's men were annihilated, Hussein himself was decapitated, and the war between Shia and Sunni has gone on ever since. Of 1.3 billion Muslims, about 10 percent are estimated to be Shia.

Unlike Christianity, Islam has had no Martin Luther and no Reformation. After the Ottoman Empire disintegrated, the Arab world, which is virtually all Muslim, was colonized and occupied by Western Christian powers, subjugating, repressing, and alienating local populations. World War I and the secret Sykes-Picot Agreement created the artificial states and boundaries of the Middle East, which largely remain permanent impediments to stability. And the pan-Arab nationalism that led to the independence of Egypt and other Arab states after World War II became fertile ground for Islamic extremism.

Saudi Arabia is central to the struggle with radical Islam for many reasons. The Kingdom of Saudi Arabia was founded by King Abdul-Aziz ibn Saud as a Sunni monarchy in 1932. Infused with the Wahhabi theology—at best a highly conservative, if not radical, form of Islam—as part of the union in 1902 that set the Sauds in power, Saudi Arabia became petro-rich. Saudi Arabia's conservative philosophy has enabled the ruling family, now consisting of some two thousand princes, to retain tight political control. But Saudi Arabia is vulnerable to charges of hypocrisy from many directions.

Sharia law governs the Kingdom with a strict interpretation of Islam. The role of women has by Western standards been stifled. Public executions for violation of Sharia law are not uncommon. Religious police, enforcing the law, are ubiquitous. And the Saudis have exported Wahhabism embraced by terrorist and other radical groups, especially in Pakistan. The Saudis reject this claim. But Osama bin Laden came from an important Saudi family and believed he was advancing jihad when he set off for Afghanistan to fight the Soviets. And most of the September 11 suicide bombers were Saudis.

Iran, a Shia state, is Saudi Arabia's bête noir, reflecting not only petro- and geostrategic rivalries but the intense Shia-Sunni hatred. Riyadh has been aggressive in supporting the anti-Assad, anti-Alawite opposition in Syria as a counter to Iran and, of course, in support of the repressed Syrian Sunni majority. And because of the U.S. decision not to intervene in Syria, U.S.-Saudi relations have deteriorated.

The Arab-Israeli-Palestinian conflict united the hostility of both Sunni Arabs and Persian Shia against Israel and "Zionist occupation." September 11 was a catalyst, bringing all of these antagonisms and animosities together into many simultaneously lurking crises. From the Mediterranean to the Bay of Bengal, a surfeit of potential archdukes and virtual bullets are in play. What the cause celebre may be for a new June 1914 is unpredictable. But it is present.

One result of the decline of the Westphalian system and of the diffusion of power is that radical Islam has become empowered. Because governments have failed and are failing to address many grievances, including political exclusion and economic desperation, Islamic extremism has spread. Terror has been the weapon of choice. As extremism and terror expand, so too do the dangers of Islamic fanaticism intensify.

The West fails to understand the power and attraction of fanaticism and martyrdom. Jihad, in the minds of the believers, will lead to the imposition of both Sharia law and a new caliphate. In essence, and ironically, history has come full circle. The jihadis have become tenth-century crusaders a millennium later.

The word *jihad,* meaning religious or holy war in the name of Allah, has become a surrogate for defining Islamic extremists. Unfortunately, because jihad is an expression of reverence within traditional Islam, using it to label terrorists offers legitimacy and elevates individuals and groups to far greater status than is deserved. And nonstate actors, such as al Qaeda and the Syrian al Nusra, embrace jihad as a call to arms in their recruiting of fellow Muslims to do battle against the infidels.

To true believers, fanaticism expressed in holy war is the only way to break the iron grasp of Arab and capitalist infidels in Mecca and on Main Street who control politics. Part of bin Laden's motivation was that, having been disowned by his family and banished by the royal family, he despised and dismissed Saudi leaders as both hypocrites (with their dual standards of morality, different at home and abroad) and supporters of the decadent West, and so he sought to overthrow them. Ayman al Zawahiri, bin Laden's successor, shares this vision.

The late Harvard professor Samuel Huntington two decades ago presciently coined the concept of the "clash of civilizations." Now the once-latent hostility aroused by Western colonial rule and later the formation of the state of Israel in the Arab world has been fed a concoction of geopolitical and economic steroids.

Many arose with September 11 and U.S. occupation of two Islamic states. With 1.3 billion Muslims, recruiting even a tenth of 1 percent into radical causes provides a potential pool of 1.3 million would-be jihadis, or a group about the size of the current U.S. military. And Arab and Islamic resentment and hostility to the West reach from the Levant to the Bay of Bengal.

The dangers posed by Islamic extremism are apparent and destructive. Terrorism claims tens of thousands of lives a year in suicide and other attacks. September 11 led the United States to arguably the greatest strategic miscalculation in its history. The Iraq intervention not only cost more than a trillion dollars and many, many lives. It was a twenty-first-century equivalent of Gavrilo Princip. This time, the bullets lit the fuse on the explosive mixture of hatreds, disparities, and geopolitical time bombs latent in the Arab and Muslim worlds.

While Osama's al Qaeda may have been neutralized and many of its leaders killed, its plan of action has been copied by many so-called affiliates. The ideology and attraction of jihad and martyrdom are as magnetic for many as was the Pied Piper. Training in and learning to wage jihad is to many exciting and glamorous, as well as offering the opportunity to visit exotic (if not very hospitable) locales. Terror is a highly effective tool aimed at a major vulnerability of the West—that is, to disruption.

The shift of the strategic paradigm from assured destruction to assured disruption reflects exploitation of an immense societal weakness, whether for states (no matter how backward) or for people in general. The disruption of lives and society through terror is a powerful tool.

Disruption is the strategic center of gravity for terrorist and nonstate actors pursuing some form of Islamic extremism. September 11 was the best example of the power to disrupt. Cyber has become a new domain for terror and radical groups to exploit, alongside conventional explosives.

These extremist and terrorist organizations have another advantage in their favor—cost-exchange ratios that bleed their enemies. IEDs have cost the United States billions and the terrorists very little. As cyber becomes a more ubiquitous battlefield, at very little cost, networks and systems will be disrupted. Suppose the intrusion in Target, Neiman-Marcus and E-Bay had been the work of terrorists. The cost-imposition ratio would have been dramatically in their favor.

The notion of establishing a caliphate looms large in the propaganda and belief systems of Islamic radicals. While popular films and novels dine on these scenarios, it is far from inconceivable that some group, such as ISIS, could permanently control substantial tracts of land from which to operate. The Taliban, surely practitioners of a more extreme form of Islam, wrested control of Afghanistan from the Soviets and competing warlords and factions. But the Taliban had no external agenda threatening international peace and stability.

Would or could insurgents mount successful coups in Iraq, Syria, Pakistan, or even Saudi Arabia and from there declare a caliphate? The chances are remote. No uniting figure has emerged to integrate Islamic extremists into a single coherent organization. More likely are continuing attacks, and the absence of cohesion will not prevent them. The cumulative weight of kinetic and cyber attacks is unlikely to yield further takeovers of a state or seizure of a substantial landmass. But one Western goal is preventing the establishment of a united Islamic radicalism and at least keeping extremists divided and unable to form a coherent mass.

Countering Islamic extremism can profit from the medical analogy of using pathology in the prevention and treatment of disease. In medicine, cures focus on causes, while relieving symptoms, such as pain and fever. The current war on terror reverses that and focuses on symptoms, not causes. A terrorist is a symptom. Killing or neutralizing him or her does not address the cause.

At this stage, the seriousness of this extremist-caused disease may not be as life threatening as cancer or the staph infection MRSA. A bad case of the flu or a badly broken arm or leg is a better analogy. However, if the disease or injury is not treated quickly, it will fester and get worse. But the United States has no antidote, basic plan, or organization for tackling and removing the causes of extremism or attacking its ideological basis. In terms of a countering narrative, in today's jargon "strategic communications," the United States is unarmed.

For all the treasure invested in the ill-named and badly executed war on terror against Islamic extremism, the United States is not winning and could be losing. Yes, a Department of Homeland Security and an Office of the Director of National Intelligence were put in place. The Transportation Security Authority (TSA) is meant to keep travel safe. The Federal Bureau of Investigation made counterterrorism its highest priority, and coordination with the CIA was taken to a new level. No major terrorist attack against the United States has been launched from abroad since September 11.

Homegrown Islamic terrorists, such as Army psychiatrist Maj. Nidal Hassan, whose killing rampage at Fort Hood in 2009 claimed eleven lives, exist. Some have gone to Syria, Yemen, and other terrorist hotbeds for training. Whether these individuals will prove more dangerous than the snipers who terrorized the Washington, D.C./northern Virginia area nearly a decade ago or the outbreak of school and mall shootings remains to be seen. However, America's responses have a huge strategic flaw that has not been identified or redressed.

Cyber offers a good analogy. In cyber, offense has overwhelmed defense. In terror, the United States is playing defense. It can be argued that renditions and drone attacks against suspected al Qaeda and other Islamic extremists are taking the battle to the enemy—but only the battle, not the war. As the United States became fixated on winning battles, not wars, so too is the lack of a real offensive strategy crippling.

In the first place, where is the strategy for discrediting, delegitimizing, and disrupting these Islamic groups? Why has no attempt been made to identify an Islamic version of Martin Luther or to rally the 99.9 percent of all Muslims who eschew violence and reject terror?

Second, where is the strategy of disinformation and deception to discredit and delegitimize these extremists? Stuxnet was used to disrupt Iranian centrifuges. Where is the equivalent for taking on extremists? And where is the plan for turning groups against each other, as al Qaeda has apparently disowned al Nusra?

Third, where is the strategy to rally friends, allies, and others, such as Russia and China, who have vital interests in stopping terrorism, especially from Islamic extremists?

Finally, why has no strategy or overarching policy been developed, and why has no one in government at senior levels suggested this approach?

The Benghazi attack that killed Ambassador Christopher Stevens and three other Americans underscored the lack of an overall strategy. In the aftermath, the White House went on a verbal offensive, characterizing the attack as an unplanned and spontaneous reaction to a video, fraudulent and highly offensive to Islam, that had made its way to YouTube. Republicans immediately attacked the White House for making false claims and for not providing appropriate security for the ambassador.

An Accountability Review Board, headed by the distinguished Ambassador Thomas Pickering and highly regarded former chairman of the Joint Chiefs of Staff Adm. Mike Mullen, found plenty of fault at the State Department but laid none of the blame on then–secretary of state Hillary Clinton. Partisans screamed cover-up, and the House and Senate have held and will hold countless hearings and issued reams of statements. Some have called this incident the worst cover-up since Watergate. Perhaps the release of Sgt. Bowe Bergdahl from his Taliban captivity and the huge controversy over the circumstances will overtake Benghazi as a political cause celebre.

The House and Senate Select Committees on Intelligence released reports on the attacks. The Senate report, issued in January 2014, drew the shocking but convincing conclusion that the attack had been preventable. The report listed many warnings and briefings within the military and intelligence community that should have been heeded. As before September 11, they were not. The report confirmed the administration's position that military forces could not have been deployed in time to make a difference. In fact, Ambassador Stevens had declined military offers to bolster security.

The absence of coordination in Libya, the intelligence community, the State Department, and the Pentagon contributed to this tragedy. Ambassador Stevens' own aggressive attitude placed him in harm's way at the wrong time. As with counterterrorism, many of the critical assessments and warnings were present. They had no effect. For dealing with al Qaeda and fellow-traveler terrorist organizations, many capabilities and countermeasures exist. But they exist without a strategy that has an offensive component. And the critical part of that offensive component would be an effective strategic communications plan.

None of this is news. In 2004, the Pentagon's Defense Science Board was tasked to study the state of this country's strategic communications. It concluded, and advised the secretary of defense in its letter forwarding the report, the following: "The United States cannot win the war on terror if it does not win the war of ideas. And it is losing the war of ideas."

What have we done since regarding strategic communications? The answer is very little. Osama bin Laden did and his successors continue to issue fatwas, or religious edicts, when they have absolutely no authority or status to do so. Similarly, Iran's current Supreme Leader has the equivalent of a high-school theology "degree." Yet where are the leaders of Islam who stand up to provide accurate representations of their religion or encourage others to do so to counter that propaganda? These are the people whom a new strategy and mind-set must identify.

The State Department has a small strategic communications office. But it is directed at converting and convincing relatively junior members of extremist groups, such as the Taliban, to come in from the cold. The president and secretary of state can make grand speeches, such as in Cairo five years ago. Yet, a speech is neither action nor follow-up.

Crafting a sound strategic communications plan and a powerful narrative to counter radicalism is vital. But a plan and a narrative are not sufficient alone, and we cannot delude ourselves that so simple a solution to a complex problem will work. Western democratic values such as free speech and the role of women in society abut against opposing and strongly held religious views. Friends such as Saudi Arabia harbor ideologies not consistent with ours in the form of Wahhabism. Taliban regularly shoot or stone women to death for adultery. In Pakistan, an eleven-year-old girl with Down syndrome, who cannot read or write and probably has the mental capacity of an infant, was sent to an adult prison for allegedly destroying a page in the Koran. The charge was later found to be false, yet she was allowed to linger in jail. Few in the West understand how these and other travesties are allowed to recur.

Sadly for the United States, producing a strategic communications plan for this struggle against violent extremism and injustice is not on the agenda. Hence, when the next incident occurs, which it will, and riots against America or the West break out, we should reread and take seriously the Defense Science Board's warning—we are "losing the war of ideas!"

One of the key causal factors that empower Islamic extremism is economic despair. Rather than spending hundreds of billions fighting the war on terror, it would be more cost-effective to buy the loyalty of citizens of Islamic states with hard cash to stave off recruitment by extremists. Clearly, economics is key.

Foreign aid and assistance will never be enough. Nor should it be. Instead, foreign aid should be replaced by economic assistance to enhance the economy and thus create opportunities for improving lives in a particular society. Many obstacles—such as corruption and graft, lack of oversight and fair distribution of resources, and foreign laws—are formidable. That does not prevent assessing what such a transition in priorities to economic assistance would achieve.

Perhaps the greatest economic leverage can be achieved through creating national infrastructure banks for many of these countries. Because many states are unstable or not subject to oversight and suffer from corruption and payoffs, collateral for investment is critical. Debt-equity swaps—that is, exchanging loans for equity conversions—have been successful. These and other financial instruments to cover collateral will be needed.

Reducing the deprivations of economic shortcomings, no matter how long in the making, is an essential part of any strategy designed to take the offensive against Islamic extremism.

Countering Islamic extremism demands a new mind-set. A strategy that favors offense to discredit and impeach the bases for extremism, as well as providing for defense against attack, is needed. The aim is to win the struggle, not just individual battles. A dynamic and well-conceived strategic communications plan is central to success.

While finding an Islamic Martin Luther will prove difficult, influencing Islamic clergy to support reform and reformation that outlaws and ends the influence of extremism is crucial in this struggle. Success in keeping Iran from obtaining nuclear weapons and, even more, in resolving the Arab-Israeli-Palestinian conflict will strike a decisive blow against Islamic extremism. Saudi Arabia is crucial to any solution.

Whether or not the United States is capable of producing a strategy to fit these realities will be a test for its government. But unless Islamic extremism goes the way of the hula hoop and vanishes, a real strategy is vital. A mind-set for the twenty-first century is the first step in getting that strategy.

11

Environmental Calamity and Climate Change

S uperstorm Sandy, which ravaged New York and New Jersey in 2012; the super snowstorms that blanketed much of America in 2013 and 2014; drought in California; and unprecedented rain and floods throughout England in early 2014 may be harbingers of climate change. It is the power, force, and frequency of these events that differentiate each from the past. Should more such events occur, the issues of environmental calamity and climate change will have to be regarded even more seriously.

About environmental calamity and climate change, there are two certainties. Environmental calamities, both acts of man and nature, will occur. If climate change does lead to greatly increased global warming, the consequences for much, if not all, of the planet will be catastrophic. Beyond that, it is impossible to predict where, when, or what type of environmental calamity will strike. Nor has political agreement on where climate change is headed, irrespective of the bulk of objective scientific analysis that points to danger, been possible so far.

Environmental calamity strikes with minimal or no warning. That uncertainty, paucity of resources, and the physical realities of geography and infrastructure often limit preventive action. Earthquakes in remote or inaccessible locations in China or Pakistan cannot be responded to quickly. Many nuclear reactors, such as the ones at the Dai-ichi plant in Fukushima, Japan, store spent fuel on top of their buildings, for security reasons. Hence, the reactors are vulnerable to tidal waves or surges that engulf buildings. In New York, both electrical-power generators and subways are underground and thus were put out of action by Superstorm Sandy's extraordinary flooding.

First, it is useful to review the history of major environmental disasters to get a sense of the magnitude, impact, breadth, costs, and recurrence of these calamities, beginning with acts of nature. Natural calamities include earthquakes, droughts, hurricanes and typhoons/tsunamis, and other weather extremes, as well as disease and floods; they can be measured in deaths, numbers injured and displaced, and costs imposed by each disaster.

In 2013, according to the *International Business Times*, earthquakes in Lushan and Fitow, China, in April and October respectively cost about $25 billion. Droughts in China and Brazil cost about $20 billion in losses. Hurricanes and typhoons—particularly Haiyan, which hit the Philippines with 250 mph gusts—cost about $15 billion. And flooding in Central Europe (May), Canada (June), and China (July and August) recorded losses of about $40 billion.

Historically, the most destructive of earthquakes occurred in Tangshan, China, in 1976, taking between a quarter and three-quarters of a million lives. The 2005 earthquake that struck northern Pakistan killed at least 75,000. While droughts remain common, the most costly were in China in 1900 (a half to three million dead), 1931 (two and a half to three million dead), 1936 (five million dead), and 1941 (three million dead).

Hurricanes, typhoons, and tsunamis measured over the past decade are increasing in numbers and intensity. In 2004, a massive tsunami struck Indonesia and other states, killing about a quarter of a million people and displacing over two million. The Indian Ocean earthquake/tsunami of 2010 was the third-largest recorded, measuring 9.1–9.3 on the Richter scale. About 250,000 perished. In August 2009, Hurricane Katrina struck the Gulf Coast, doing nearly $200 billion worth of destruction, as well as destroying the credibility of the Bush 43 administration, owing to its failure to respond.

Disease and pandemics have claimed more lives than any other natural calamity. About fifty million died in the Spanish flu epidemic of 1918. The SARS epidemic of 2002 and the H1N1 flu epidemic several years later killed relatively few people. But the fact that disease could spread so quickly across oceans and continents, largely carried by airline passengers, demonstrates one of the downsides of globalization.

Disease that kills livestock and crops is also potentially calamitous. In 2003, BSE (mad cow disease) struck England, where hundreds of thousands of cows had to be slaughtered. Only a few human deaths were attributed to BSE. The British army was called up to take charge. And elsewhere, as noted, the psyllid virus threatens Florida's citrus crop.

A final example of an environmental disaster was the London smog crisis of 1952. Weather caused a massive and persistent layer of smog covering London for five days. This was the first recorded case of a pollution-induced environmental crisis. About 12,000 Londoners perished. Today, China is experiencing pollution-induced environmental destruction of the air, water, and ground, a major challenge for the government to address, especially as economic growth demands greater consumption of energy, which in turn leads to greater production of greenhouse gasses and pollutants.

Man-made catastrophes are plentiful. On December 3, 1984, shortly after midnight, a poisonous gas cloud was released from a Union Carbide India Limited (UCIL) pesticide factory in Bhopal. The cloud contained fifteen metric tons of methyl isocyanate (MIC), and it covered an area of about thirty square miles. At least 4,000 local residents died instantly, and another 500,000 people were affected; the cloud ultimately killed some 15,000 of these and caused chronic disease in others.

Regarding nuclear disasters, several are significant, although only one caused massive loss of life. On April 26, 1986, tests were conducted in Nuclear Reactor 4 of the Chernobyl nuclear-power plant in Ukraine, eighty miles from Kiev. Design and personnel errors forced a shutdown of the reactors. But the shutdown failed, and the reactor melted down, releasing approximately 185 to 250 million curies of radioactive material and killing thirty-one workers instantly. Chernobyl was evacuated. It is estimated that over a half-million suffered radioactive poisoning that could prove fatal.

The other major nuclear disasters were the responsibility of the U.S. nuclear-weapon-test series known as Operation Castle. Castle Bravo was the first test of a dry-fuel hydrogen thermonuclear bomb. On March 1, 1954, the bomb was exploded on Bikini Atoll in the Marshall Islands. Due to errors, the explosion reached 15 MT, almost double what had been expected. The resulting radiation from the nuclear weapon needed to detonate the fusion weapon caused the largest contamination in history.

The United States has had some major nuclear-weapons accidents (nuclear-submarine accidents, including the losses of USS *Thresher* and USS *Scorpion*, are not included—the Soviet Union and Russia have had far worse submarine safety records). On January 17, 1966, A B-52G bomber collided with a KC-135 tanker during midair refueling. All of the tanker's crew members were killed. Seven of the ten crew members of the B-52 safely bailed out. The conventional explosives in two of the bombs detonated on impact on the ground, spreading plutonium. A third landed intact. The fourth fell in the sea, where the U.S. Navy was able to locate and retrieve it.

During the Cold War, there were at least two incidents of accidental nonnuclear detonation; two nuclear bombs dropped accidentally (March 1957 and April 1958); one lost in the sea of Japan in December 1965, when an A-4 Skyhawk armed with a nuclear weapon accidentally went overboard from an aircraft carrier; and an accidental explosion in September 1980 in a Strategic Air Command launch site in Arkansas, propelling a Titan II warhead about a hundred feet from the silo, demolishing the complex and killing an airman.

The best known U.S. civilian accident was the Three Mile Island reactor explosion on March 28, 1979, in Dauphin County, Pennsylvania. The partial meltdown was the worst in U.S. commercial nuclear-power history. While the damage and contamination were contained and no immediate deaths resulted, Three Mile Island is still the poster child for opposition to nuclear power.

Oil has been the source of many environmental catastrophes. Four are of consequence: *Amoco Cadiz; Exxon Valdez;* the British Petroleum *Deepwater Horizon* spill in the Gulf of Mexico; and the oil fires in Kuwait in 1991 and Iraq in 2003. In March 1978, SS *Amoco Cadiz,* flying a Liberian flag, grounded off the French coast of Brittany, sending about 220,000 tons of oil into the English Channel. On March 24, 1989, *Exxon Valdez* ran into Bligh Reef, in Alaska, spilling about 750,000 barrels of crude oil into Prince William Sound. It was the largest oil spill in history, costing Exxon about $4 billion, or about $12 billion in current dollars.

The largest disaster was the *Deepwater Horizon* spill in the Gulf of Mexico in April 2010, caused by an explosion on and the sinking of an oil platform. About 270 million gallons of oil escaped, contaminating the whole Gulf coast and reaching up as far as Florida's east coast. The costs to BP are estimated at $40 billion.

Finally, Saddam Hussein was guilty of being the worst polluter in history. In 1991 as Iraq was being ignominiously expelled from Kuwait, Saddam ordered setting fire to Kuwait's oil wells. In 2003 as the coalition forces raced north to occupy Baghdad, crushing the Iraqi army in the process, Saddam extended the favor to Iraq's oil wells. The environmental damage was horrific, and Iraq's oil production capacity is affected even today.

The reason for this excursion is to demonstrate the range and magnitude of environmental catastrophes that have occurred. Many are beyond the ability of man to prevent. Earthquakes, tsunamis, droughts, and other major weather events are among them. We can hope that with nuclear-arms reductions that limit both the United States and Russia to 1,550 deployed warheads and caution on the part of the other nuclear powers in keeping their weapons secured, the stunning number of Cold War accidents will not be seen again.

Of course, North Korea, tensions between Pakistan and India, and what Iran does regarding its nuclear-weapons ambitions require close attention. Hence, expanding the U.S-Russian arms-control and reduction dialogue to all nuclear states is essential. Two Nuclear Security Summits focused on preventing terrorists from acquiring fissile material. However, bringing together all the known nuclear powers in the equivalent of the G-20, perhaps named the "N-8 Plus One" (Israel), to discuss relevant issues makes sense and would expand the mission while narrowing the participants.

The most dangerous of these calamities in terms of potential harm is disease. The possibility of a new version of the Spanish flu, a drug-resistant virus or bacterium, or some other evolution in disease such as Ebola poses huge danger. Of course, nothing may happen.

One key is climate change, which has the potential to affect or make more likely many of these natural disasters, from drought and heat wave, to flooding and pollution, to the creation of deserts and of new bodies of water that previously were dry land. Debate over whether global warming is man-made or a hoax has been contaminated by the extremes of left and right, who argue that this is a zero-sum game—"my way or the highway." For the time being, within broken government, resolving these disputes will remain difficult if not impossible.

Several actions are needed. Response to environmental catastrophe requires a great deal of international cooperation and coordination. For militaries, this translates into humanitarian assistance, much of which is addressed as part of the training and international coordination that is ongoing. NATO lists humanitarian assistance as part of its capability. Raising the priority of the humanitarian mission and using it to coordinate and integrate broader whole-of-government solutions will strengthen alliance capacity by engaging agencies not always connected with security and establishing closer contact with NATO. Humanitarian assistance also can improve interactions with the EU.

As NATO develops its international partnerships, humanitarian assistance can reinforce this purpose. The NATO Response Force (NRF) can be more useful if NATO assigns this mission a higher priority. The SCO could be part of these partnerships, as well as ASEAN. Perhaps the most useful potential partner is the UN Office of Coordination of Humanitarian Assistance.

Inside the United States, while many lessons were learned from the catastrophe arising from the failed response to Hurricane Katrina, which devastated New Orleans and the Gulf coast, the Department of Homeland Security (DHS) could stand a major reorganization. The Federal Emergency Management Agency (FEMA) should be divided between response and administration of assistance. The operational-response portion would be folded into the Coast Guard and the new organization assigned to a new undersecretary dual-hatted as commandant. The operational experience of the Coast Guard, combined with the emergency-response capability of FEMA, would produce a powerful asset. Given that the Coast Guard has an international role, other countries could be involved.

Another viable solution is bilateral executive agreements with major countries, such as China and India, that are dependent on economic growth to balance population growth. These two and other countries will continue to modernize. Modernization requires massive amounts of energy, most of it derived from hydrocarbons. In several years' time, with a combined population of three billion people, how many more cars, buses, and means of transport, including new highways, will be needed by China and India? And what will that consumption do to production of greenhouse gases?

In many ways the wildest of wildcards is environmental calamity and climate change. It also may prove the most difficult to reconcile, in the face of broken government, competing economic policies that ratchet up tension between growth and pollution, and divergence of ideologies over the dangers posed by climate change and between the advanced countries, which can "go green," and advancing ones, that need to consume far more energy to grow.

12

Mind-Set Myopia

The Failure of Strategic Thinking

Four examples reflect the current state of American strategic thinking: Washington's focus on winning battles, not wars; China, the pivot to Asia, and allegations of U.S. decline; Europe and NATO; and Russia and lessons from the Soviet Union.

Exacerbating and demonstrating the limits of its strategic thinking is America's geostrategic Achilles' heel: preoccupation with winning battles, not wars. The North Vietnamese famously boasted, "America won every battle and lost the war." In Afghanistan and Iraq four decades later, the same critique applied. America and coalition allies won virtually every battle. But if winning the war meant establishing a safe, secure, and stable state under the rule of law, by any definition, America and its allies have lost in both countries.

How did America's strategic thought process arrive at favoring the winning of battles over the winning of wars? First, it is often easier to focus on battles, reasoning that as battles were won, so too would be the wars. Second, in conflicts not fought against like conventional forces, metrics for victory or winning simply do not exist. Third, presidents, especially inexperienced ones, are seduced by the tactical prowess of the American military, power that obscures the absence of or deficiencies in other policy tools. By default, or as the least path of resistance, tactics overcomes strategy or becomes strategy.

The United States wrested independence from England not because it won every battle, which it did not, but by winning the war—a strategy purloined by North Vietnam. America could succeed because it understood that Britain had a greater interest in defeating France than the colonies. Other than the War of 1812 and the Civil War, until 1917 America's external wars were fought against weak adversaries, from ill-equipped Indians in the west to the Spanish in Cuba and the Philippines.

In World War II, America set the unconditional surrender of the Axis powers as its wartime goal. America and its allies did not win every battle—merely enough and at the right times and places so that its overwhelming economic and industrial might (and two nuclear bombs) overpowered the enemy. While veterans of that war would continue to serve in high office for more than four decades, mission creep gradually metastasized into the fixation with winning battles and not wars.

Korea marked the beginning of the fixation on battles, not wars, and preference for the tactical over the strategic. The aim of that war became reestablishing the border between north and south at the thirty-eighth parallel. In the Cold War, the concept of winning wars was constrained by the massive societal destruction that would follow an "unthinkable" conflict that escalated to use of thermonuclear weapons. Because of the destructive costs of nuclear war, deterrence had to work, and that became the battle.

The United States inched and then plunged into Vietnam under Presidents Kennedy and Johnson with generals who had served in World War II and Korea. In those wars, the battlefield tactic had been to employ overwhelming firepower to destroy the enemy. In Vietnam, search-and-destroy missions relied on firepower from artillery and fixed-wing fighter-bombers and helicopter gunships to defeat the largely invisible and elusive Vietcong and North Vietnamese army. Body counts became the war's metric, and the obsession of winning battles to attrite the enemy was the strategy. Killing one's way to victory rarely works. And the United States lost.

After the Vietnam War and as the Soviet Union built up its conventional forces, the United States turned to technology and precision, or "smart," weapons to offset conventional numerical inferiority. Winning "the first battle" became doctrine, because if the first battle were lost, the belief was, the Soviets would quickly overrun and occupy western Europe.

The two wars in Iraq in 1991 and 2003 and in Afghanistan in 2001 were indeed fought as extensions of the concept of winning the first battle. Saddam's army was twice eviscerated and the Taliban routed in matters of hours and days. George W. Bush's White House, unlike his father's in the first Gulf War, became infatuated with winning the battle and failed to think about winning the war. So, as in Vietnam a generation earlier, every battle was won, and both wars were lost.

This failure to focus on winning wars was not unique to Republicans. Bill Clinton did no better in Serbia in 1999, when it took seventy-eight days to force a tin-pot dictator to withdraw from Kosovo—a battle that if fought as a war should have taken hours to win. Yet, NATO had no stomach for even threatening the use of ground forces until week ten of the conflict.

Over the past decade, as the strategic paradigm has shifted to assured disruption, adversaries, with malice or by luck, have been able to exploit this American fixation on battles. The Obama White House has succumbed to this policy of fighting battles, not winning wars. Libya was a battle. Protecting citizens of Benghazi led to the toppling of Qaddafi. The war and strife still continue.

Syria, Iran, and North Korea remain crisis spots. Limited uses of force—no-fly zones and safe havens in Syria and preemptive air strikes to eliminate Tehran's nuclear facilities—are routinely debated as options. This tactical preference reinforces the failure to define strategy in terms of the broader objectives—which involve, once again, winning the war and not battles. A corollary or consequence is that after Korea, in every war America has started, it has either lost or failed to achieve its goals.

The second example of the absence of strategic thinking is the combination of perceptions of American decline, the rise of China, and the pivot to Asia. In relative terms, the U.S. strategic and economic comparative advantages are diminishing. Without a profound improvement in governance, the standards of living of and future expectations by the majority of Americans will decrease, even though opportunities for the lucky few will persist. However, that relative decline will not consign the United States to the famous Marxist "rubbish dump of history"—far from it. The size of the American economy and the virtues of a free market will still promote and provide competitive advantages even as other states close the economic gaps.

Too often, predictions about American decline are put as simplistic sound bites reflecting superficial thinking. Such arguments go like this: exhausted by two unsuccessful wars, with an economy that is fragile and could become recessional, and facing a rising China and India, the United States is following the trajectory of other great, spent powers that have exceeded their sell-by dates. Reinforcing this declinist argument is the inability of a broken government to deal with the nation's economic and financial crises. In this toxic political condition, both parties fall prey to the influence of their extreme wings. Compromise, vital to the smooth workings of a system based on balance of power, is considered a weakness or an abandonment of principle.

Taken further, this argument is distorted into the specter of a massive American decline or implosion. Circumstances that led to the fall of the Roman Empire or the catastrophic Grecian wars between Athens (read America) and Sparta (read China) are likened to America's. Other bleak scenarios posit the prelude to World War I as context for today. China is portrayed as the emerging and aggressive Germany. The United States is the declining great power Britain. Modern-day Japan plays the role of France. And Gavrilo Princip is embodied by historical hatreds and conflict over specks of land in the China seas. While China may be "rising" and America losing its absolute lead, disaster need not follow, despite the failings of government—provided common sense prevails.

Allegations and presumptions of China's ascent and America's decline must be balanced by logic, reason, and fact—that is, in plain terms, by strategic thinking. For example, if the wealth and success of a neighbor grow, does that automatically diminish everyone else, unless the neighbor uses those gains to the detriment of others? The United States still has, by a factor of two, the largest economy in the world. It is the leader in entrepreneurialism and the forming of new businesses. Its established businesses have become models of productivity and efficiency, notwithstanding the failure of its government to govern.

To take this line of thought even further, neither the United States nor any other state could remain the world's colossus and dominant power forever. The end of World War II, with the destruction of Europe and Asia, granted the United States a unique moment in history. However, an ascending Soviet Union ultimately checked its unilateral authority and influence. The inevitable diffusion of all forms of global power, along with the rebuilding of Europe and Asia, made it impossible for any state to exist as the world's sole superpower.

Unfortunately, too many who long for the days of American dominance refuse to understand that the current realities, in which all forms of power are diffusing, are also creating new and different opportunities. These opportunities can be readily exploited, provided the United States is prepared to shed rigid beliefs about the past and the virtues of unilateralism for a new and more relevant mind-set. "Provided" remains the operative word.

In absolute terms, American power is broadly expanding, certainly economically. In relative terms, American power has been diluted. Comparative advantage and the growth of other economies have enhanced global competition. Burgeoning economies have magnified the need for energy, enriching oil and gas producers, whose treasure chests have in turn created huge financial and investment leverage. These trends augur well for the United States if it chooses to understand and respond to them and not bemoan the decline of its dominant status.

Meanwhile, over the last decade, America's unchallenged military power has proven strategically ineffective in waging war against adversaries who lack armies, navies, and air forces. In Iraq and Afghanistan, nation building and economic development could not be pursued or achieved by force of arms alone. Cyber threats transcend fixed boundaries once enforced by departments and ministries of defense. And another shortcoming must be faced.

Metrics for defining measures of power and influence in this post-state-centric universe are still in adolescence. Harvard's Joseph Nye has been credited with inventing the concepts of "hard" and "soft" power. Yet, both terms are qualitative, not quantitative, and thus susceptible to psychological, emotional, or political interpretation. Further, distinctions between hard and soft do not offer solutions or policy prescriptions, only descriptions that may or may not be relevant.

In business, when conditions change, organizations must respond if they are to succeed. That IBM no longer builds computers and Xerox no longer is synonymous with copying machines are salutary examples of change. So too, American policy must recognize that the emergence of new power centers creates opportunities as well as challenges.

In the Pacific, tensions over territorial claims in the various China seas involve several states. Fortunately, the chances for outright war are low. China is increasing its defense spending and its military capability. But China is also surrounded by states who are not all friends or allies. Many of China's neighbors are well armed and possess or could possess counterbalancing forces. India has a large and nuclear-equipped army. Japan and South Korea have substantial forces. China has suffered militarily at the hands of Vietnam on more than one occasion. And Putin's Russia is still a Pacific and nuclear power. The $400 billion, forty-year energy deal between China and Russia underscores this point.

Against this background, concern in Europe over the Obama eastward pivot is palpable. Tepid economic growth, uncertainty over the future of the euro, and the huge debt of southern-tier states remain important issues. Most NATO members, including the United States, are cutting back on defense spending. And Russia's Crimean incursion has been unsettling.

The United States has removed two brigade combat teams from Europe, compensating with increased naval deployments and the stationing of antiballistic missiles, in what has been agreed to by NATO as the Phased Adaptive Approach, to defend against potential Iranian rockets. Russian intentions and needs post-Ukraine do not coincide with Europe's or America's, raising the prospect of a resurgent mini–Soviet Empire. How then should the United States respond? Can strategic thinking be applied to these interrelated challenges and potential dangers? The starting point must be a comprehensive strategic approach.

Establishing new metrics for measuring and understanding power is a good initial step. Those who see China eclipsing the United States use GDP as a single, simplistic measure. At some future date, China, with a population four times larger than America's, may achieve a larger GDP. But what does that signify? Using GDP alone as the measure of power is akin to basing an assessment of an individual's health solely on height, weight, temperature, or another single index.

Application of strategic thought and common sense works this way. The total assets of the United States, less its natural resources, are currently estimated at about $100 trillion. Deducting public and private debt of about $30 trillion, that leaves net assets at the $70 trillion level. With an annual GDP currently of about $18 trillion, the aggregate wealth of the United States is between $80 and 90 trillion.

What is China's net worth? Even given an equivalent GDP—and today China's is about half of America's—China is light-years away from overtaking the United States in net asset value. The point is not whether this metric fits. It makes the point that new measures are needed to evaluate relative and absolute power.

China is building up its military. That is one reason for the pivot. But what nation would exchange American for Chinese weapons? If strategic thinking is ruthlessly applied, the Cold War trap of grossly exaggerating and misunderstanding the nature of the Soviet military threat can be avoided, despite the pressures from domestic lobbies and groups who benefit from making China into an adversary. Other initiatives can help reduce misunderstandings and miscalculations

In 1972, Secretary of the Navy (later Senator) John Warner presided over the Incidents at Sea (INCSEA) Agreement between the U.S. and Soviet navies. These navies often interacted at close range, where a collision or unintended incident could have provoked a major crisis. Suppose that during the Cuban missile crisis of 1962 Soviet and U.S. warships had collided or inadvertently exchanged fire.

Who knows what might have transpired and whether another archduke experience would have arisen?

The INCSEA Agreement was meant to lessen the chances of miscalculation and escalation. It and the ABM Treaty and Strategic Arms Limitation Talks (SALT), which limited nuclear forces, much reduced the chances of the Cold War becoming hotter. China may or may not be interested in a new version of INCSEA. However, informal discussion is essential. With progress, engagement of other interested states with naval forces, such as South Korea, Japan, the Philippines, and even Taiwan, might be possible, as was the earlier agreement with the Soviet Union.

Partnerships beyond trade and investment are part of a brains-based approach to strategic thinking and to a new mind-set. Applied to China, in security terms, expanding the reach of NATO to engage the Shanghai Cooperative Organization can build relationships and overcome cultural ignorance. Despite the intense reverberations of Edward Snowden's revelations about American surveillance and spying, new efforts for cooperation in cyber and counterterror must be undertaken.

Obama policy toward NATO is a third example of the absence of strategic thinking by the United States. NATO has been the most successful military alliance in history. Perhaps NATO's time has passed, given the strategic pivot to, and the growing importance of, Asia. Perhaps a quarter of a century without an existential threat in Europe and weariness with the conflict in Afghanistan have contributed to strategic amnesia. Whether or not Russia's Ukrainian intervention has provided the needed "wake-up call" to the alliance is by no means clear, nor was the impact of the ISIS onslaught into Iraq in affecting NATO perceptions of danger (refer back to the wildcard predictions made earlier). Indeed, what was meant to be a summit directed on setting a course for the alliance post-Afghanistan had been highjacked by events.

The Obama administration planned to focus on reinforcing Article 5 of the Washington Treaty as proof and reassurance of American commitment to Europe. Second, the administration intended to call for all NATO members to meet the minimum spending commitment of 2 percent of GDP. Finally, the ability to "export security"—that is, to continue to build capacity in partners and other states outside NATO's Guideline Area—was a third priority. Missing however from the discussion was the gap in thinking and in action to deal with the absence of NATO capacity to deal with the types of political-military-propaganda dangers exposed by Russian annexation in Crimea and by spillover from the civil wars in Syria and Iraq.

President Putin exercised Leninist tactics and strategy in Ukraine and in Crimea. Ironically, Lenin had attempted a similar takeover of Estonia in 1924, which failed. Using troops and agents in place; a propaganda campaign to support and legitimize Russian actions; intimidation, using troops massed on the border and cyber attacks; and economic leverage, such as Ukraine's dependence on Russian energy supply, Moscow successfully annexed Crimea.

Meanwhile in Syria and Iraq, ISIS and other terrorist organizations were in the process of creating an ultimate nightmare scenario—a Jihadi Islamist takeover of a large slice of territory that could be turned into the equivalent of a sovereign region, exporting the most despicable and dangerous forms of Sharia law and terror. While that threat may be a long way from being existential to the West, "blowback" from well-trained Jihadi-Islamist terrorists into NATO states was no longer a theoretical fear. Unfortunately, because these threats did not fall under the same category of Article 5 protection in that they eschewed direct military invasion and attack in favor of violence, subversion, and other means to advance an ideological cause, they have fallen into a no-man's land regarding responses.

Subversion, terror, propaganda, intimidation, violence, cyber, and other forms of advancing a hostile ideology are inherently difficult by themselves. These also have been extremely difficult for NATO—a military alliance after all—to confront directly. As noted, NATO does not have its own intelligence capability, depending instead on the contributions of individual members. Countering terror has largely been the purview of individual states, not NATO. And the alliance has been unable thus far to come up with specific and consensus actions to deal with the threats of cyber, energy security, infrastructure protection, and terror. This gap should have been the strategic center of gravity for the September summit.

That said, this is what should have been preparation and actions for the summit. The summit will have taken place after this book has gone to press; perhaps some of these recommendations will have been used.

First, withdrawal from Afghanistan and the 2014 NATO summit of heads of government offered an opportunity for adjusting NATO's strategic concept adopted at the 2010 Lisbon summit. The most important action was reinforcing Article 5. The United States almost certainly would have made the strongest possible statement reaffirming that an attack against one was an attack against all, in light of Ukraine. However, events in Syria and Iraq should have had greater impact in filling in this strategic gap in NATO's thinking and planning.

Second, barring extraordinary events, including an explosion in Ukraine, further defense cuts and declines in capability were inevitable. "Tough love" to cajole or coerce the allies to spend more on defense could not work for the long term. The use of good strategic thinking would acknowledge that the alliance still spends about three-quarters of a trillion dollars on defense and musters over two million people in uniform. NATO has the most advanced military technologies in the world. Three of its members have nuclear weapons. This is not 1938! And NATO is far from being the proverbial ninety-eight-pound weakling. Hence, NATO still maintains the strongest military capacity in the world, even if all of its members do not spend more money.

Third, NATO must react to the strategic gap in its thinking and capacity to deal with the threats posed by Ukraine and now the Middle East. In 1968, NATO approved the so-called Harmel Report, which transitioned it from a strategy of massive nuclear retaliation to one of flexible response. NATO needs to expand its strategic aperture beyond simply military defense to engage the newer threats of the twenty-first century. That means that the traditional focus of a military alliance must be expanded to a political-military alliance. That transition must start now. The summit could and should have been the starting point. If not, NATO must begin this process now!

Fourth, "smart defense" and "connected forces initiatives" to achieve maximum effectiveness and efficiencies in the use of resources must give way to a brains-based strategic approach in which we think (as we cannot spend) our way clear of danger.

Fifth is a simple fix. During Jimmy Carter's administration, Defense Secretary Harold Brown appointed Ambassador Robert ("Blowtorch Bob") Komer as his special advisor for NATO. Komer had had a long and distinguished career in public service, ending as ambassador to Turkey. Interestingly, the day he arrived in Turkey, his car had been caught in a riot and burned. Komer had joked that Turkish rioters were not responsible for setting his limo afire, but his staff, anticipating the new ambassador's well-deserved reputation as Blowtorch Bob.

A new American special advisor would have sufficient rank, experience, and access to impress European and NATO allies. Such an official would provide a direct link between Washington and Brussels, a link having the visibility and credibility to reassure allies. Perceptions and psychology are crucial, perhaps more than adding a handful of forces to Europe or spending a few more pennies on defense. NATO and Europe must be made to feel critical to the defense of the West. One person, as Bob Komer famously showed, can make a big difference.

Sixth, for years, NATO employed an operational Standing Naval Force (SNF). The concept for this force was to strengthen the ability of member navies to operate together at sea and thus be prepared to support a variety of contingencies. Notwithstanding cuts in naval forces and budgets, a rejuvenated SNF could be reestablished on an experimental or trial basis.

The SNF would train and operate with partner navies globally and, on a small scale, prepare for many contingencies, to include noncombatant evacuation operations (NEOs) and antiterror, antipirate, antiproliferation, and other activities. In cases where the SNF lacked the capacity, the United States could augment. In this process, partners could be strengthened and thus be better prepared for regional and local contingencies. The United States would provide the enablers, such as lift, logistics, ISR (intelligence, surveillance, and reconnaisance), and other capabilities, when needed.

Partnerships would also be expanded to work more closely with the SCO. Perhaps the Chinese navy (the People's Liberation Army Navy, or PLAN) might be encouraged to operate with the SNF as a means of improving mutual understanding through military-to-military ties. Certainly, the NATO-Russia Council is a partnership that could be better exploited.

The original agreement establishing that council called for a command-and-control relationship to be established between NATO and Russia. That was never finalized. Perhaps the escort of seaborne transport of Syrian chemical weapons by NATO and Russian warships could have been expanded into a broader relationship.

Despite the requirement for consensus—meaning unanimous agreement by all twenty-eight members—and other bureaucratic and political constraints, such as diverging national and alliance interests, NATO has a surprisingly wide array of resources to exploit. Among these are eighteen national "centers of excellence" established and paid for by individual states to generate cutting-edge solutions to operational challenges, from countering IEDs to enhancing air defenses. Presided over by Allied Command Transformation in Norfolk, Virginia, these centers could be coordinated and chartered to take the lead in generating brains-based approaches and new answers to current problems.

Finally, NATO needs a good "elevator" speech to justify its importance to its publics and politicians. British general Lord Ismay was NATO's first secretary general. Ismay liked to quip that the purpose of NATO was "to keep the U.S. in, Russia out and Germany down." Today, this Ismayism can still apply. The purpose of NATO is to keep Europe safe, danger out, the United States in, and Russia in check.

None of these proposed initiatives necessarily costs more money. What is required is the will to act. And will is the only way to pivot back to our longest-standing allies in Europe.

A last example about the failure of U.S. strategic thinking deals with Russia, first about its future and then about its past. Unfortunately, too much American strategic thinking about Russia still rests in the last century and the specter of a recrudescent Soviet Union. The Crimean intervention, of course, rekindled fears of a new cold war. But on the current trajectory, Russia will not be immune to many of the forces that provoked the so-called colored revolutions in adjacent states and even the misnamed "Arab Awakening." A third revolution could be unfolding.

The key questions are: Will that revolution reach a critical mass? More important, will the forces of autocracy or pluralism carry the day? Russia has experienced two twentieth-century revolutions. The kaiser's Germany provoked the first by sending Lenin back to Russia from Switzerland on board the famous sealed train in 1917. Lenin and the Communist Party would ultimately overthrow the Kerensky government and murder the tsar and his family after signing the Treaty of Brest-Litovsk, which ended the war with Germany and allowed the Bolsheviks to consolidate power.

The second revolution came about some seven decades later. The causes were a corrupt and fundamentally dishonest political system kept in place by a disciplined central leadership and the dictatorship of the party. But control required able, or at least competent, leadership. Instead, the ruling Politburo had become a gerontocracy headed by sick, old men. Leonid Brezhnev took years to die and was replaced by general secretaries in even poorer health. In the mid-1970s, William Colby, then CIA director, repeatedly predicted Brezhnev's demise. Finally, in 1982, Colby's forecast came true.

In the succession process, younger members were elevated to the Politburo. Because of the succession of superannuated leaders, Mikhail Gorbachev found himself moving from post to post after his appointment to the Politburo in 1979. In each post, he realized afresh that the Soviet Union was an empty shell. Each department was grossly mismanaged and underperforming. Six years later, when he became general secretary, Gorbachev was determined to save the Soviet Union by reforming and modernizing its failing system.

Gorbachev's tools were *glasnost* (openness) and *perestroika* (restructuring). The floodgates of reform were fully opened, and the old and unworkable system could not bear the strain. By 1991 the system had imploded and the Soviet Union was no more.

In the decades since, Vladimir Putin has emerged as the iron man of Russia. In the process, Russia has become what is viewed by many as a kleptocracy, ruled by a few who have pillaged national wealth for their own benefit. His is what in the United States Republicans and Democrats alike see as a government of and by thugs.

Human rights have been violated. Dissidents and members of the press have been arrested. And opponents of the Kremlin have been subjected to purges and show trials leading to long prison sentences. Instead of the prospect of a democratic and friendly Russia, most knowledgeable Americans view the country as falling back to the autocratic rule that had existed for centuries.

Russia's immediate neighbors to the west are worried about a more aggressive Russian bear, especially in light of Crimea. Spreading its influence and control by manipulating oil and gas resources and prices for political purposes and by military maneuvers designed to intimidate neighbors, Russia is stoking these fears. Cyber attacks, principally against Estonia, reinforce the perception of a neo–Soviet Union under the leadership of former KGB colonel Putin. Putin's commitment to greater military spending and his unwillingness to accept NATO's missile defenses raise darker possibilities. The $50 billion Sochi Winter Olympics were billed as Putin's and Russia's latest coming-out party, asserting Moscow's growing role and influence.

Within Russia, however, and despite Putin's rise in popularity, discontent and discomfort have been growing among many citizens. Outright oligarchical theft and greed have gone too far. Persecution of any political opposition is particularly vexing. And the health and longevity of a declining population reflect more than harsh winters and excessive consumption of vodka. Indeed, the Kremlin faces a very limiting factor on Putin's intent to ramp up his military: 90 percent of all Russian youth are currently unfit for military service. Of course, standards can be lowered.

It is very likely that the Crimea grab could be Putin's undoing. Had he moved farther west, the resources required to provide for the citizens of illegally seized territory would prove huge. Given the Western response and the cost of annexing Crimea, that gambit may yet become Russia's second Afghanistan in terms of what Moscow will end up paying for in its occupation.

Unfortunately, the West in general, and the United States in particular, has never been very good at Kremlinology (or indeed in understanding foreign cultures at all). Whether Putin is aware of the ticking time bombs over which he presides or not, Russia is still important to Western interests. Syria and Iran are two major crises where Russian support is important.

But exploiting the possibility of a third Russian revolution requires skill, patience, comprehension, and wisdom—not always Washington's strongest suits. The analogy of triangular politics invented by the Nixon administration, in which reconciliation with China was a strategic lever to use against Russia, has some relevance provided we substitute Putin's domestic problems as the new lever.

Clever statecraft is essential. Putin must be worried about Russia's future economic prospects, given the reductions in exports of gas and oil, which will contract yet further. Another "reset" is not the solution. But a hardheaded evaluation of Russia's potential weaknesses and vulnerabilities is.

The failure and implosion of the Soviet Union provide a few lessons for the United States and a few interesting observations. The Soviet political structure was based on fundamental philosophical and practical contradictions in which fact and truth were the first victims. Gorbachev's *glasnost* and *perestroika* are relevant.

The United States could surely use a large dose of openness and restructuring regarding its own political system. Part of that effort could embrace a major and comprehensive examination of the nation's political health. That examination must start with national security and the application of strategic thinking based on a new mind-set. And it must start now.

In war, uncommon valor is often a common virtue. In simplest terms, sound strategic thinking is the application of an uncommon amount of common sense to a problem. For the purposes of this book, strategic thinking entails an accompanying mind-set. That mind-set must be focused on the present and future; it cannot be trapped in the past, ignoring, dismissing, or downgrading the impact and effect of change. This mind-set must be agile, flexible, and subtle, not confusing symptoms with causes and attuned to broad objectives rather than narrow, single issues. The repeated metaphor is winning wars, not necessarily individual or single battles.

Strategic thinking must impose a process that is highly disciplined, analytical, rigorous, and self-critical, designed to dissect and then provide solutions to particular problems or problem sets. Self-criticism is essential. Aims and assumptions, as well as proposed courses of actions, must be challenged— hard, and as often as needed. On occasion, Eisenhower's advice to make the problem "bigger" surely applies.

Leadership is vital, but without constructive and innovative application of intellect to solve problems, it is not sufficient. Thinking, and emoting or wishing, our way clear of danger mandates a brains-based approach. Such an approach could rejuvenate American strategic thinking, provided it is a serious and not casual undertaking.

Since George Washington was America's first commander in chief, successive administrations have been accused of either lacking a strategy or of having one that did not work. Major exceptions were the policies of unconditional surrender by the Axis powers during World War II and those of containment and deterrence that ultimately prevailed over the Soviet Union. The debate in those periods focused more on means than on ends.

Unfortunately, the success of the Cold War perpetuated a twentieth-century mind-set for national security, one predicated on a Westphalian, state-centric model that cannot and will not work in the twenty-first century. Until a relevant framework and paradigm is created or unless unlooked-for luck occurs, future policies almost certainly risk being flawed and ineffective. Critics will, sadly, prove correct in assailing the inability to "think strategically."

The reasons why twentieth-century thinking no longer fits are clear. For centuries, national security and strategy were based on the Westphalian state-centric system of international politics, a system predicated on force as the ultimate arbiter of conflict. Indeed, from Sun Tzu to Clausewitz, strategic thinkers have used this paradigm in protecting the state from threats and challenges to its existence.

That mind-set has been overtaken and bypassed by the diffusion of all forms of power, further accelerated by globally instantaneous and interconnected communications, from the Internet to social media and other creations of the information and electronics revolutions. This diffusion of power has had many transformative consequences. The empowerment of individuals and nonstate actors is among the most dramatic.

During the twentieth century and certainly before, it was difficult for individuals and nonstate actors acting alone to exert global influence. Exceptions persisted, from Martin Luther on. And certainly, the Bolsheviks of a relatively tiny but highly disciplined Communist Party could launch a revolution and seize control of Russia in 1917. A geriatric, exiled Iranian cleric could foment a revolution that toppled the shah in 1979.

But it was not until these cadres wrested control of their states' power and legitimacy that they could exert influence beyond national borders. Now, virtually anyone with the skills and intent and who owns or has access to a smart phone or desktop computer can potentially have global impact. A lone Tunisian fruit vender sparked the Arab Awakening by setting himself afire and becoming a legend on the Internet.

The reality is that major threats and dangers are not always amenable to state-centric solutions predicated on the utility of military power. If failed and failing governance is the major impediment to global peace, prosperity, and stability, no army or navy will alter that situation. If economic despair, disparity, and disloca-tion constitute the bases for terrorism or revolution, similarly, military force will not relieve the desperate condition of many millions of Egyptians living on two dollars a day.

Economic despair, disparity, dislocation, and other forces provoke, empower, and legitimize radical ideologies. In turn, religious extremism amplifies and exploits this empowerment and uses terror and violence to turn a perverted vision into action. Under these circumstances, state-centric strategies will fail. The Vietnam War was a harbinger of this transformation (although some will assert that is was the cutoff of funds by a soured American Congress that allowed Hanoi to win). However, Iraq and Afghanistan have demonstrated the absolute failure of twentieth-century thinking applied to twenty-first-century crises and conflicts.

Miscalculations come from both inexperienced leaders and the inherent dif-ficulty and often intractability of the issues confronting global security writ large. This produces misplaced strategic thinking, exacerbated by focus on winning bat-tles and not wars. Leadership is a precious commodity. And exercising leadership in a broken political system tests the skills, luck, and patience of even the greatest statesmen.

The power of interest groups, from pro-Israeli and anti-Cuban (and Florida's twenty-nine electoral votes) to anti-Iranian factions, influences decision making, neutralizing or preventing sound strategic thinking. The intent of Congress in passing legislation to impose crippling sanctions against Iran should negotiations fail amounted to strategic insanity, not strategic thought. Eliminating these realities of the political process will be impossible—reducing their impact must be the goal. And understanding the value of America is essential.

America is not just a powerful country with the world's largest economy. It is an idea. Its values as enshrined in its founding documents are the heart of democracy.

But not to question or challenge the flaws, faults, and downsides of democracy is to reject the duties of citizens and good Americans.

During the Cold War, the West was populated with many strategic thinkers and statesmen. Bernard Brodie, Zbigniew Brzezinski, Herman Kahn, and Henry Kissinger come to mind on this side of the Atlantic, Raymond Aron and Michael Howard, among others, in Europe. Today, identifying and compiling a list of eminent strategic thinkers is far more difficult.

In part, this dearth of thinking arises from the failure of governance. Politics, especially in the United States, is no longer about governing. Politics is about winning—winning elections, winning campaigns, winning on issues at any cost, when the most effective means to succeed is negative and destructive advertising. No matter the issue, one is either for or against—or is at grave risk of retribution for disloyalty in abandoning the party line.

In this politically poisonous atmosphere, it is no accident that strategic thinking has become a casualty. The only solution, absent the elusory White Knight or a catalytic crisis, is to be found through what could be the slim reed of academe. Think tanks and universities must respond to the challenge of changing antiquated mind-sets—a daunting task when raising money has become a principal occupation of many of these great institutions. And taking the king's shilling usually means serving that particular king and not a more noble or contrarian cause.

How then can and should the United States endeavor to ensure sound strategic thinking is inherent in its decision making? The first step is creating a mind-set that understands the realities of the twenty-first century.

The second is creating a process that applies common sense and self-criticism and is prepared to challenge the aims and assumptions of any decision before it is made.

The third is establishing mechanisms to make permanent this process through bureaucratic, organizational, regulatory, and educational changes and incentives.

One relatively inexpensive yet bureaucratically frightening solution is transforming the federal government's educational process. Instituting a permanent thirst for and pursuit of knowledge and learning, using case studies of both sound and flawed strategic thinking, in both private and public sectors, is a critical requirement.

But developing a new mind-set will be a Sisyphean labor. Part of that labor requires injecting new ideas into government, often more difficult than exorcising old ones. Getting elected leaders to lead in a broken or failing system defies the pull of political gravity, especially when winning, not governing, has become the de facto aim of politics today. Further, part of any sound mind-set is a firm appreciation of what America is and what it is not. Consider several astounding statistics of where the United States ranks worldwide, statistics that temper this appreciation.

In most global surveys, the United States ranks first in GDP and numbers of billionaires and the superrich. It ranks first in military power. It also ranks first in incarceration rates and deaths by violence. It is no better than 17th in education, 24th in literacy, 26th in infrastructure, 49th in life expectancies, and 125th in per capita GDP growth. And a third of its population is obese. Most Americans would not wish to trade places with citizens of other countries. However, America and Americans must understand that in many critical areas, the United States is far behind other states and that its status cannot be defined only by its economic and military strength.

To make the case for a new mind-set, what is vitally needed is a thorough examination and assessment of the health (and weakness) of the U.S. national-security capacity. As common sense leads people to have annual physical examinations, so too does this nation need the equivalent of a comprehensive physical. National security is a good starting point.

Unless the ship of state is righted, American global leadership will be increasingly ignored, downgraded, or barely tolerated. The United States will remain the world's strongest economic and military power. However, translating that power into effective and relevant leadership to protect U.S. interests will be far more difficult.

Conclusions

Needed—A Brains-Based Approach

A hundred years have elapsed since the archduke's murder. But, surprisingly, even a century later the legacies of that assassination are having profound and lasting impact on society and on America. A striking example of that legacy for the United States is that the al Qaeda attacks of September 11, 2001, have become a twenty-first-century version of June 28, 1914, and Osama bin Laden is this decade's first Gavrilo Princip. The "global war on terror" that followed was the culmination of American misunderstanding of the impact of globalization and the diffusion of power that have eroded the Westphalian state-centric system and unleashed the new Four Horsemen.

Had the archduke not been killed and World War I so avoided, who knows how history would have been changed? The Soviet Union and the Third Reich might never have existed. World War II, Japanese aggression, the Chinese Civil War, and the Cold War might have been prevented. Perhaps globalization and the diffusion of power would have had far different and possibly more positive consequences. But they did not. And in essence, both have led to a transformational and even revolutionary time in history.

Revolutionary and transformational periods are often better understood in retrospect. The year 1776 and the American Revolution, 1789 and the French Revolution, 1848 and the European revolutions, 1917 and the Russian Revolution, 1949 and the victory of the Maoist revolution in China, and 1989 with the fall of the Berlin Wall all marked great turning points in history. September 11, 2001, while not a traditional revolution, has altered the course of history.

The United States is arguably at a point of inflection as marked as at any time in its history since 1776 or 1861. How this process of transformation and change will play out is far from certain. Unlike 1914, a spark is unlikely to ignite world war.

191

But a spark could easily ignite a regional conflict with global ramifications and consequences. And, in any event, the global economy remains fragile.

In a perfect world, the United States would be capable of creating an objective and comprehensive strategy for dealing with these changes and dangers. A new mind-set would be an essential first step. However, the limits of a failing government and the breakdown of the two-party system must be overcome or reset if the United States is to be successful in advancing its general welfare and its common defense. This failure, fortunately, is not existential. But failure will mandate at best a decline in standards of living for most Americans and a lowering of expectations of future generations for better lives than their parents and antecedents had.

In developing this mind-set, Americans must also be brutally frank about the strengths, weaknesses, and perceptions of their democratic system and the performance and effectiveness of government. That frankness begins at home. Openness and reform are essential. Unfortunately, they are unlikely to happen. One reason is that even with the strongest incentives for change and penalties for inaction, overcoming the status quo is not easy and perhaps impossible short of crisis.

A second reason for inaction is the reality that money and politics make bad bedfellows. Continuous pursuit of dollars for campaign financing butts against every principle of good government. So too has the overlay of a parliamentary majority of the majority in the Republican-controlled House of Representatives been crippling to checks and balances. But the really devastating blow has been the disenfranchisement of the broad middle class by extreme groups of left and right. Ideology has trumped reason. And facts have become obsolete and intermingled with opinions.

Sadly, temporary legislation that defers tough debate and decision is not governance. It is not even crisis management. It is an admission that the system no longer works, that it is broken.

Meanwhile, both political parties are out to defame each other. No holds are barred. Civility and decorum have no place in these political wars. When the Republican Party shut down the government toward the end of 2013, the White House sat back, relishing the GOP's self-destruction. Then the revelation of the NSA surveillance programs reversed the favor. The prize was 2014 and control of both houses of Congress. But no matter who wins, divided government will persist, which means that the order of the day will be no government.

Can anything be done? Obviously, a bold, charismatic, and forceful leader could emerge from the ashes. And tomorrow we could all be rich. But investigative commissions will not work. The inertia of the political status quo, made even more ponderous by gerrymandered electoral districts and irrational campaign financing laws, will block any disruptive change.

Popular movements, from Vietnam-era protests to change government to Occupy Wall Street, have had and will have marginal effects. The way to end mourning for America as a permanent part of our society begins with leadership. And leadership must have new and bold ideas and the will to implement them.

Leadership means recognizing that the United States is currently ignoring or abandoning many of its political, economic, strategic, and moral responsibilities. That will not come out well for anyone. Indeed, whether in Europe, the Middle East and the Persian Gulf, or Asia, and for good or ill, America's standing and influence are in decline.

American credibility and honor have been stained and have metastasized into a political form of AIDS. The ill-named and badly waged war on terror, "black" interrogation sites, questionable internment practices embodied by the Guantanamo Bay prison, lack of clear due process in targeted assassinations by drone, and the NSA imbroglio over security and privacy have done great harm to the United States.

These misdeeds, missteps, and charges of American hypocrisy have raised the cynical question of whether this country is a democracy or not. To many, that may seem a naïve question. It is not naïve, even though most Americans believe the United States is the greatest democracy in the world and value so-called American exceptionalism.

The case for American exceptionalism was inspired by the Declaration of Independence and the Constitution. Both injected into law and into the nation's DNA values that preserve and defend individual liberties, freedoms, and rights and that guarantee the pursuit of happiness. Where else, in what other democracy, could the son of a Kenyan goat herder aspire to be and become the nation's president? And why have so many immigrants sought refuge, protection, and the opportunity offered by the United States?

But many global citizens still ask, "Is America still a democracy?" Critics usually cite allegations of American hypocrisy and the many contradictions in its policies, stemming from inconsistencies and abuses in using human rights and democratic values as justifications and covers for policies and for uses of force. Policy toward Israel is one such case, the NSA leaks another. In a deeper philosophic vein, the Constitution, the rule of law and regulation, terrorism, and technology also are bases on which to question American democracy.

Regarding the Constitution, and despite universal suffrage, Americans still do not elect their president directly. An unelected group of Electoral College officials determines who wins office. Two hundred seventy, the majority of electoral votes needed to win, not a majority of votes cast, is the crucial number and the single determining factor in presidential campaigns.

Further, given this constitutional structure, campaigns in the electoral cycle fixate on about a dozen "swing" states. Hundreds of millions, if not thousands of millions, of dollars are spent on these select dozen states. On a historical basis, Ohio is the most important. To make a cynical point, why then not excuse the rest of the nation from voting and allow the people of Ohio to go to the polls and elect the president? That would save everyone (except Ohioans) time and money.

The constitutional requirement for an Electoral College is long past its sell-by date. Amending the Constitution either to end the college and let the popular vote elect the president or to make the college proportional instead of winner-take-all would be a giant step toward democratizing the process. All fifty states and the territories would be in play, not a handful. That the prospect of such an amendment is more remote than outer space reinforces the need to examine the nature of our democracy.

The rule of law likewise raises doubts as to just how democratic America is. The size of America's prison populations, the world's largest, is a disgrace, more than just an embarrassment. Mandatory sentencing, a narrow slice of which regarding minors was ruled unconstitutional, is a large contributor to the incarceration rate, especially regarding illegal drugs. Hence, the proportion of jailed black and Hispanic minorities is obscenely high.

Regulations impinge on democracy, especially when aimed at trying to regulate human behavior. The Sarbanes-Oxley and Dodd-Frank laws regarding corporate governance and finance impose major costs and penalties on the private sector; they add little or no value and in some cases are ludicrous. Hand in hand with the notion of democracy is the need for free markets, provided there is proper accountability and oversight. There are better ways to achieve both, through more sensible laws and regulations that do not impose and intrude so deeply on freedom and democracy.

Perhaps the most grievous assaults on democracy arise from the interaction of terrorism and technology. Because of the war on terror, drones and targeted assassinations have become weapons of choice. Credible and visible due process is essential for democracy and its legitimacy. The killing of Anwar al Alwaki, an American-born Yemeni cleric who was a senior al Qaeda leader, may have been justified. But the precedent of killing an American citizen without a visible or transparent reference to due process is both a stain on the notion of democracy and a chilling precursor of more to come.

Similarly, enemy combatants are fair game if the targeting process is considered legitimate by the publics where drone strikes are being employed. Collateral damage, the killing of innocents, must be eliminated and not just minimized. Imagine if the Russians used drones to kill Chechen terrorists in France or, more boldly, if Mexico were to use drones to target drug kingpins inside America—one can imagine U.S. reactions.

Technology presents another challenge to democracy and another aggravation of the tension among national security, privacy, and due process. Snowden's revelations now render the notion of cell-phone privacy ancient history (as Assistant Secretary of State Victoria Nuland discovered when her cell was tapped by the Russians and recordings put on the Internet). Indeed, intrusive airport security searches violate, by many standards, the spirit of the Fourth Amendment, as well as specific prohibitions against illegal search and seizure. Unless Americans admit to the imperfections of the political system, along with its many benefits, any new mind-set will be incomplete.

On the current trajectory, the world may or may not be more dangerous. It certainly will be more unpredictable and more susceptible to violence and instability. At home, unless the United States takes action (or is exceedingly lucky), future generations—technology withstanding—will not be better off than their predecessors.

Part of that trajectory has been excessive use of American exceptionalism and addiction to the export abroad of the American concept of democracy and values. Since the end of the Cold War, both excesses have invariably made the United States less safe and less secure. As the world heads toward a post-Westphalian era in which assured disruption and not assured destruction defines the new strategic framework, a more relevant model is needed. As Lenin famously asked, "What is to be done?"

During World War II, the strategy demanded unconditional surrender of the enemy, establishing as the first priority destroying the Nazi war machine and occupying Europe, and then defeating Japan in the Pacific. Following the end of the war and the Allied victory, what Churchill called the virtue of being magnanimous in peace was translated into the Marshall Plan, and the United States began to rebuild both the allies devastated by war and the crushed Axis powers. During the Cold War, the West's dual strategy of containment and deterrence outlasted the Soviet Union—the USSR ultimately imploded.

Today, aside from "pivots to Asia," preventing Iran from obtaining nuclear weapons, and a variety of other platitudes or sound bites passing for strategy (such as drawing "red lines" and ordering despots to stand down), a real American strategy is, to put it politely, elusive. Tactics and specific policies, however well crafted, cannot substitute for the absence of a viable and comprehensive strategy. Confusing the winning of battles with the winning of wars does not help.

To develop such a comprehensive strategy, a better mind-set is desperately needed. Otherwise oldthink risks repeating many past blunders and mistakes that led to disaster in Afghanistan and Iraq and to the financial crises of 2008. That new mind-set would be well advised to embrace the construct of peace, prosperity, and stability through partnerships.

Peace is more than an absence of war. Peace means reducing the chances for major conflict to as low a level as possible and containing conflicts that may have serious repercussions for U.S. and allied interests. That does not mean that all conflicts must be contained or fought.

This mind-set must also take into account that the political system and the organization for national security, like the international structure, reflect the twentieth and not the twenty-first century. Both are inadequate for keeping up with the challenges, threats, dangers, and uncertainties facing mankind. At a time when the most powerful armies in the world cannot defeat by themselves enemies that lack armies, the strategic paradigm has shifted from the Cold War's assured destruction, in which thermonuclear weapons posed existential threats to society, to one of assured disruption, in which the aim of the adversary is disruption, not necessarily destruction, to achieve political ends.

Further, a new definition of "winning" is essential for the twenty-first century. That definition begins with understanding that the United States has lost or failed in all the wars it has started after 1945. Absent a direct state-on-state conflict in which one side is forced (or persuaded) to accept the adversary's terms, winning may be any of a range of outcomes as diverse as preventing a humanitarian catastrophe, establishing the rule of law, eliminating a dangerous or potentially dangerous threat, or coming to the assistance of a needy state to prevent instability or worse. In any of these and other conditions of "winning," military force may or may not be needed. Thus partnerships, promoting and creating the other tools needed, are essential.

In that regard, the United States should take a page out of the unofficial motto of the Royal Canadian Mounted Police: "Never send a man where you can send a bullet!" The proxy meaning is that indirect, subtle, and thoughtful leadership by which others are persuaded or convinced to assume certain regional and security responsibilities is a clever, effective, and essential way of ensuring that American interests are kept safe.

With that background, what are the specific bases for this new strategic mind-set? In addition to being "brains based," this mind-set must start at home. Failed and failing government is the single greatest threat to society at large. This mind-set must help overcome the effects and causes of broken government identified in chapter eight.

Over the past twenty-two years, the United States has not elected a president who was fully prepared, qualified, or experienced enough for the job on taking the oath of office or for some time thereafter. Given the condition of the political process, it is uncertain that this condition will change in 2016. And few administrations or Congresses have understood the vast cultural differences that separate the United States from the rest of the world.

Specific recommendations were made earlier about correcting failing government and need not be repeated in full. But universal voting, allowing a third presidential term, extending the terms of House members to four years, reorganizing the national security structure, prequalifying national security appointees, and transforming education to focus on knowledge and learning are the most important.

Next, this mind-set must combine three principal foundations. The first principle is explicit and unambiguous statement of the aim of achieving greater peace, prosperity, and stability through partnerships.

Second is achievement of these aims through a twenty-first-century version of the Nixon Doctrine of the 1970s, one that assigns security responsibilities based on shared or common interests among the United States and its "partners," consisting of regional states and international organizations.

Third is strenuous challenging of the aims and assumptions underlying policy choices at the very outset, prior to decision, to uncover possible flaws and to ensure that cultural understanding has been appropriately integrated into the process.

To work, this mind-set must incorporate an uncommon application of common sense. For example, those who predict the end of the American era and a major decline for the United States are entitled to their opinions. But these dire forecasters misunderstand the current forces reshaping international and domestic politics.

China's GDP may ultimately overtake America's. However, that statistic alone means little. Al Qaeda and religiously motivated terror remain real threats. But through common sense these realities and dangers can be countered, constrained, and contained, provided the United States responds with sound judgment and intellectual objectivity. The words "but" and "provided" are the strategic centers of gravity that will define America's future, for good or ill.

Handled badly or bungled, China, terror, the environment, and possible wildcards will have negative, even calamitous consequences for not merely the United States but the world at large. At home, politicians and publics must appreciate that without sound policies, aspirations and expectations about the future, along with standards of living, will decline for the majority of Americans. Failing government only ensures these outcomes.

The most important recommendations regarding economic despair, disparity, and dislocation are the establishment of national and regional infrastructure banks and the transformation of foreign assistance into economic aid.

Response to ideological extremism and religious radicalism demands concentrating on causes, not symptoms, and mounting a comprehensive and unyielding public-diplomacy campaign to discredit and delegitimize the perversion of Islam and to protect the vast majority of Muslims who reject violence and terror.

Environmental calamity and climate change offer unique political and perceptual roadblocks. Improved coordination for the former is essential. And until some crisis strikes, dealing with greenhouse gases and climate change will be a rough ride at best.

The most important partnership for the United States is that with NATO and Europe. A rejuvenated NATO is the best mechanism for the United States to use in developing relationships on a broader basis. And where NATO partnerships may be missing or need support, the United States might respond on a unilateral basis.

Prosperity can be attained through the concept of national infrastructure banks. Surely, oil-rich states can be helpful in their regions. Regional development banks likewise can be induced to support these infrastructure advances. And the United States should shift to economic assistance rather than foreign aid, so as to develop indigenous businesses and industries as the best means of advancement.

Stability is by far both the most difficult ideal to fulfill and the most perplexing outcome to achieve. In a perfect world, resolution of the Arab-Israeli-Palestinian conflict and the Indo-Pak standoff would have the highest priority. By the time this book is printed, Iran's nuclear ambitions should have clarified. In that regard, Nixon's triangular politics toward China and the Soviet Union have relevance. The tension here is between Iran and Saudi Arabia. Without referring to Iran or Saudi Arabia as equivalents of either China or the Soviet Union, leverage between the two can be put to advantage. That requires sophistication, subtlety, and luck.

If the negotiation produces a verifiable agreement, that alone will be a great success. Should Iran be induced to rejoin the international community, that too, if handled properly, could be a game changer. It is not beyond possibility that a non-nuclear Iran might be disposed to end its hostility toward Israel. And Iran might be used as a lever for inducing Saudi Arabia to support a lasting peace agreement between Arabs and Israelis.

If Iran procrastinates and prevaricates or the negotiations fail, the most dangerous recourse would be a military attack to destroy or degrade its nuclear facilities. While the administration may not like the term "containment," a policy of deterrence and prevention will work. As noted, extending the nuclear umbrella to the Gulf states could strengthen the region and with it American interests. If America can think strategically as well as smartly—a big if—Iran's truculence can strengthen partnerships in the region and possibly move the Arab-Israeli peace process forward.

Similarly, resolving the Indo-Pak conflict would be a game changer. Resolution of these crises will relieve huge pressures for conflict and remove a certain number of Gavrilo Princips from positions in which they might trigger another crisis.

The United States is far from becoming a Gulliver tied down by Lilliputians or a Goliath overcome by a David. But if the last twenty-two years of history repeat, the next president is unlikely to be ready or qualified for the office. The nation's political process is broken and is unlikely to be repaired soon. And the international situation is filled with crises and potential time bombs.

The challenge is first understanding and appreciating the current situations at home and abroad. Second is deciding to act. And third is fashioning strategic policies and brains-based solutions that are smart, objective, decisive, and comprehensive.

But who will listen? And who will lead? Until these questions are answered in in helpful ways, more than just a handful of bullets threaten peace, prosperity, and stability. A new Gavrilo Princip, or indeed a replacement for Osama bin Laden, may appear. But in what form or shape? No one knows. That must not be allowed to happen. That is why a new mind-set for the twenty-first century is desperately needed.

Appendix I

A Letter to the Secretary of Defense

Dear Mr. Secretary;

As you know better than anyone else, every administration since George Washington's has been accused of having no strategy or the wrong strategy. There have been few exceptions, the administrations during World War II being the most notable. Much more recently, the problem in America has been less the lack of strategy than the absence of strategic thinking.

In the conflicts since Korea, we have focused on winning battles, not wars. We have too often substituted symptoms for causes. And sound bites have become surrogates for strategic principles.

In my view, what is needed is a process by which the aims, objectives, and assumptions underlying strategy are rigorously challenged through a Hegelian dialectical process and then assessed against proposed courses of action. This will be difficult, because for the department and services, any challenge to certain "sacred doctrinal cows," central to the military ethos, will understandably provoke negative responses and resistance. However, if we are unable to generate the intellectual fortitude to undertake these challenges, we will be jeopardizing in most serious ways the future fighting ability and morale of our forces. For the Department of Defense, this proposed process might proceed as follows:

The Department of Defense faces three major challenges, challenges that in my view have been understandably downplayed in the Quadrennial Defense Review (QDR). These challenges are indeed crises. In terms of priority, these crises are over people, strategy, and money. Unfortunately, we have not sufficiently analyzed the nature of these crises or the underlying assumptions from which proposed solutions have been fashioned.

About people—after more than a dozen years of war, combat operations are finally ending. This means that the department will be transitioning from a deployed and highly ready combat force to a largely deployable force faced with the vagaries of peacetime and not the urgencies of war. This transition will be exceedingly difficult, as virtually every aspect of the people issue will come under intense scrutiny, from pay and benefits, incentives for recruitment and retention, and the often mundane aspects of peacetime duty to ethical, moral, and performance matters ranging from sexual harassment and abuse to criminality. Indeed, the future of the all-volunteer force may have to undergo fundamental reexamination, no matter how politically volatile the attempt may be.

Regarding strategy, the QDR reflects the president's strategic pivot to Asia, renamed by the department "rebalancing." But events in Ukraine, as well as in the Middle East and South Asia, overshadow and could overwhelm the reasons for the pivot. Beyond that, many of the assumptions underpinning the QDR have not been fully or even partially challenged or tested. This means that potential flaws and erroneous bases for planning the future joint force may be lurking, even in plain sight. Of course, even a suggestion of reviewing the White House's strategic pivot will draw a stern rebuke and even direction not to proceed. But the wars in Vietnam, Afghanistan, and Iraq have been depressing reminders of initial and persisting strategies that were wrong and needed serious change if they were to succeed. Sadly, while the jury may still be out over Afghanistan, Vietnam and Iraq were costly losses, the latter the worst geostrategic disaster since the end of the Cold War.

Last, the QDR, no doubt by presidential directive, did not fully and frontally address the money realities. The proposed presidential defense budget for FY 2015 is around $600 billion, when all the components are included: a base of about $496; the opportunity fund of $26 billion; and a placeholder of about $70–80 billion for Overseas Contingency Operations (OCO). Congress will not approve a budget of that amount. Worse, as will be noted, if the planned active-duty force of just under 1.3 million is to be kept at current levels of capability and readiness, annual budgets of $550–600 billion will be required. Absent a major crisis, that level of funding is unlikely.

There is a further predicament about people. During the dozen or so years of war now ending, the force has wanted for naught. That the nation could spend about $70 billion on counter-IED (improvised explosive device) systems for force protection and about eight hundred dollars a gallon for transporting bottled water to Afghanistan suggests how well supported the force has been. But this spending largesse, along with public acclaim, has bred in the military a sense of entitlement. Beyond the huge financial and logistical outlay on its behalf, the nation holds its military in very high regard. Servicemen and -women, whether they have seen combat or not, are routinely thanked for their service—something that never happened during World War II and certainly not during Vietnam.

Pay, benefits, retirement, and health-care spending must be curtailed. For obvious reasons, Congress will resist. The political argument that our service personnel deserve the best makes for great rhetoric, even if unaffordable. Far less money will be available for training, readiness, weapons systems, and other support that have been taken for granted in recent years.

Many peacetime duties that have been performed by civilian contractors, from providing base security and performing guard duty to feeding troops, will have to be assumed by military personnel. For the fairly small percentage of the total force that served in harm's way, where preparations for and participation in combat provided a certain adrenalin rush and incentive, peacetime duty will seem boring and tame. Many will leave the service. Recruitment and retention could become critical issues.

The spate of ethical and moral lapses that have resulted in many sexual-abuse cases among the most junior ranks to the most senior are nontrivial. Cheating in the nuclear forces (in part a result of a zero-defect mentality), criminal activities (outright theft and bribery), and other misdeeds require a great deal of command attention. Appointing a two-star advisor on ethical conduct may not be the complete answer. The answer rests in the service four-stars, who must be the guardians of ethics and good conduct.

Regarding strategy, six of many possible examples illustrate the need for and the difficulty in rigorously challenging the assumptions underlying the department's strategy and force structure and confronting certain articles of faith strongly held by each of the services. First, the number-one mission of the department is the physical defense and protection of the homeland. That is too limiting (and reminiscent of the period from Jefferson to FDR when coastal defense was given that priority). The Departments of Homeland Security and

Justice should be charged with direct protection of the homeland. Defense has far broader responsibilities and challenges.

The purpose of the Department of Defense should be to protect the interests and security of the United States and of its allies and friends (and possibly to deter aggression and prevent the use of weapons of mass destruction)—far more expansive objectives.

Second, department planning is based on seeking "balance"—balance among and between the services, missions, readiness, capacity, and capability. Balance may not be the best measure. In some cases, imbalance is more important. For example, regarding Special Forces, those that you have must be ready. But the whole force need not be equally ready. Hence, "balance" can mitigate the need for tough choices and prioritization.

Third, the Army is basing its force structure on brigade combat teams (BCTs). But is that the best unit on which to build an army? A BCT consists of about 4,500 personnel. It is a powerful force, best suited to high-intensity operations. When it is deployed, another 4,500–5,000 logistical personnel are essential to provide food, ammunition, water, fuel, batteries, lift, and other support for sustained operations. In all likelihood, more fixed-wing aircraft are also needed. Experience in Iraq and Afghanistan suggests that perhaps another 5,000 civilians are also needed for support. Thus, to deploy a BCT may require 10,000–15,000 people, the equivalent of a small division.

Yet, for many operations, especially building partnership capacity and presence, where lower-intensity and noncombat operations are needed, a battalion-, company-, or platoon-sized force may be more appropriate. Hence, the assumption that a BCT is the basis for developing future force structure can be self-limiting, as well as implying that high-intensity operations are the best sizing construct for the Army in virtually all circumstances—something we know to be untrue.

The Navy has a predilection for nuclear power. Nuclear power obviously provides virtually unlimited endurance. Yet nuclear power is enormously expensive in dollars and personnel. About three-quarters of the Navy's maintenance budget goes to the nuclear submarine and carrier force.

For a nuclear aircraft carrier, being able to steam around the world for dozens of years before refueling makes little difference if it needs to rearm and refuel its aviation detachments as often as every three days when engaged in combat operations. Diesel submarines with air-independent propulsion (AIP) are quieter than their nuclear sisters while still having a fairly good underwater endurance capacity. Thus, why is nuclear power needed for every attack submarine and for the ballistic missile fleet, whose D-5 Trident missiles have exceedingly long range? Given that no state has or will have the long-range antisubmarine capacity to locate ballistic-missile submarines in areas where they operate, why is nuclear power still relevant for every submarine?

The Air Force adheres to the mantra of the nuclear triad and the need for a replacement bomber with penetrating ability, meaning stealth. But the triad is not sacred. In fact, the triad really did not come into being until the 1960s. For the first decades of the Cold War, B-29s and B-36s formed the backbone of the strategic force.

Intercontinental ballistic missiles (ICBMs) entered service in the late 1950s, Polaris submarines in the 1960s. If air-breathing nuclear systems are needed, it would seem that cruise missiles and large cruise-missile-carrying aircraft, which need not be all that expensive, are better alternatives. Hence, the assumptions of the need for a traditional triad and an advanced manned bomber (or new land-based ICBM) must be challenged and reexamined.

The U.S. Marine Corps sees the mission of forcible entry through amphibious assaults as central to its ethos. It is self-evident that naval forces must have an amphibious capacity, one adequate to send troops ashore in large numbers. The issue is whether the landings are largely in permissive or in highly contested situations where forcible entry is essential. The last forcible-entry amphibious operation took place more than sixty years ago at Inchon, Korea. And because that assault completely surprised the North Korean army, it was more "administrative" than forcible.

Given advanced technology and the lethality of modern weapons, an opposed assault would most likely be accomplished by outflanking the enemy rather than through a direct attack. And where forcible entry might be needed is not obvious. It is unlikely the United States will have to mount an amphibious assault against China or North Korea; the South Koreans maintain a large, powerful, and well-prepared military. Thus, while a significant amphibious capacity is vital, forcible entry need not be the basis for force design.

Last is the money crisis. Whether or not sequestration is in effect, to maintain the projected force of about 1.25 million active-duty personnel at current levels of capacity and capability an annual budget in current dollars of about $550–600 billion is required. Beyond that, inbuilt and uncontrollable cost increases for personnel, health care, retirees, and weapons systems are running at an annual rate of between 5 and 7 percent or higher. At 7 percent, costs double in real terms in about ten years.

Future defense budgets are likely to range between $400 and 450 billion a year in current dollars. That means by the end of the decade, if major action is not taken over the next year or two, the choice will be cutting the active-duty force by about two-fifths or more or buying virtually nothing for it. The QDR does not take these fiscal realities into account. Worse, even if sequestration were abolished, the inbuilt cost growth could turn the projected military into a hollow force or worse.

Many, of course, will reject these dire warnings. The services will be uncomfortable at best, recalcitrant at worst, in even reconsidering some of the most strongly held views—articles of faith that, however valid in the past, may not have stood the test of time. Others will argue that drastic or major change is impossible to implement, because of immovable and irresistible vested and constituent interests. Congress will be seen as the source of reprieve and relief. Congress will not and cannot be. And this situation will worsen when interest rates begin to rise, which inevitably they will. Even at 5 percent, interest on the national debt will amount to just under a trillion dollars a year, or more than double the defense budget.

Setting up a small internal group to examine the basic assumptions underlying defense regarding people, strategy, and money is essential. Politicians, and any White House, will resist such an effort, because the consequences could be so dire. However, someone must act, and someone must lead.

Over to you!

Appendix II

A Future Maritime Force

How can naval forces respond to what Adm. James Stavridis has called not a brave, new world but "a new, new world"? In July 1970, at age forty-nine, Adm. Elmo "Bud" Zumwalt became the youngest Chief of Naval Operations (CNO) in history. We forget that Zumwalt assumed office at a time of raging and frequently violent domestic protests against the Vietnam War, fear over growing Soviet military strength, and the start of huge cuts in defense spending. In response to what he saw as grave crises to the nation, Zumwalt would set three overriding objectives as CNO.

Top priority was modernizing the U.S. Navy to counter an increasingly capable Soviet adversary. Second, Zumwalt agonized over the prospect that racial unrest within the service combined with the backlash against the Vietnam War could become mutinous at worst, highly destructive at best, and had to be addressed immediately. And third, the new CNO saw the exploitation of technology as a game changer in fielding a modern fleet.

The result was an extraordinary planning effort, called Project 60, to remake the Navy. The name came from the number of days Zumwalt gave for the project's completion (although, in fact, a little more time was required). Project 60's most sweeping recommendation was to decommission nearly half of the some nine hundred ships then in service, discarding obsolete veterans of World War II, in order to recapitalize and build a modern fleet. This modern fleet would carry out four missions: deterrence, power projection, sea control, and presence. And personnel policies to control explosive racial issues were put in place.

Project 60 also created the first of many of today's space-surveillance and intelligence programs; introduced new classes of ships, cruise missiles, and other advanced weapons systems into the fleet; and increased the numbers of carrier battle groups and nuclear submarines—all through savings generated by the whole-sale force reductions, even at a time when the Nixon administration was cutting defense spending. Clearly no plan was perfect. But Zumwalt's came pretty close.

As the next Quadrennial Defense Review unfolds, the question arises, is a Project 60–like effort needed? If so, why? We are in 2014, not 1970. But, in many ways, today is an even more disruptive and challenging time. Three reasons, laid out earlier in this book, make this case and are restated here.

First, the international and domestic environments are undergoing tectonic changes as profound as (and even potentially more than) the threat and then demise of the Soviet Union. Driven by globalization in general and by all forms of the diffusion of power in particular, these dynamics have altered the nature and character of the major threats and dangers to global security but so far have been largely hidden in plain sight. This diffusion has empowered individuals (such as Edward Snowden and Bradley Manning) and nonstate actors (such as al Qaeda) at the expense of states. In simple terms, the major threats and dangers to global order and security are no longer state-centric, despite claims about Chinese or Iranian ambitions.

The four greatest threats of the twenty-first century directly affect far more people than did the potential destructive danger of the Soviet Union: failed and failing government, including, and especially, our own; economic despair, disparity, and dislocation; ideological and religious radicalism; and climate change. None is susceptible to a military solution alone.

Second, defense spending is entering a period of what will become draconian budget cuts, far harsher than post-Vietnam. Even without $500 billion of reduc-tions through sequestration over ten years, greatly escalating personnel, health-care, weapons-systems, and pension costs will, unchecked, cut the buying power of the current defense budget in half by 2020 or sooner. In blunt terms, on the current trajectory the Department of Defense will be forced by budgets alone to make cuts equivalent to at least 40–50 percent in force levels and associated weapons systems.

Compounding the budget problems, when interest rates go up—and they will—a larger share of nondiscretionary spending will mandate even greater cuts to discretionary accounts. Defense will be vulnerable. So far, the gravity of this situation has not been fully absorbed on either side of the Potomac.

Third, the international structure for global security and our own national security decision-making apparatus date back to the end of World War II and the Cold War, and they have not kept up with the profound changes to order and stability. Nor are the grammar and syntax of the twentieth century capable of dealing with these twenty-first-century threats. And the old strategic calculus of the twentieth century, encapsulated by the danger of massive destruction in an all-out thermonuclear war, has been replaced by the actuality of massive disruption that is now part of daily life. The attacks of September 11 and the common use of terror more globally seize on the vulnerabilities of societies to disruption.

Fourth, after a dozen years of war, the all-volunteer force has become extremely expensive (and some say overly pampered, even spoiled). For many of the servicemen and -women engaged in combat, "capture or kill" missions have had profound impact, physically and psychologically, and not all for the best. After withdrawing from Afghanistan by the end of 2014 (with possibly a smaller although undefined force left behind), the Pentagon will have to transition to missions and operations based on routine peacetime tasks that are often boring and mundane to people who have experienced the demands of actual combat. Transitioning the force to a far different and probably far less challenging operational environment brings a new set of complications.

Further, as Afghanistan and the ill-named global war on terror sadly proved, the best armies, navies, and air forces in the world are hard pressed to defeat adversaries that possess no armies, navies, or air forces and instead use terror and violence as weapons of choice. And, even more sadly, the necessary tools for bringing peace, stability, and prosperity to these and other states through nonmilitary means are lacking.

What should the Navy and Marine Corps do in response? Four general propositions set the context for specific recommendations.

First, given threats that are not amenable to military solutions, definitive strategies will be difficult to create. Instead, the U.S. military must be ready and able to carry out on short notice a variety of missions directed by the president that require agility and flexibility. They will also require intellectual innovation, as many missions, such as dealing with the disposal of Syrian chemical weapons, will not be part of any standard playbook.

Second, given the likely operating environments and threats, force size, and structure, trade-offs among readiness, modernization, and deployment should be based on maintaining a smaller, highly ready, and capable force with global access—although on this point there will be heated debate. That force clearly must be coordinated and integrated with those of allies and other partners through more extensive interactions among flag and general officers, combined exercises and operations, and far greater personnel exchanges. This means that old partnerships, such as NATO, must be qualitatively strengthened and rejuvenated and new partnerships put in place. The quality and not the quantity of these interactions will become the critical metric. Given the forward-deployed status of naval forces, partnership building is a foregone conclusion.

Third, people are the most vital assets and must be treated as such. Because spending will decline, the military will not be provided the same generous levels of pay, benefits, and other perquisites that have tacitly become accepted as entitlements. Nor will budgets allow massive spending to meet all operational requirements. As with Project 60, new personnel policies are essential to deal with these cutbacks and the mundane rigors of peacetime rather than the challenges of wartime deployments to dangerous regions.

Fourth, as Churchill reputedly quipped, "Now that we are out of money, we will have to use our brains to think our way clear of danger." The Navy and Marine Corps can achieve this by embarking on a revolution in military education, in which the goal of greater understanding can be obtained through emphasis on continuous learning and on knowledge that extends beyond professional duties and responsibilities to greater regional, technical, and other expertise required by this changing operational environment. This also means recognizing that the twentieth-century notion of a defense industrial base must be expanded to become a twenty-first-century defense intellectual property and industrial base.

Devils and details are incestuous. Obviously, many force-structure options exist. My leading criterion for fielding future forces is that readiness and modernization must be kept high, at the expense of numbers. Today, of an active-duty force of about 1.3 million, the United States has about 100,000 troops forward deployed in the Pacific; 80,000 (headed down to 68,000) in Europe and the littorals; and, after the drawdown in Afghanistan and assuming war with Iran does not break out, perhaps 10,000 in the Persian Gulf and associated regions. Wildcards cannot be discounted, however, from operations in Libya and Mali to what may or may not happen in Syria. And Iran.

Maintaining a joint force of 150,000 on each coast, both deployed and deployable units, for a total of 300,000 would seem sufficient to cover two concurrent contingencies, including Korea and the Persian Gulf. A further 300,000 troops would be in rotational training and preparation for deployments and would serve as a reserve should contingencies demand more forces. Another 200,000–300,000 would be in a stand-down status, performing routine peacetime duties at home as well as undergoing training, education, and other assignments, with an eight-to-ten-month time frame for returning to fully active status. And a strategy for regeneration and reconstitution both of forces and infrastructure is vital to providing for unforeseen contingencies that require greater numbers and capabilities.

Over time, this approach would lead to a total active-duty force of 800,000–900,000, with equivalent reductions in the reserves and National Guard (understanding that the Navy has assigned certain critical skills, such as medical, to these components). One significant change will be to place more units in cadre or "reserve" service, with skeleton manning, as part of a strategy for reconstitution and regeneration to restore numbers. It is pointless to decommission ships, especially aircraft carriers and their aviation squadrons or nuclear submarines that still have years of service life left, when they can be placed in this status for contingencies and other eventualities.

Six to eight active carrier strike groups and six to eight amphibious ready groups would form the core of immediate naval power, with perhaps three or four of each category in some form of reserve or cadre status. Fewer active nuclear-powered attack submarines (SSNs) would be needed once cadre programs were in place, given a viable program for bringing cadre ships back in case of contingencies. While less new construction would follow, some funding would have to go into maintaining a minimal intellectual-property and defense industrial base for regeneration if needed. And it may well be that due to budget cuts, far fewer F-35s will be procured. But as with the Polaris and Trident fleets, "blue and gold" squadrons could be formed in which pilots, not aircraft, would rotate.

Clearly, maintaining a strategic deterrent is crucial. Given advancing technology, diesel-electric submarines could be an alternative to nuclear power and should be examined. Such a notion alone will precipitate a tsunami of opposition, for reasons that are well understood. But with the range of the D-5 missile and the absence for the foreseeable future of adversaries with long-range, oceangoing antisubmarine capability, the risk is low and the cost savings high.

Adm. Jonathan Greenert, CNO, and Gen. James Amos, commandant of the Marine Corps, appreciate the need for anticipating these ambiguous circumstances and agree that, given the evolving international environment, the Marines have become in many ways the main battery of naval forces. Yes, should diplomacy break down and military strikes are necessitated against Iran's nuclear facilities, cruise missiles and naval aviation will be in the van. But the operational implications of this new world—from humanitarian to antipiracy missions and, more important, partnership-capacity building—mean that strategic centers of gravity are shifting ashore. Having a highly ready force means, however, that when or if these centers of gravity change, the Navy must be able to adjust rapidly.

One consequence is that the Marine Corps will have to reexamine its core mission of forcible entry through direct amphibious assault and downsize accordingly. The cost of advanced landing vehicles is high, while the likelihood of their wartime use is low. The last major forcible-entry operation was the Inchon landing in 1950, and that was largely unopposed. Hence a much smaller forcible-entry force as well as other tactics (such as air assaults and outflanking gambits) must be considered. Given the theological reverence in which forcible entry is held, such thinking will not come easily.

If a Project 60–like effort is undertaken, a careful assessment of foreign capabilities will be vital to determine application here. The Royal Navy is building a new Type-26 warship. The ship has large volume and hence can be outfitted for a variety of missions beyond those of the U.S. Navy's Littoral Combat Ship (LCS).

The Swedish navy has for over a decade deployed a stealthy *Visby*-class corvette. While U.S. law makes purchasing foreign warships difficult, a larger version of the corvette could be an alternative to the much more expensive LCS. The point is that the United States does not have sole ownership of good ideas and military capability.

Obviously, far greater personnel exchanges between staffs, units, squadrons, and war colleges for both enlisted and officers must be part of the naval kit bag. Interestingly, this is what happened before World War I and, of course, during the interwar years; operating with others is perhaps one of the most effective paths to greater knowledge of and learning about the profession. And the personal relationships over time can become irreplaceable, especially as peers move up the chain of command to positions of higher responsibility.

Space precludes a fuller amplification of a viable force structure, but the guidelines are clear. Such a total force is probably sustainable on a defense budget of $400–450 billion a year, provided there is stability in that budget. If more money is available—though the best guess is that it will not be—larger forces and more procurement could follow. A Navy of 180–225 ships (including those in cadre), provided they are the right ships, could be sustained, along with a Marine Corps of about 140,000–150,000.

Currently, no senior officers or civilian appointees in the Pentagon have much experience in defense build-downs. During the past decade, defense spending has dramatically risen. Meanwhile, the major threat of failed or failing government is manifest in the United States. No rational government would consider imposing sequestration on its military and mandate it be applied "equally," meaning evenly—as if 90 percent of a bullet, missile, or aircraft could be built. White Houses have become even more political over the years, and fewer appointees (or members of Congress, where the turnover rate is the highest in decades) are fully credentialed in defense and national-security matters. And perhaps more daunting than conducting dangerous operational missions is coping with exploding social issues, such as sexual misconduct and tragic shootings, such as those in the Washington Navy Yard and Norfolk, Virginia—challenges that consume huge amounts of energy.

Superregulation and the legions of lawyers who have added "lawfare" to the lexicon prevent achieving greater efficiencies and rationality in the world's largest bureaucracy. Interestingly, while the dangers and risks of World War II and the Cold War were far greater than today's, ability and agility to act and react were then far greater. Because of the complicated nature of government and its failure to allow efficiency and effectiveness to become meaningful metrics for assessment, vital and long-overdue reforms, especially in management and acquisition, are unlikely ever to receive more than lip service.

These environments are pernicious and deeply hostile to new and innovative thinking. Bud Zumwalt came into office at a time when the nation was being torn apart by Vietnam and was threatened by the growth of Soviet power and ambition. Yet, Zumwalt was able to bring immense intellectual breadth and innovation to those times.

The dangers today are not existential. Disruption, not societal destruction, is the reality. While terrorism is on the rise, Western and advanced societies are not threatened with annihilation, despite the presence of chemical, biological, and nuclear weapons.

In this world so transformed by the diffusion of power and by the electronic and information revolutions, U.S. military forces in general, and especially naval forces, have vital but new roles to play. Fighting wars has been their traditional raison d'etre, and the U.S. military must be prepared to do just that. But more subtle uses of military power—to reinforce national interests, protect citizens, and maintain access to regions not only for resources but to engage people—are the new normal.

The challenge is great and the opportunities greater. Whether or not a new Project 60 is undertaken, one conclusion is strikingly obvious. In a more complicated, complex, and interconnected world, given budgets that will only shrink, and with fewer armies, navies, or air forces to fight, the point is to use brainpower, rather than firepower, to ensure security. The Naval Academy motto, *Ex Scientia Tridens*, could not apply more—"Through knowledge, seapower."

Index

Affordable Care Act, 25, 41, 55, 120, 128, 132

Afghanistan: Basic Security Agreement (BSA) in, 25, 115, 116, 139; chaos in, 49; civil war in, 115–16; cost of security in, 25; cost of war in, 28, 41, 126; cultural understanding, failure of, 49, 118; defeat of Taliban in, 48, 50, 51; economic situation in, 32; funding for war in, 39, 40; government in and governing of, vii–viii, 9, 31, 42, 71, 115–16; ideologies and outcome of war in, 13; invasion of, 110; military assaults in, 39; mismanagement of war in, 41, 45–46, 48–52, 129–31; Pakistan and security in, 73–74; potential crises in, 63, 64, 71, 81; security forces in, 115–16; Soviet invasion of, 37; success in and Afghanistan-Pakistan study, 53; troops for war in, 21, 51, 113, 115, 116; winning war in, 28, 40, 49–50, 174, 209; withdrawal of U.S. troops from, 49, 71, 139

Africa: government in and governing of, 42; potential crises in, 78; violence in, 24, 61, 105

Agnew, Spiro, 37

Air Force, U.S.: Air-Sea Battle, 54, 76; nuclear threat and aircraft for, 205

Air-Sea Battle, 54, 76

Aldrich-Vreeland Act, 18

Alexander, Keith, 96

Allen, John, 53

alliances, avoidance of permanent, 125

Angell, Norman, 16

Arab Awakening, 11, 14, 22

Arab-Israeli-Palestinian conflict and peace process, 64, 67, 112–13, 160, 199

Army, U.S.: force strength of, 19, 26; force structure, 204

Asia: governments in and governing of, 42; instability in, 1; U.S. pivot to, 22, 54, 63, 119, 177–79

assassinations: of Archduke Franz Ferdinand and Sophie, vii, ix, 1, 7, 8, 9, 14, 17; impact of assassinations of heads of state, 1; legacies of assassination of archduke, 1–5, 191

Bank for International Settlements, 90

Benghazi attack, 66, 163–64, 175

Biden, Joe, 52

bin Laden, Osama: Abbottabad raid, 46; Pashtun protection of, 114; replacement for, 200; September 11 attacks, expectations about response to, 47; September 11 attacks, role in and influence of, 3, 39, 191; world-changing influence of, vii, ix, 47

Bremer, L. Paul "Jerry," 52

budgets and spending, U.S.: annual deficits, 88–89; balanced budgets, 126, 133; budget cuts, 26, 120; defense spending and military budget, 18, 20, 24, 26, 55, 125–26, 137, 139, 140, 202–3, 205–6, 208, 213; education spending, 18, 20, 24; entitlement programs, 37, 40, 88, 126, 128, 155; failure of spending as

About the Author

Harlan K. Ullman is a strategic thinker and innovator whose career spans the worlds of business and government. He serves on the advisory boards for Supreme Allied Commander Europe and Business Executives for National Security (Washington, D.C.) and is senior advisor at the Atlantic Council. Chairman of several companies and an advisor to the heads of major corporations and governments, he was the principal author of the military doctrine of "Shock and Awe." A distinguished graduate of the U.S. Naval Academy, he skippered a swift boat in Vietnam and a destroyer in the Persian Gulf. He holds a Ph.D. from The Fletcher School of Law and Diplomacy as part of a joint degree program between Tufts University and Harvard University. He lives in Washington, D.C.

The Naval Institute Press is the book-publishing arm of the U.S. Naval Institute, a private, nonprofit, membership society for sea service professionals and others who share an interest in naval and maritime affairs. Established in 1873 at the U.S. Naval Academy in Annapolis, Maryland, where its offices remain today, the Naval Institute has members worldwide.

Members of the Naval Institute support the education programs of the society and receive the influential monthly magazine *Proceedings* or the colorful bimonthly magazine *Naval History* and discounts on fine nautical prints and on ship and aircraft photos. They also have access to the tran scripts of the Institute's Oral History Program and get discounted admission to any of the Institute-sponsored seminars offered around the country.

The Naval Institute's book-publishing program, begun in 1898 with basic guides to naval practices, has broadened its scope to include books of more general interest. Now the Naval Institute Press publishes about seventy titles each year, ranging from how-to books on boating and navigation to battle histories, biographies, ship and aircraft guides, and novels. Institute members receive significant discounts on the Press's more than eight hundred books in print.

Full-time students are eligible for special half-price membership rates. Life memberships are also available.

For a free catalog describing Naval Institute Press books currently available, and for further information about joining the U.S. Naval Institute, please write to:

Member Services
U.S. NAVAL INSTITUTE
291 Wood Road
Annapolis, MD 21402-5034
Telephone: (800) 233-8764
Fax: (410) 571-1703
Web address: www.usni.org